745.1
M

Mebane, John, 1909-
    Collecting nostalgia; the first guide to
the antiques of the 30s and 40s.   New
Rochelle, N. Y., Arlington House [1972]
    367 p.   illus.   25cm.

    Bibliography: p. [353]-358.

    1. Art objects--Collectors and collect-
ing. I. Title.
NK1125.M352

COLLECTING NOSTALGIA

THE FIRST GUIDE TO
THE ANTIQUES OF THE 30s and 40s

JOHN MEBANE

COLLECTING

NOSTALGIA

THE FIRST GUIDE TO
THE ANTIQUES OF THE 30s and 40s

ARLINGTON HOUSE

New Rochelle, N.Y.

Library of Congress Catalog Card Number 72-77644

ISBN 0-87000-173-6

MANUFACTURED IN THE UNITED STATES OF AMERICA

My book and my heart are for
HANNAH

ACKNOWLEDGMENTS

ASSISTANCE in the preparation of this excursion into the past has come from far and near, and the author is indebted to many individuals, businesses, and institutions for both encouragement and generosity.

Special thanks are due to Martin Gross, Senior Editor of Arlington House, Publishers, who conceived the idea for the book in the first place and who kept the author supplied with an abundance of pertinent information about those dear, dead days that are not yet quite beyond recall. The writer is also greatly indebted to Jimmie Fitzpatrick of Dunwoody, Georgia, and Don Howard of Atlanta (a growing suburb of Dunwoody some 10 miles hard to the south), who took many of the photographs for this book.

Acknowledgment also is made of the help of the following, who provided guidance, illustrations, permissions, or other assistance of a tangible nature:

American Motors Corp., Detroit; Americana Interstate Corp., Mundelein, Ill.; Professor William E. Atkins, Texas Christian University, Fort Worth; Don Barber, Television Station WQXI, Atlanta; Bennett Brothers, Inc., Chicago; Maurice D. Blum, of John J. Greer–Maurice D. Blum Associates, Washington, D.C.; Dick Bristow, Santa Cruz, Cal.; Buick Motor Divison, General Motors Corporation, Flint, Mich.; Campbell Soup Company, Camden, N.J.; Chevrolet Motor Division, General Motors Corp., Detroit; The Coca-Cola Company and The Archives, Coca-Cola, U.S.A., Atlanta; Columbia Broadcasting System, New York; Mrs. Theodore Davidov, Bethesda, Md.; Walt Disney Productions, Inc. and David R. Smith, Archivist, Burbank, Cal.; M. Thomson Fagan, Rutland, Vt.; Finch College Museum of Art and Elaine Varian, Director and Curator of the Contemporary Wing, New York; Ford Motor Co., Dearborn, Mich.; Fostoria Glass Company, Moundsville, W. Va.; Harry Greenwold, Wallenstein-Mayer Company, Cincinnati; Ted Hake, Philadelphia; Barry Hardin and The Collectibles Corp., Atlanta.

Also, International Silver Co. and E. P. Hogan, Historical Librarian, Meriden, Conn.; Miss Joann Janzen, Wichita, Kan.; Lucien Lelong Corporation, New York; Charles L. Leonard, Cincinnati; Lenox, Inc., Trenton, N.J.; Tom Mahoney, Poughkeepsie, N.Y., and New York; Herman Miller, Inc., Zeeland, Mich.; Minneapolis Institute of Arts and David Ryan, Curator of Exhibitions, Minneapolis; Barbara R. Mueller, Jefferson, Wis.; National Antiques Show, Madison Square Garden, and Pearl Winick, New York; National Broadcasting Company, Inc., New York; Oneida Ltd., Silversmiths, Oneida, N.Y.

Also, Parke-Bernet Galleries, Inc., New York; Bill Poese, Route Four, Jefferson, Ohio; Ovaltine Food Products Division, Sandoz-Wander, Inc., Villa Park, Ill.; Kenneth W. Rendell, Inc., Somerville, Mass.; Paul C. Richards, Autographs, Brookline, Mass.; Charles L. Schaden, Trio Enterprises, Chicago; Sears, Roebuck & Company, Chicago; Van Camp Sea Food Co. Division, Ralston Purina Co., St. Louis; Montgomery Ward & Company, Chicago; and Paul A. Straub & Co., Inc., New York.

The author is also grateful, as are many persons who write about collectible objects, to those businesses that issued illustrated and descriptive trade catalogs in years gone by, for these volumes help preserve a part of our history. Pertinent to this book are those issued by such businesses — in addition to those mentioned above — as the American Wholesale Corp. Division of Butler Brothers, Baltimore, that offered almost everything from household necessities to toys, Western Auto Stores, with establishments around the country that provided motorists with so many items that today constitute a collector's field in themselves, and others whose catalogs constitute treasure-houses of information about the wonderful world of "antiques" of a generation ago.

CONTENTS

COLLECTING NOSTALGIA
THE FIRST GUIDE TO
THE ANTIQUES OF THE 30s and 40s

1 THE INCREDIBLE ERA

THERE was little to distinguish the dawning of January 1, 1930 from the dawning of January the year before or, in fact, from the onset of most Januaries in the 154 years of United States history that preceded it.

True, three members of the United States Cabinet, including Secretary of the Treasury Andrew Mellon, predicted on this date — with an inaccuracy that has seldom been rivaled — a year of "progress and prosperity."

On the same date, Professor James MacKaye of Dartmouth offered a startling new radiation hypothesis of the universe that differed radically from Albert Einstein's widely acclaimed theory of relativity, but interest in his pronouncement was limited largely to academic and scientific circles. The man-on-the-street concentrated his attention on more mundane matters, such as flagpole sitting, which Shipwreck Kelly had originated in the 1920s and which by 1930 had tempted many a hopeful to better his records. Or marathon dancing, originated by one Milton Crandall and offering physical and mental torment to adventurous couples who, by 1930, were shuffling around not only for weeks at a time but sometimes for months on dance hall floors in the cities and hinterlands, taking only one 15-minute break each hour. Or listening to the crooning of Rudy Vallee, the Yale graduate who became an overnight sensation by warbling through a megaphone from coast to coast, thanks to radio.

But the banker, the financier, and the businessman had other matters on their minds, centered primarily on the extraordinarily puzzling question of what in hell was happening to the economy. (You will forgive the expletive, but "hell" was the word commonly in use in 1930 and the years immediately following.) Their attention was concentrated on the preceding October, a month that became the tormenting harbinger of a new and incredible era. Though that month may be for those children of the forties who already are well on their way to becoming the "older generation" in the 1970s as remote as the flight of the Wright Brothers at Kitty Hawk or the sinking of the *Cumberland* by the Confederate ironclad *Merrimac*, it remains for their parents the blackest October ever to be entrapped by the tentacles of their memory.

On October 24, 1929, the stock market had begun the plunge that was to lead to panic and disaster. General Electric plummeted $32 a share; other stalwarts of the economy followed suit. Twenty days later the Dow-Jones stock average, which had soared the month before to an all-time high of 381, stood almost 182 points lower. Hoover prosperity for all practical purposes was dead even then, although the average man still clung to the belief that somehow the President who had promised them two chickens in every pot would at least pull a rabbit out of the hat for them to gnaw on.

The engineer who had graduated to politics did indeed try, but the economy, except for a few minor huffs and puffs, failed to respond either to his ministrations or his exhortations.

Businesses began plunging into bankruptcy, banks to failure, and individual fortunes were disappearing. Before long, many financial geniuses and community leaders, shocked beyond human endurance by the swift and almost inconceivable torrents of adversity, were to leap to their deaths from their offices in tall buildings or, in the stark solitude of their homes, to die from overdoses of drugs or by swifter routes to suicide.

As the months passed in this new decade of the 1930s economic diagnosticians toiled valiantly but in vain to determine the causes of the tragic malady that had engulfed the nation. Markets were destroyed and workers by the thousands were laid off their jobs. In the light of subsequent developments, it seems unbelievable that the nation's businessmen could have told President Hoover on January 24, 1930, that the general business situation had been such that "no unusual methods need be considered for the stimulating of business beyond the policies of progress which ordinarily mark American industry" — and yet they did.

In September 1931, bank panic began spreading in the United States and 305 banks closed during that month; by the end of December, more than 1,300 had shut their doors. During the following year the number of unemployed reached 13 million. In January 1932, the Reconstruction Finance Corporation was established to advance loans to failing banks, farm mortage associations, building and loan associations, railroads, and insurance companies. But this did not stem the tide of trouble.

In the midst of the financial turmoil, the 20-month-old son of Colonel and Mrs. Charles A. Lindbergh was kidnaped on March 1, 1932. His lifeless body was found on May 12, and the heart of the nation, troubled as it was, went out to the man who had conquered the skies over the Atlantic in a solo flight in his monoplane, *The Spirit of St. Louis,* in 1927, and to his wife, Anne Morrow Lindbergh.

Another tragedy was narrowly averted after the "Bonus Army" arrived in the nation's capital on May 29. Things were hectic everywhere.

Having lost faith in the Republican Administration, the voters turned to the Democrats, and on November 8, Franklin D. Roosevelt won the Presidency by a landslide, carrying all states except seven. The "New Deal" was born, and auspiciously.

In 1933, the Roosevelt Administration demanded and was granted unprecedented powers that led to the creation of a host of new federal agencies charged with the responsibility of regulating private industry and finding jobs for the unemployed on government-sponsored projects. Roosevelt brought to Washington a remarkable crew: men with theories, workable, unworkable, heretical, impulsive, rational, impossible, possible. But their goal was a common one: to cure or pluck out the cancer of depression from the belly of America.

The day following his inauguration, Roosevelt proclaimed a National Bank Holiday, and eight days later banks began to reopen. By the end of March, three-fourths of all banks were operating again.

In May, the Agricultural Adjustment Act was passed, creating the AAA to restrict the planting of certain crops and to pay farmers for uncultivated acreage. On May 12, Congress passed the Federal Emergency Relief Act with an appropriation of $500 million for the Federal Emergency Relief Administration, and on May 18 the Tennessee Valley Authority was established to control the floods on the Tennessee River and to develop a program of rural electrification.

The National Industrial Recovery Act, establishing the National Recovery Administration and the Public Works Administration, came in June. Named to head the NRA was the zealous and tempestuous General Hugh S. Johnson, while Harold L. Ickes was selected to head the PWA. And in November the Civil Works Administration, with Harry L. Hopkins as administrator, was set up to provide work for about four million unemployed.

The names and probably the original purposes of many of the innumerable government agencies and boards created chiefly in 1933 to deal with the nation's worsening problems have dimmed for many with the passage of time, and those that are recalled today are perhaps best remembered by their initials rather than their precise names, such as, in addition to those already mentioned, the CCC (Civilian Conservation Corps), FCA (Farm Credit Administration), NLB (National Labor Board), and others.

Yet during that year and two or three to follow there flowed from Washington to individual businesses a vast array of orders, directives, posters and placards, insignia, report forms, bulletins, and memoranda, most of which today, as a part of what all individuals who can remember the era fervently hope is the American *past,* are collectible and constitute a part of our history.

The NRA assigned fair practice codes to every industry in the country and created disciplines for them. Thousands of businesses displayed and utilized in their advertisements the NRA member insignia with its blue eagle and the slogan "We Do Our Part." Placards and other original materials with this insignia are now fetching cold cash on the collectibles market. The NRA operated until 1935 when the code systems were decreed unconstitutional by the United States Supreme Court — a decision that threw Administration thinking into a heady though short-lived tailspin.

Much of the ephemera of the 1930s as represented by paper is relatively scarce today because, being both transitory and fragile, it has been subject to the normal ravages of time. Nevertheless, it can be found and in sufficient quantity to constitute a display of historical interest and importance. And among the items the collector might want to seek are pieces of scrip. Ah, scrip! What memories it brings back!

I came to maturity in the clamorous days of the thirties. Fresh from the university, I applied simultaneously for two jobs — one on a newspaper in my home town and the other on a newspaper in a nearby community. The homefolk offered me $20 a week and their nearby competitor offered $22.50. I accepted the job away from home: The extra $2.50 a week loomed large in those days. And I set forth, not bright-eyed but probably bushy-tailed, as a cub reporter in September 1930.

My first realization that something was wrong with the economy (college students in those days were sheltered from the hard facts of life) occurred the following year when my salary was abruptly cut from $22.50 to $20. But the worst was yet to come. A few months later I began receiving my compensation not in cash but in scrip — scrip good only for the purchase of merchandise from specified advertisers in the newspaper. Happily, these included the grocer and the shoe merchant.

But millions of others around the country were not so fortunate. The apple vendors on the street corner, many of them war veterans, became a common sight: A nickel for an apple could buy a loaf of bread in turn. Some of the more affluent citizens purchased popcorn wagons, popped their own corn, and vended it for a nickel a bag. The popcorn wagons were mobile affairs, and they were not uncommon sights in many neighborhoods. And for those who didn't care for popcorn, there were peanuts.

Some of these popcorn wagons are preserved today in museums and recreated country stores. They are particularly collectible for those who enjoy popcorn.

Porcelain and fine crystal table services were high-priced, certainly for the thirties, so new and inexpensive services were created for those hard hit by the depression. These included colored glass wares in the form of plates, serving dishes, cups and saucers, tumblers and other adjuncts of dining. This glass was decorated with etched or molded designs and was turned out by the carload in green, pink, blue, an opalescent white, yellow, purple, and shades of those colors as well as in clear glass. Many of the patterns bore fancy names such as English Hobnail, Lorain, Sandwich, Vernon, Pear Optic, and Madrid, and they were sold in the ten-cent stores and by some of the chains. Suddenly as the 1970s dawned, we rediscovered this glass and called it, appropriately, "Depression glass."

Numerous other inexpensive wares and gadgets also made their appearance in the 1930s for those who had to count their pennies — and most everyone did. They ranged from decorative adjuncts such as wall plaques and table ornaments for the home to toys and games and perhaps the most fascinating array of trivia ever created in any decade.

Hundreds of these objects have become eminently collectible today, even though they are a far cry from legitimate antiques, and the reader will encounter many of them in the pages of this book.

The 1930s was *the* era of the comic book and of objects fashioned in the likeness of comic book and comic strip characters or named after famous or notorious personalities of the day. It was the era of the radio (there were well over 11 million sets in homes in 1930), and of radio premiums that ranged from Frank Buck good luck coins to Orphan Annie decoders, all of them now avidly sought by a growing host of collectors. The 1930s and the decade that followed constituted the era of wacky songs that could somehow trace their ancestry back to several that had flourished in the 1920s, among them *Yes, We Have No Bananas* and *Icky Wicky Woo.* The offspring included a motley group — *The Music Goes Round and Round, Three Little Fishes, Old Man Mose, Mairzy Doats,* and a plethora of others, some of which will be considered in a subsequent chapter of this book.

That was the era of the sound film, Three-D, and the wide screen, of television's infancy, of some remarkable books and plays, of sports records, of functional furniture, of women's skirts whose hemlines dropped and ascended with dizzying speed, of pinup posters (some created especially for the men in military service), and of Walt Disney.

It was also the era of model planes and tin windup toys, of travel by air, of a host of drink-hoisting adjuncts that crammed the market following the repeal of Prohibition in December, 1933 of the exploits and death from an FBI bullet of Public Enemy No. 1 John Dillinger, of the Dionne Quintuplets, and, of course, of a new World War.

It was the era of Father Charles E. Coughlin, the radio priest whose beguiling voice and overweening ambition netted him hundreds of thousands of followers before his downfall when they awoke to the realization that he was a bulwark of the pro-Nazi organization in America and a baiter of Jews.

It was the era of the exposure of Aimee Semple McPherson, whose contralto voice had comforted the weary and the overburdened in the 1920s but whose tempestuous private life was subsequently laid bare in the courts, thanks to an incredible number of lawsuits brought against her. (The final headlines in September 1944, reported the coroner as recording her death as due to a kidney ailment and an overdose of barbitual compound.)

The thirties, too, marked the true beginning of the commercial air age and of individual exploits that included a circumnavigation of the globe by Wiley Post and Harold Gatty in June 1931, in slightly less than 16 hours; a second expedition to the South Pole in 1934–1935 by Admiral Richard E. Byrd, whose "Little America" had been established there in 1929; and a flight by Douglas Corrigan, without benefit of permit or passport, from Brooklyn to Dublin, Ireland, thereby earning for him the moniker "Wrong Way Corrigan," since he claimed he had originally set out for his home in Los Angeles.

The 1930s and 1940s marked an era of heroic achievements, but they also marked one of fads and follies. It was the era of not only the flagpole-sitter but of the tree-sitter, of "bunion derbies" and marathon bicycle riding, of the chain letter craze that promised fortune to the gullible, of Francis E. Townsend's plan for "old age revolving pensions" of $200 a month for everyone over 60, and of goldfish-swallowing. We are not yet past the age of fads and follies but we would be hard pressed to match some of those in the two decades under discussion.

This book concerns the collectible adjuncts spawned in profusion between 1930 and 1950. The collecting of them has just begun, really, and may not reach its climax for a few years to come. Meanwhile, prices are almost certain to ascend, because so many collectors are getting into the act. The connoisseur will look down his nose at these trifles, for indeed many of them are trifles; but they also are a part of the history of a fascinating and a compelling period in America. And although many of these collectible objects may be purchased for only a dollar or two, many others will come substantially higher. Who would have thought, in the 1930s, that a Mickey Mouse watch would be fetching $125 or more today, that some pieces of ten-cent-store Depression glass would be bringing $10 and $15, or that a Buck Rogers water pistol would be priced at $55?

This, then, is not a book for the connoisseur. It is a book for the average collector for whom the beautiful but rare is out of sight but who is intrigued by the originally inexpensive objects, gadgets included, that held a certain fascination for his parents. The reader *will* find herein a discussion of a number of articles of intrinsic merit and more than casual value, particularly in the chapters dealing with furniture and household furnishings, ceramics, glass, and autographs. But, by and large, the things presented here are still

easily and inexpensively available for those who must pursue a
hobby on a limited budget.

In a book of this sort, a certain amount of overlapping seems
inevitable. Separate chapters have been devoted to certain types of
collectible objects that might be lumped together in the broad category of "trivia." These include Walt Disney character collectibles,
Coca-Cola-related collectibles, and toys. While Mickey Mouse and
other Disney character watches will be found in the Disney chapter,
other types of character watches will be found discussed in the
chapter on entertainment. Dolls in general are discussed in the
chapter on toys, but Disney dolls will be found in the Disney chapter.

Such questions arose as to what to do with the host of Little Orphan Annie objects. Since the coveted Ovaltine mugs were originally issued as promotional gimmicks, should they be included in
the chapter on business antiques? But since Little Orphan Annie
was also a radio program of the thirties, was it logical to include
these collectibles in the chapter on entertainment, which naturally
includes radio? Or, in view of the fact that this appealing little waif
originally began her career in a comic strip, should the Annie
mementos be consigned to the chapter on reading habits, which four
decades ago as now, embraced the comics? To settle these questions
for you, the orphaned tyke has been assigned to entertainment. The
decision was purely arbitrary and one that was made in an interval
between taking two aspirin tablets and sweeping a debris of miscellaneous clippings off the floor.

The same questions arose with relation to a variety of other collectible objects of the two decades herein discussed, and they were
all settled by the same method — arbitrariness. If you wish, you are
at liberty to clip categories from one chapter and paste them in
another, though this will do the value of this book no particular
good.

However, to make things much easier for readers who want to find
the discussions of specific objects quickly, there has been included
an alphabetical index that will indicate at a glance on what pages
each object and each subject included in this volume may be found.

Those who have attained the proper maturity will remember
many of the things about which I write herein — the Charlie
McCarthy souvenir spoons, depicting Charlie as Sherlock Holmes;
the Coca-Cola trays featuring such lovelies as Frances Dee and
Madge Evans; the 1939 New York World's Fair bronze coins; the
Mickey and Minnie Mouse bisque toothbrush holders; the Shirley

Temple dolls and mugs; the Roy Rogers wristwatches; the Captain Midnight decoders; the Dick Tracy secret compartment rings, and perhaps scores of others.

The more commonplace of these fascinating and often delightful mementos of an incredible era are also now becoming familiar to a widening circle of collectors, so great is the interest being awakened in them. But we also have included herein many equally intriguing collectible objects of the two decades that indeed may not be familiar to many of you, even those who grew up in the thirties and forties. The research for this book has taken me from thousands of magazines and merchandise catalogs of the period to garrets and basements of friends and strangers alike; and I have uncovered numerous quaint and useful and beautiful objects that are discussed for the first time within these covers. Some of these may become "hot" collectors' items, and in the near future at that.

A veritable deluge of articles that perhaps would have fitted somehow into other chapters have been included instead in one entitled "Collectors' Miscellany." This may constitute one of the book's more interesting chapters. At least I had fun with it and suspect many of my readers may encounter therein objects they either did not know existed or at least did not realize were collectible.

This book is not a price guide, but a good many current prices have been included so that readers may have some approximate idea of the values of these new "antiques." I didn't dream these prices up. They have been taken from advertisements, dealer lists, and from quotations given by shop proprietors. You are likely to find many of these articles selling at prices higher or lower than those quoted. So rapidly, in fact, are some prices ascending that it is entirely possible that some included here may seem quite low by the time you read them. So use sensibly the prices cited — only as a rough guide to approximate values as established by a number of knowledgeable dealers.

For those who wish to read at greater length about many of the subjects discussed here, the Selected Bibliography at the end of this book will prove helpful.

Welcome, then, to the Age of the Jumping Jive and the equally jumping Art Deco; the age of the drive-in theatre — the greatest boon to necking since the rumble seat; the era of Clark Gable and Carole Lombard, of William Powell and Myrna Loy, of Mickey Mouse and Donald Duck; the sounds of Rudy Vallee, Bing Crosby, and the boy wonder Frank Sinatra. Welcome, too, to the airborne dialogue of tear-jerking soap operas, the soothing music of great symphonies conducted by maestros whose names will yet become legend, and the gravel voices of Amos 'n' Andy.

Yes, and welcome to the days of the five-cent cup of coffee, the nickel head of lettuce, and bacon at a quarter a pound; the heyday of gin fizzes and tournament bridge; the glory days of Lou Gehrig, the Dionne Quintuplets, and Burns and Allen.

I hope that this book will generate a pleasant and warm nostalgia for my older readers and that it will whet the curiosity of my younger ones about those fabulous years with which their parents or their grandparents lived so intimately. The collectibles of the 1930s and 1940s constitute a fairyland of wonders and marvels for the uninitiate. We may never make a fortune by investing in the things described within the covers of this book — but we can have a tremendous amount of fun pursuing them.

Three signs of the times. **Top Left:** a combination peanut roaster and popcorn popper wagon of 1932. **Top Right:** NRA membership emblem. **Below:** "Prosperity" clock of 1933 reflected growing confidence in the new administration.

2 TRAVEL HURRIES ON

AND it came to pass in the days before the Trojan War that Minos, King of Crete, imprisoned the inventor Daedalus and his son, young Icarus, who, longing again for freedom, set about devising a way of escape. Daedalus was no mean inventor. He had contrived the fabled labyrinth in which Minotaur, that half-man, half-bull offspring of the wife of Minos, devoured many a youth and maiden sent by the Athenians as tributes to the king who had conquered them in battle. (Theseus slew the monster, thereby ending this sorry affair.) Daedalus had also invented the axe, the plummet, and the thread that Ariadne, daughter of Minos, gave to Theseus to enable him to find his way out of the labyrinth after dispatching Minotaur to a well-deserved fate.

So it was no great wonder that Daedalus, imprisoned, perfected a pair of wings intended to enable him and his son to escape. He attached the wings to Icarus, who soared from a hilltop into the skies, headed for Sicily, as his father had instructed him. The wings worked admirably — but Daedalus had made one fatal mistake: He had fashioned them of feathers and wax. Icarus — alas! — flew so near the sun that the wax melted, the wings fell apart, and he plunged into the waters that were to be named after him, the Icarian Sea.

For three millennia thereafter man scowled at the sky he could not conquer, struggling with the yearning to fly but stumbling constantly against the demon frustration.

It was not until the 18th century that man ascended again successfully into the sky. The vehicle was a captive balloon devised by the brothers Joseph Michel and Jacques Étienne Montgolfier of France, and the passenger was one Jean François Pilâtre de Rozier, who soared to a height of 84 feet.

The balloon made progress through the decades. The first free flight with passengers was made on November 21, 1783, just a little more than a month after de Rozier had ascended. More feats were accomplished in the 19th century and in July 1901, Professor Arthur Berson and Dr. Reinhard Süring ascended to the remarkable height of 34,500 feet — an altitude record that stood until 1935.

The first successful dirigible was perfected in 1852, and the forerunners of navigable airships appeared late in that century. But it was not until a blustering December 17, 1903 that the brothers Orville and Wilbur Wright, bicycle-mechanics-turned-inventors, made the first self-powered airplane flight in history above the sand dunes of Kitty Hawk, North Carolina.

The airplane played its role in the first World War, and the rigid airships *Los Angeles* and *Graf Zeppelin* subsequently made history. The 1930s, however, ushered in air travel for the masses and helped pave the way for the flights to the moon. Encouraged by the wildly-acclaimed feat of Charles A. Lindbergh in flying alone from Roosevelt Field in New York to Le Bourget in Paris on May 21–22, 1927, other hopefuls in the thirties racked up records. In 1932, Amelia Earhart Putnam flew from Newfoundland to Ireland (and she made it from Honolulu to California in 1935 before her mysterious disappearance that still has the world baffled). In the same year, Clyde Pangborn and Hugh Herndon, Jr. flew nonstop from Tokyo to Washington, and James A. Mollison made a successful flight from Ireland to Penfield, N.B.

Early in the thirties, too, barnstormers were flying all over the countryside, earning a few dollars here and there by taking aloft passengers who were brave enough or brash enough to take a chance on making it upstairs and down again safely.

The feats of the *Graf Zeppelin,* named after its German designer and commissioned in 1928, captured the public fancy after this remarkable ship made 109 trips to North America and to Europe in 1930. In 1935 she flew more than 222,000 miles. Remarkable, too, were the achievements of the *Hindenburg,* the zeppelin which flew from Lakehurst, New Jersey, to Frankfort, Germany, in 1936 but whose exploits climaxed in stark tragedy in 1937 when she was destroyed by fire, with a loss of 37 lives, while landing in Lakehurst. (In the early thirties accidents were to be expected. The intrepid Frank Hawks, who had set a coast-to-coast nonstop flight record on January 30, 1930, wrecked the plane in which he had made it, at West Palm Beach, Florida, on an attempted takeoff for New York.)

In 1928, there were only slightly more than 14,000 miles of airways in this country, but commercial transportation expanded sharply as the third decade of this century got under way, and by the outbreak of World War II nearly 42,000 miles of air route were being traveled in domestic service.

This, of course, is not the place to delve into the history of air transportation or flying, but travel by air had so captivated the imagination of the public in the 1930s that it gave rise to by-products that today are eminently collectible. These range from model planes to pocket watches and from commemorative stamps to aviator helmets for the youngsters.

Postage stamps were issued to commemorate the achievements of the *Graf Zeppelin,* not only in Germany but in numerous countries that the ship visited. When this famous ship flew to the Chicago Century of Progress fair in 1933, a commemorative airmail stamp was issued, overprinted "Chicagofahrt Weltausstellung 1933." All of these special stamp issues are now sought by philatelists and by collectors of aviation memorabilia.

By 1932, the *Graf Zeppelin* pocket watch, commemorating the ship's travel around the world in 21 days in 1929, was on the market. It was reported to be the same model as carried by a member of the ship's crew on its around-the-world trip. The nickel-plated case contained a 37-hour American stem-wind movement, and it was offered by Montgomery Ward & Company at 98 cents with a plain dial or $1.48 with a luminous dial. The price also included a leather fob with a metal charm.

In the same year, Montgomery Ward offered for the same prices a Trail Blazer watch commemorating Admiral Byrd's Antarctic Expedition. In 1928 Byrd had led an expedition to that region and established his camp, "Little America," on the Bay of Whales. From there he flew to the South Pole and back in 1929, becoming the first man to reach both the North and the South Poles by air. The Admiral went on to further achievements as aviator, explorer, and scientist. The watch was Ward's exclusive design and the movement was reported to be an exact duplicate of one carried by a member of Byrd's Expedition, "who stated that it kept wonderful time."

Both watches will make valuable additions to the collections of aviation enthusiasts or those who seek exploration mementos; but, unlike the Mickey Mouse watches produced in such profusion for many years, they are scarce; and they will bring substantial prices when found, just as many of the Mickey Mouse watches currently do.

Capitalizing on the mounting interest in the conquest of the skies, manufacturers turned out a number of model planes in the early 1930s, many of them collectible.

In its 1932-1933 catalogue, Montgomery Ward offered several build-it-yourself kits — one for the Lockheed Sirius monoplane, one for the Curtis Army Hawk pursuit plane, and a third for an autogiro model that would fly and make vertical landings. The Lockheed Sirius, when assembled, had an 18-inch wingspread, a retractable landing gear; it sold for just 89 cents. The Curtis had a 24-inch wingspread and cost $1.79, while the autogiro with its 21-inch wingspread and 12-inch length sold for 89 cents. Also available from Ward at $1.79 were materials for building the British S.E. 5 pursuit plane.

Boys' magazines of the period published illustrations of various planes, and Ward had available at $1.79 a kit of wooden pieces that would enable the purchaser to make from four to six of these.

Other model plane kits were made by various manufacturers and offered through numerous outlets. The tin windup planes were a hit of the early thirties too. In 1933, Sears, Roebuck and Company offered a Marx tin plane that was powered by a strong gum rubber motor. This one, 9½ inches long and with an 11¾-inch wingspread, was wound and then took off from the ground. If the plane crashed into an obstruction, the wings and undercarriage detached themselves, thereby averting catastrophe! This Marx toy sold originally for 59 cents. Try to find one for that now.

Recognizing the advances being made in transportation of all kinds, Ward's made available early in the thirties a miniature transportation building of 22 pieces that included three airplanes and a landing field, plus ocean liners, a steamship dock, railroad station, and other vehicles and adjuncts of transportation, even including an airplane beacon light. The boxed set retailed for $1.89. The same company presented a flying zeppelin equipped with a Marx motor, which caused the propeller to whirl, thereby propelling the ship in circles after it had been suspended by a cord.

For the tiny tots there were pull-toy planes of metal, and plane-shaped toy metal vehicles with propellers. One of the latter, the "Curtis Hawk," boasted a revolving propeller and a rudder that turned with the rear wheel. An aviator's helmet was thrown in for good measure at Ward's price of $8.98. These vehicles were capable of accommodating a small child, and many of them were produced after 1930.

There were also "whirl" planes with metal fuselages that were swung into the air with a string. And for the adults there were airplane novelty lamps. One of the latter was a chrome-plated replica of a plane attached to a 7x3¾-inch base. The plane was 12½ inches long and had a 13-inch wingspread. The light was transmitted through glass windows in the ship's cabin. One couldn't do much reading with the aid of its light, but it was ideal for young courting couples.

Definitely collectible are any of the scores of postcards illustrating these early planes, and a veritable "slew" of these were issued in the early 1930s picturing the *Graf Zeppelin* and the *Hindenburg.* These are considered choice collectibles at $5 to $7 each today. Also collectible are photographs of the early airplanes and dirigibles, some of which will fetch as much as $10.

Autographed photos of pioneer fliers will bring even more, some scarce ones being worth $30 or over. Envelope covers of the *Hindenburg* and *Graf Zeppelin* flights are selling for $10 or more.

Naturally any aviation mementos stemming from World War II are sought by many, and these include flying gear and instruments and even salvaged parts of battle planes.

Miscellaneous air transportation collectibles include a zeppelin token of bronze, presently valued at $25, inscribed on the obverse "Graf Ferd V. Zeppelin" and containing on the reverse a view of the zeppelin and the phrase "Gut Luft! Gluck Ab!"; and miniature dirigibles of cast iron made as Tootsietoys and now fetching as much as $15 or $20. There is also sheet music devoted to the exploits of Amelia Earhart and at least one, *Amelia Earhart's Last Flight,* issued in 1939, is now valued at $15. For those who wish to go back a few years, there are numerous pieces of sheet music heralding the feat of Lindbergh that are worth between $10 and $20 each, depending on rarity. And a cover commemorating the airship *Hindenburg*'s first flight to South America, issued in 1936 and signed by Dr. Hugo Eckener, was priced recently at $75.

There are also collectors of actual early planes, but a person must indeed be affluent to amass a hangar of these. Nevertheless, they are being sought, as recent advertisements in collector periodicals will attest. This subject is discussed in greater detail in the chapter entitled "The Impact of War."

Incidentally, the largest military museum ever built is now located at Wright Field, Wright-Patterson Air Force Base, Dayton, Ohio. The huge structure can accommodate 100 planes under its hangarlike construction. More than 8,000 artifacts of military history are on display there. The famous aircraft on display range from a 1911 Wright Modified "B" Flyer to the B–36s, B–17s, B–24s, P–47s and P–51s of World War II. There are even very modern jets and a Japanese *kamikaze* plane. The new structure, erected at a reported cost of about $6 million, replaces the old museum that during the preceding two decades had been housed in an engine repair shop.

The progress of air travel has perhaps sounded the death knell for the heyday of the train as a conveyor of passengers over long distances, in the judgment of many people. The railroads tried to fight back with new equipment, gadgets, and services, but it may have been a case of too little, too late. Early railroad mementos have been collected for years, and it now appears likely that many items relating to the trains of the 1930s will soon be avidly sought.

Railroad dining car silver is a case in point. It is now being offered by a number of dealers. The plated pieces are heavy, made to withstand abuse, and they possess intrinsic value. The initials or names of the railways may be removed from the pieces—but it would be a pity if this were done. They should be preserved more properly as relics related specifically to what was once a fabulous mode of transportation before the skies became crowded with planes and the streets made hazardous for unwary pedestrians by millions of whizzing automobiles.

Railroad china, too, is now being sought. Many pieces are of excellent quality, though heavier than similar pieces intended for home service. They were produced by several famous pottery and ceramics manufacturers.

Just what railroad silver and china will bring on today's market is reflected in the following sampling of prices in recent advertisements:

Oval silverplated tray, 12 inches long, marked "Santa Fe," $22.50; silver crumber with "BR" (Burlington Route) on handle, $10; silverplated sugar bowl, handled, marked "Seaboard," $25; coffee pot from the Pennsylvania Railroad, $35; coffee service consisting of pot, sugar, and creamer, New York Central Railroad, $90; napkin ring of hammered nickel silver with centennial emblem of Baltimore and Ohio Railroad, $35; tureen and ladle, marked "C. & N.W. Ry.," $55; chocolate pot with California Poppy design (Santa Fe), $25.

Also, New York Central Railroad rectangular platter, 7½ x 11½ inches, made by Buffalo Pottery, $20; Indian Tree pattern china plate, marked "N.Y., N.H. & H. R.R. Co.," $35; Old Ivory soup bowl made for the Union Pacific, $20; and set of three dinner plates made by Syracuse China Company for the Baltimore & Ohio Railroad, floral decor, $65.

Pullman towels are bringing $1.25 each; dining car menus up to $5; large dining car tablecloths around $25; playing cards as much as $12.50 a deck, and silver menu holders about $25.

Numerous other "artifacts" of railroading are being collected, including uniform buttons (currently being offered at four for a dollar); annual tickets and annual passes, conductors' caps and insignia, and, of course, the ponderous bells from the old locomotives as well as the smaller ones from more recent engines.

Watch for adjuncts of the railway depots, many of which have been closed or demolished in recent years. These include signs and placards, timetables, and even the brass spittoons without which no railroad station was well equipped. Switch keys have some followers as do date nails used in building the tracks. And railroad lanterns, inspectors' lanterns, and magazines are still available.

Timetables are already considered prime collectors' items. Some of the early ones were extremely interesting and contained illustrations. Quite scarce and desirable timetables will fetch as much as $50 to $75, and some have sold for as much as $100. However, the more commonplace ones will usually be found in a price range of about 50 cents or $1 to $5, with the majority of them selling at $3 to $5. One of the country's most interesting collections of timetables has been assembled over the past dozen years by Franklin M. Garrett, Director of the Atlanta Historical Society and a true railroad buff. Mr. Garrett's personal collection includes literally thousands of timetables, many of them exceedingly scarce, and he has cataloged and arranged them meticulously. His objective is to obtain one timetable for each railroad for each year the road was in existence. In addition to being a fascinating pursuit, he points out, collecting timetables can certainly enlarge one's knowledge of geography.

Finally, in the category of general railroad miscellany are calendars, individual railroad publications, lithographed letterheads, engine number plates, crossing signs, builders' plates from engine boilers, locomotive headlights, metal railroad matchboxes with cover insignia, railbed spikes, various types of oilers, conductors' ticket punches, books of railroad rules and regulations, and advertising cards.

Some of the railroad calendars are particularly fine, featuring excellent full-color illustrations. While the fledgling collector may be tempted to remove the illustrations and frame them, the experienced buff keeps the calendars intact.

And now to the automobile — that truly fantastic monster that consigned Dobbin to the pasture and made obsolete the surrey, the stagecoach, the buggy, the Conestoga wagon and a host of other horse-drawn vehicles.

The 1930s, incredible as it may seem, were the years of automobiles abundantly priced under $1,000. They were the years, too, of names unfamiliar to many of us and scarcely recalled by those in their sixties. Who recalls intimately, for example, the De Vaux, the Viking, the Erskine, the Stutz (especially the "Bearcat"), the Franklin, the Reo, the Graham, the Peerless? The number of auto manufacturers today has shrunk even though aggregate production has soared, and many in business four decades ago have gone the way of the dray cart and Old Dobbin.

The early 1930s were not years of severe changes in models. Six-cylinder engines were most frequently encountered, although the eight-cylinder engine, even during the Depression era, gained rapidly in popularity. Compared with the low-slung, streamlined models of today, the majority of cars of those years were boxlike affairs that rode high off the ground. Yet some innovations did appear, such as the Essex Speedabout, a boat-tailed roadster that was produced through 1931; the Hudson boat-tailed sport roadster of 1931; the LaFayette powered by a 75 horsepower L-head engine and priced from $585 to $745 (1934); the Ford V-8 with 85 horsepower and built-in trunk; and, on many cars, free wheeling and synchro-mesh transmissions, semiautomatic clutches, and automatic chokes.

Later in the decade came other innovations. The Nash appeared in 1936 without a rear trunk. Chrysler and other makes adopted streamlining and automatic overdrive. Hydraulic brakes became commonplace.

Today the cars of the early 1930s have become collectible and, fully restored, will often bring prices well in excess of the list prices of models of the 1970s. Some collectors own "stables" of a dozen or a score of old-timers. A 1930 Reo four-door sports sedan will sell at around $1,500. A 1931 Chevrolet or Ford sedan in good condition will often bring $1,500 to $1,750. Cars that were originally higher-priced are valued at substantially more, especially if in good condition, even though they may need some restorations.

For example, at an auction sale of antique and classic cars held in April 1971 at Radnor, Pennsylvania, successful bidders shelled out $20,000 for a 1932 boat-tailed Auburn V-8 roadster; $14,100 for a 1931 Auburn speedster with eight cylinders, and an astonishing $66,000 was bid for a tricolored 1931 Duesenberg Le Baron Phaeton, which was $2,000 under the reserve price that had been fixed by its owner. It is also interesting to note that a Cadillac owned by the gangster Al Capone fetched $14,000 at the same sale. Altogether, 48 cars were sold at the auction, bringing a total of more than $323,000.

Rare and unusual automobiles of this period are considered by many as an investment just as are stocks and bonds, because of the rapid rise in their values in recent years.

Even as late as 1937, Packard Sixes were available at well under $1,000, Buicks for under $1,300, small Chevrolets for under $500 f.o.b., Dodges at $835 up, f.o.b. Actually one had to get into the class of Cadillacs, Cords, Stutzes, and Lincolns to pay substantial — at least substantial in those years — prices for cars. In 1931, Lincoln prices started at $4,400, f.o.b. Detroit, and the Hupmobile Eight with a 133-horsepower motor was fetching about $2,100.

But to check the newspaper advertisements for automobile prices in 1930 is as mouth-watering a delight as to check the food prices: Essex with a rumble seat, $750; Plymouth Deluxe sedan, $745; Dodge Sixes, $825 up; Erskine sedan, $965; Ford Tudor sedan, $500. There were 46 American car manufacturers in that year, and more brand names than most Americans can remember. In addition to those mentioned earlier, can you remember the Durant, the Oakland, the Whippet, the Jewett, or the Marmon?

Several intriguing histories of the automobile have been written, and those who would like to wallow in the nostaglia of the 1930s will delight in Tad Burness's *Cars of the Early Thirties* (Philadelphia: Chilton, 1970), packed with advertisements of the auto makers of those days.

The majority of collectors can't afford a stable of early model cars; but for them a host of appealing adjuncts are available. These range from radiator ornaments to horns and include, in between, limousine vases, mirror—clocks, gear shifts, cigarette lighters, brand name lapel pins, license plates, radios, luggage carriers, and key chains.

The radiator cap ornament of the 1930s can provide the collector with a wide diversity of designs and materials. There were stream-lined Egyptian figures with wings; naked nymphs; sleek grey-hounds; eagles, kingbirds, and one feathered species identified as a "speedbird;" swans; golfers swinging; propellers and complete model miniature planes; geese in flight; rams; winged mermaids; and Indian chiefs.

Most radiator ornaments were fashioned in glistening chrome (plate). In those years for 39 cents, one could have purchased an ornament in the shape of a modernistic bird that more accurately resembled an airplane with a beak; a Winged Diana sold for 17 cents; a V-shaped ornament for a Ford V-8 for 23 cents; a Flying Aviator for a quarter; or a Futuristic Heron for 95 cents. For those who desired swankier ornamentation, there was a chrome-plated "Speedy" figure with a built-in heat indicator at $1.89; a winged aviator with built-in heat indicator at $1.69, or an illuminated air-plane at $1.05.

The ornament was a radical departure from the flat radiator cap, and some of them are actually miniature works of art. In fact, Eugen Neuhaus, then a teacher of art at the University of California at Berkeley, contended in his book *World of Art* (New York: Harcourt, Brace and Company, 1936) that if all the other utilitarian devices that surrounded man in his daily routine were imbued with the artistic quality of the best of the radiator ornaments, "the millen-nium in art would not be far distant."

Even the famed René Lalique designed radiator hood ornaments, and one of his, apparently originally designed for either a Rolls-Royce or a Bentley, was recently offered for sale at the rather aston-ishing price of $325.

Some ornaments came complete with bolts. Incomplete orna-ments could be affixed with bolts available for a dime. Some orna-ments were designed especially for specific cars and year models; others could be attached to almost any vehicle.

The original prices are a far cry from the $15 to $25 that some desirable ornaments are bringing today, although others are avail-able for around $10. But even flat radiator caps of the early models are now selling at $3 or more.

In the 1930s and even the early 1940s the cautious motorist sounded a horn before attempting to pass another vehicle. Turn signals were not included on most automobiles until the mid-1940s and after. Drivers were no more psychic in those days than they are today so that a blast or a honk on a horn prevented many a crash and also caused a few, due chiefly to the frightening of timid pedestrians and daydreaming motorists.

Horns were produced in as great variety as were radiator ornaments and are now among the most eagerly sought automobile accessories. Twin-type horns were favorites early in the third decade of this century, and their blare was nothing short of brazen. If they didn't warn a pedestrian or another driver, they could scare him to death.

There was a twin air-vacuum Superette with a chrome finish available at the Western Auto Stores in 1933 at $5.65, and twin musical trumpet vibrator horns in chrome at $8.89. Super Tone vacuums, said to "give a brazen blare like the tone of a war trumpet," could be mounted almost anywhere on the car and sold for $11.95.

The Klaxons were favorites, too, with many owners. They could produce diversified sounds ranging from "beep-beep" tones to loud blasts set up by electrical vibrating units. They were available at prices from as low as $1.89 up to more than $20. Tooters were equipped with a rubber bulb and a brass reed, and the tooting sound they emitted was not nearly so raucous as that of other types. More pleasing also were the two- and four-tone melody horns. There were also auto whistles of aluminum and bronze whose penetrating scream could be heard for long distances as could those tremendous blasts of the Air-Blast Trumpets, electrically-operated, that made their appearance by the mid-1930s. There were several varieties of flat horns, such as the Wizard Micro sold by Western Auto Stores, that could be mounted on the fenders or outside edges of the radiator grille, or the Trail Blazers, sold by Montgomery Ward, for in-front mounting.

In the novelty line, there was a Yelping Dog horn and one called a Torovoce that had a motor-driven sound mechanism which, when activated, extruded a deep, bass bull-like noise. There were also novel musical horns that came complete with a sheet of music showing how to finger a keyboard that enabled the operator to play several different tunes. In 1941, for $6.95, Sears, Roebuck offered one of this type upon which one could play eight different tunes. One could play on it any melody within the range of three tuned trumpets. The keyboard was mounted on the steering column.

Virtually all of the auto accessory horns of the 1930s and 1940s are collectible. Quite early bulb types with brass shafts have brought $25 to $60 on the current market. One hand Klaxon is now valued at $45.

Automobile cigarette lighters can be collected. One favorite brand was the Casco, which came on many factory-equipped vehicles The knob lit up when the lighter was ready to use. There were simple clamp-on types with Bakelite cups that sold for as little as 17 cents. The Inverto had a disc in the center that glowed when the lighter was hot, and another had an inverted cup on the end that glowed when hot. The latter type boasted an inverted heat element that prevented one burning his fingers and kept lighted tobacco from dropping on one's clothes. It was marketed by Western Auto for as little as 68 cents in a choice of red or gray-green heads.

There were fancy lighters that clamped on steering columns, and combination lighters and ash trays that could also be clamped to the dash. Other simple push-in lighters could be clamped on the dash and were available complete with brackets in 1930 for as little as 15 cents! Some types could be swung under the dashboard when not in use.

Both early auto and early radio enthusiasts will find automobile radios of interest. The auto radio was an untapped field prior to 1929 when the Automobile Radio Corporation was organized. As the year 1930 began, several manufacturers had invaded the field, and a few makes of cars were wired for radios at the factory.

Although the first radios were costly when installation was taken into account, by 1933 the Truetone superheterodyne auto radio with six tubes was being offered at $32.95. The price for this electric model included a remote control that mounted on the steering post under the steering wheel.

Among the major auto radio producers in the early 1930s were Automobile Radio Corp. mentioned above, which marketed the Transitone; General Motors Radio Corp. with its Delco-Remy; and American Bosch Magneto Corp., which produced the Bosch radio. Very soon Philco acquired Automobile Radio Corporation's Transitone and began marketing an inexpensive set for cars. Subsequently various other producers joined this growing parade.

Combination mirror-clocks, designed for rear viewing, became popular in the early 1930s. The clocks were inset into the narrow, rectangular mirrors of nonglare plate glass and were equipped with 30- to 36-hour movements as a rule, although deluxe models came with jeweled eight-day movements. Clocks with both stem and pull winds were available. Some of these combinations originally retailed for less than $1.50. Rear-view mirrors, without clocks, were abundant at a 25 cents with bracket.

Auto clocks were also available separately for mounting on dash or overhead with New Haven and Westclox among the favorites. Prices started at under $1.50.

Gearshift balls and ornaments provide another intriguing category of automotive adjunct collectibles. These were produced in a great variety of shapes, primarily of Bakelite or other plastic or composition materials. There was an oval type that featured a picture of a pretty girl in the top center, and this one undoubtedly cheered many a male driver on a lonely trip. Another was made in the form of a dice cube. Others imitated striped marbles, balls of onyx, or had built-in thermometers. In a similar category were the steering wheel spinners, which enabled a driver to spin the wheel with one hand while backing into a parking space. These remained popular over many years. They clamped to the steering wheel and the majority were made of plastic. Sears and Ward sold some for as little as 16 and 17 cents. Nine cents would buy a gearshift ball at Western Auto Stores in 1937.

Some of the luxury car models came equipped with limousine vases, many of them of colored glass, that fitted into a bracket and were intended to hold roses or other long-stemmed flowers to impart the elegance of the parlor to the back seat of a sedan. The vases, tapering to a point at the bottom so they would fit snugly into the bracket, are especially desirable when made of carnival and opalescent glass, and will bring $5 to $10 each.

Folks who wanted to identify their cars easily in crowded parking areas affixed car initials to their hoods or radiators. They were inexpensive and easy to install; and one's initials are much easier to remember than a license plate number.

Also utilized over a period of many years were gas tank lock caps to prevent tampering with the gasoline supply. Siphoning gas not only was a favorite spare-time occupation of the otherwise idle in the early days, but still is. Most lock caps were chrome-plated; some boasted reflector tops that could double as a rear end parking signal. There were also spare tire locks, especially useful in those days when spares were mounted on the exterior of the car instead of being safely locked inside the trunk, and radiator cap locks, also useful since petty thieves of earlier days had a particular penchant for radiator caps and spare tires.

Luggage racks and carriers are among the auto accessories now sought. Most were made of steel with a baked enamel finish, and there were several kinds: running board carriers that were attached to the running board with thumbscrew clamps; racks that could be attached to bumpers; and those with folding guard rails that prevented luggage from sliding off and that could be folded out of the way when not needed. There were also accordion-type running-board racks that would accommodate a single piece of luggage and could be easily removed when not in use. And there were complete auto trunks—rumble-, rattle-, and rust-proof—that could be accommodated on the luggage carriers; some of them snuggled between the back of the car and the spare tire. Deluxe models were made with tool compartments that could be detached and converted into space for hats and thermos bottles and with compartments for carrying fish and game. Other types were designed for permanent installation at the rear of the vehicle.

While the previously mentioned accessories are among the prime automobile adjunct collectibles, they by no means comprise the entire list. Other things that are being or can be collected include driving goggles, robes, miscellaneous tools, curtains, tire covers, outside mirrors, windshield visors, license plate "jewel" fasteners, ventilating eaves and visor vents, windshield cleaners, tire gauges, motometers, spare tire carriers, early jacks, tool boxes, hub caps, traffic signal reflectors, headlamps, spotlights, trouble lamps, stop and tail lamp lenses, running board step plates, compasses, safety reflectors, fender guides, key chains, door handles with crests, and brochures and printed material of all kinds.

Naturally the true automotive addict will not stop here but will pursue radiators, exhaust controls, and a score or more of other accessories and parts that were associated intimately with the automobile of four decades ago.

Lapel pins and clips handed out by automobile dealers and lettered with snappy phrases will be collected by many. These began to appear in the 1930s and continued into the 1940s and included Hudson's pin "Ride the Green Lane to Safety in a New 1939 Hudson," Plymouth's "1940 Plymouth, Hotter than a Firecracker," and World War II Packard's "Work to Win, Packard, Count Me In."

There are various organizations of collectors in the broad transportation field, and there are also museums. Some of the best automobile museums are in Dearborn, Mich.; Sarasota and Silver Springs, Fla.; Cleveland, Ohio; Harrisburg and Huntingdon, Pa.; Luray Caverns, Va.; and Los Angeles. The Antique Automobile Club of America, which was founded in 1935, has since been joined by numerous others, including clubs whose members are dedicated to the collecting of specific makes of cars. The Antique Automobile Club of America has more than 20,000 members. Many clubs and associations publish their own newspapers. The oldest of the non-club newspapers is *Hemming's Motor News,* published in Quincy, Ill.

As for air transportation, there is a new group called The Zeppelin Collector. Information about this group may be obtained from George W. Hoffman, 1830 Petersburg Avenue, Lakeland, Fla. 33803. Those who collect stamps may be interested in The American Air Mail Society. Information about this society may be obtained from Herman Kleinert, 213 Virginia Avenue, Fullerton, Pa. 18050.

There is also the National Railway Society, Inc., with chapters around the country. A large chapter is located in Atlanta, Ga., and it is now engaged in creating the Southeastern Railway Museum on a 12-acre site in nearby Gwinnett County that was donated by the Southern Railway System. The chapter now owns more than 40 pieces of railway equipment, including steam locomotives and Pullman sleepers. Plans call for a big circular railroad track inside the museum so that the cars can be moved around.

You may be interested in a sampling of prices other automobile accessories and adjuncts are now fetching. They include: brass tire pressure gauges, $5 to $8; a Kessel brass hubcap, $16; a Hawkes cut glass auto vase with hobstar cutting, $20; wooden gasoline dipsticks, $3 to $4; brass tire pumps, $8 to $10; advertising brochures for models made during the 1930s, $5 to $10; operator manuals for the same period, up to about $25; and sales catalogs, $7.50 up.

Children's vehicles in airplane form were highly popular in the thirties.

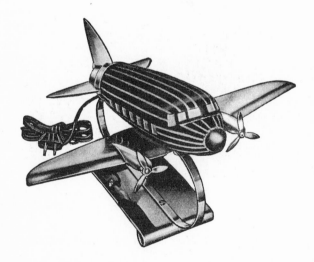

Top: Popular with the youngsters as the thirties opened were such gems of aviation fiction as *The Girl Aviator* series, *Radio Boys in the Flying Service*, and the *Aeroplane* series. Center: The air age also influenced children's headgear, as witness this Ace Flyer Cap with attached goggles (1930). Below: This novelty chrome-plated metal lamp (1940) transmitted light through the glass in the ship's cabin. Its wingspread was 18 inches, its wholesale price $4.80.

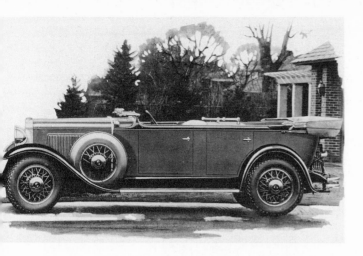

Top: This Slim Jim was Nash's Model 498 (1930). Nash Motors also introduced an eight-cylinder engine in 1930. **Center:** The 1930 Essex Phaeton, body by Biddle & Smart. **Below:** This is the 1935 LaFayette, Model 3512, selling for $585. Nash Motors' LaFayette line in 1935 ranged in factory-delivered price from $580 to $720. (*Photos courtesy American Motors Corp.*)

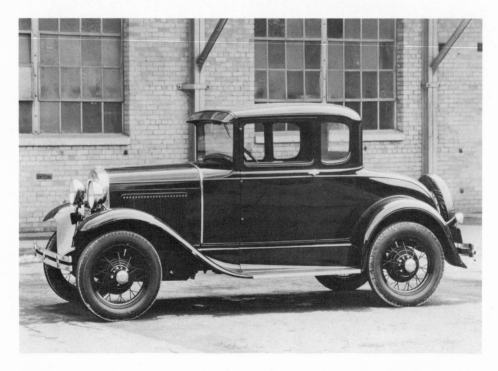

Two chic symbols of the thirties. Lady Astor steps out of a 1933 Terraplane, a six-cylin-der convertible coupe. (*Courtesy American Motors Corp.*) **Below**: 1930 Model A Ford, five-window coupe. (*Courtesy Ford Motor Co.*)

Top: 1930 Model A Ford roadster. (*Courtesy Ford Motor Co.*) Center: 1931 Chevrolet with spare tire in fender well. Below: Cars were becoming longer, sleeker by 1938, as shown by this Chevrolet. (*Chevrolet photos.*)

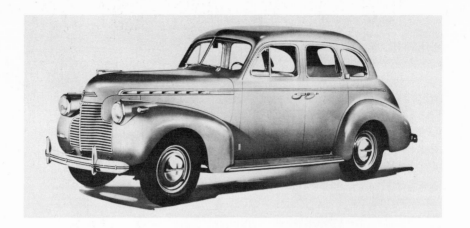

Top: Note the door handles on this roomy 1940 Chevrolet. (*Chevrolet photo.*) Center: Buick's five-passenger, four-door Special sedan of 1930 with a 132-inch wheelbase. Below: 1931 Buick roadster Model 8-64 with well for spare tire and luggage carrier on back. (*Courtesy Buick Motor Division, General Motors Corp.*)

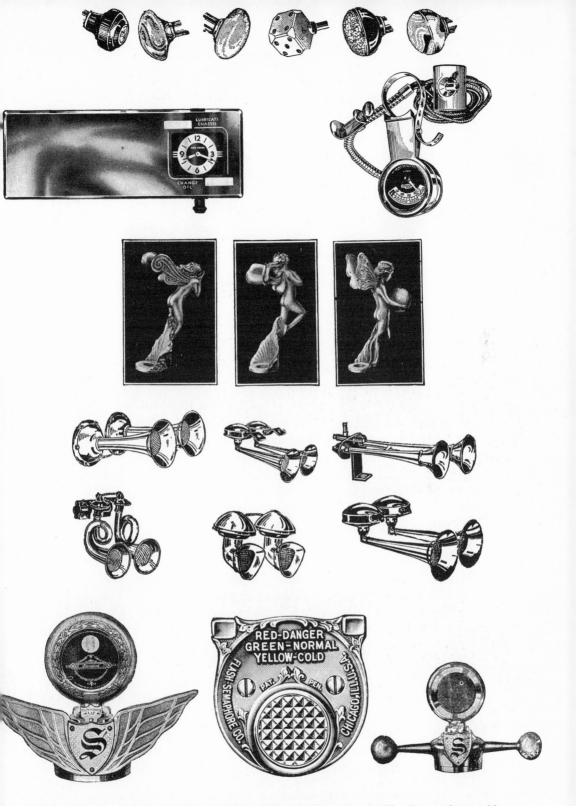

Top: 1930 gearshift knobs. The Oil Meter (right) had speedometerlike figures that could be reset to remind driver to change oil. Second Row Left: Streamlined New Haven auto clock, 1940. Second Row Right: A choice 1930 Boyce Motometer. Third Row: These 1930 radiator ornaments were finished in nickel, wholesaled for $3 to $6 each. Fourth Row: Auto horns popular in early thirties included Straight Trumpets, Curved Trumpets, etc. Below: Monogram wing radiator cap (left), flash semaphore temperature indicator (center), and Monogram Royal Onyx radiator cap, all of 1930 vintage.

3 SYMPHONIES, SOAP OPERAS, AND HOPALONG

WHATEVER else the 1930s were, they were not years of boredom for the masses. From the two decades 1930 to 1950, there gushed from the airwaves, the movie screens, and the bells of saxaphones and trumpets undoubtedly the greatest diversity of entertainment ever scrambled together within a similar period of history.

These decades brought the talking picture, the color movie, the wide screen, 3-D, the soap opera, Amos 'n' Andy, *The War of the Worlds,* Mickey Mouse, the Lone Ranger, Frank Sinatra, Kay Kyser, Walter Damrosch, and the advent of television. They brought the drive-in-theatre, *Mairzy Doats,* Buck Rogers in the 25th Century, Marlene Dietrich, Shirley Temple, the $109 Atwater Kent console, Rudy Vallee, Phil Spitalny, Stoopnagle and Budd, Graham McNamee, Clark Gable, Hedy Lamarr, and the prettiest pair of legs that ever graced silk stockings. The legs belonged to Betty Grable.

The movies offered something for everyone during those exciting years. The advent of the talkies doomed many a former screen idol and many a curvaceous cutie, and not solely because of their voices. The talking pictures demanded acting ability and — alas! — revealed the lack of it among some whose names had graced the marquees in the years of the silent movies. But bright new talent filled the void, the shoes, and, in more than one case, the stockings. Although the first all-talking picture, Warner Brothers' *Lights of New York,* had made its debut in July 1928 (*The Jazz Singer,* starring Al Jolson, which had appeared shortly before, was largely silent, although Jolson sang and spoke a word or two), it was not until the early 1930s that the talkies came to stay.

As the decade opened, a handful of studios controlled the bulk of American film production. The giants were Metro-Goldwyn-Mayer, Fox, and Paramount. But others were to appear before long. Mobsters were still abundantly with us at the outset of the thirties, and a host of gangster films appeared in rapid succession. Who, now in mellow years, will ever forget Edward G. Robinson in *Little Caesar* or that constantly-gesticulating tough guy James Cagney?

Worthy comedians followed Charlie Chaplin (who was still to make a few more films in the 1930s and 1940s). Harold Lloyd scored solid successes in *Movie Crazy, The Catspaw,* and *Welcome Danger.* The Marx Brothers perfected the zany comedy and a nation shook with laughter at *Animal Crackers, The Coconuts, Monkey Business,* and *Horse Feathers.* The late Stan Laurel and Oliver Hardy were unforgettable, bringing reactions that veered from guffaws to tears.

The talkies were a boon to the irascible, gravel-voiced W. C. Fields, who, without the sound of that unbelievable voice, would have been just another comedian. And one of the most appealing comedians of them all, Mickey Mouse, arrived in the thirties, offspring of the fertile brain of Walt Disney. Other beloved animated cartoon characters, that will be considered in greater detail in a subsequent chapter, arrived about the same time.

The sex symbols became more exciting than ever. Theda Bara and other languorous, almond-eyed vampires made way for sirens who beckoned with more than their eyes and lips. Pola Negri could be reached only by a Valentino, and Mae Murray only by a Jack Gilbert, but anyone could come up and see Mae West; and Jean Harlow was the Blonde Bombshell that exploded to the delectation of the male masses and the anguish of the female. Marlene Dietrich, whom Americans discovered in *The Blue Angel,* awakened slumbering desires in many a male breast throughout the 1930s and 1940s. And today, although a grandmother, Marlene still generates envious glances from far younger members of her sex. Born Mary Magdalene von Losch in Berlin in 1904, she teamed in her first American picture with another all-time great of the movies, Gary Cooper. She not only set the pace in the movies but also in the field of fashion, introducing in 1932 a new style for the ladies — that of wearing pants, an abbreviated (exterior) version of which became the hot fad of 1971.

The 1940s saw the luscious flowering of Hedy Lamarr, who could have enticed an automaton into the Casbah; Lana Turner, who actually was discovered in a Hollywood drug store; Paulette Goddard, who obtained her start as a Ziegfeld Girl and married Charlie Chaplin, though not for long; the "Oomph" girl, Ann Sheridan, whose toothsome figure graced posters and billboards from one end of the country to the other; Dorothy Lamour, who made the sarong more famous overnight than the natives of the Malay Archipelago had in decades; and Rita Hayworth, who caused more panting among the males than the hundred-yard dash.

There were male sex symbols, too, chiefly the swashbucklers who imitated the feats of Douglas Fairbanks, Sr., though perhaps less adeptly. These included Errol Flynn, that handsome roustabout with a flair for costume; the charming Frenchman, Charles Boyer, who went on from mere romantic parts to roles showcasing his real acting polish; Tyrone Power, who demonstrated considerable versatility by the time he reached his zenith in the late 1930s and early 1940s; and Clark Gable, whose first significant role costarred him with Norma Shearer in *A Free Soul* in 1930 and who rose to become one of the top box office attractions for men and women alike.

Some extraordinarily talented actors emerged during the two decades. Their names remain fresh for even the younger generation of today, because some of them are still making pictures. Among the more notable were Fredric March, whose early 1930s starring roles included *Dr. Jekyll and Mr. Hyde* (with Miriam Hopkins), and *A Farewell to Arms* (with Helen Hayes, Gary Cooper, and Adolphe Menjou); Paul Muni, whose first major success was in *I Am a Fugitive from a Chain Gang* and who subsequently essayed with remarkable finesse such roles as those of Émile Zola, Louis Pasteur, and Benito Juarez; Bette Davis, unsurpassed in her roles of imperious women; the polished Englishman, Leslie Howard; the versatile Henry Fonda, who brought alive John Steinbeck's *The Grapes of Wrath* and made Jesse James a human being; Barbara Stanwyck, who could be as tough as hardtack; Orson Welles, the multifaceted genius, who could do everything from acting to writing and directing; Katharine Hepburn, who converted mannerisms into a career; Gary Cooper, who became everyone's hero; the consummate actor Spencer Tracy, who went from the stage to the movies in 1930; the tough guy, Humphrey Bogart, whose movies are still favorites as television reruns; and actors of such diverse talents as Greer Garson,

Jimmy Stewart, Ingrid Bergman, Gregory Peck, Cary Grant, and John Wayne.

A delightful nostalgia emerges with the remembrance of William Powell and Myrna Loy, costarred in *The Thin Man* series and many other films; Wallace Beery and Marie Dressler; Claudette Colbert, Fred Astaire, Joan Crawford, Greta Garbo, and Dick Powell. Of course Bob Hope and Bing Crosby are still very much around, and the monsters whose roles were portrayed with such gruesome perfection by the late Boris Karloff can still chill many a warm night.

The child stars of the period and the cowboys managed to generate for today's collectors a host of objects named after them which are now sought in antiques shops, attics, and basements. Who, indeed, will *ever* forget Shirley Temple, Judy Garland, Mickey Rooney, Margaret O'Brien, or Deanna Durbin? And who is likely to forget Bill Boyd as "Hopalong Cassidy"; Roy Rogers and his horse Trigger, or Gene Autry, the singing cowboy?

Shirley Temple was everybody's darling. At the age of six, in 1934, she appeared in the astonishing total of seven motion pictures and won millions of hearts. She was truly an overnight sensation, and the most fervid desire of brides throughout the land was that they would have a baby who would become exactly like Shirley Temple.

Perhaps the next best thing to having Shirley Temple in one's home was to have a Shirley Temple doll, and such dolls began appearing in profusion in the mid-1930s. In 1935, Curtis Publishing Company was offering a 13-inch-tall Shirley Temple doll, clad in a plaid frock, in exchange for four one-year subscriptions to the *Ladies' Home Journal* or only two one-year subscriptions to *The Saturday Evening Post*. Since subscriptions to the former cost $1 a year and those to the *Post* cost $2, this placed the value of the doll at $4.

The same offer was continued through 1936, and in the fall of that year, Curtis offered the doll with a special outfit that included a party dress, print dress, coat and hat, pajamas, an extra set of underwear, and a pocketbook in exchange for four one-year subscriptions to the *Post* or seven to the *Ladies' Home Journal.*

Shirley Temple dolls of both composition and of vinyl made their appearance in stores around the country too. The composition dolls were produced by Ideal Toy Co. By 1940 there were Shirley Temple dolls with moving and sleeping eyes and wearing a celluloid button with her name on it. The name also was impressed on the back of the head. These came in sizes ranging from 13 to 27 inches tall and originally were sold in a price range of from about $4.50 to $18. In

1940, also, a Shirley Temple cowgirl doll made its appearance in a series ranging from 11 to 27 inches high and selling for around $5 to $25. This doll was clad in a plaid shirt, khaki shorts, brown stockings, high brown boots, a leather jacket, and leather chaps. The outfit was topped off with a red bandanna, a sombrero, and a pistol holster! Paper doll outfits were produced, too.

Shirley Temple dolls are now selling at $25 to $40 for the smaller sizes and $75 to $100 for the 27-inch composition.

But mementos of this lovable little tyke were by no means limited to dolls. There were Shirley Temple creamers of blue-flashed glass, now selling for $6 to $7.50; pink plastic pitchers with the star's face on one side (one was recently offered at $12); a three-piece bowl, mug, and pitcher set, which has recently brought $25; coloring books, now selling at $3.50 to $10; 4½-inch-high ceramic figures, bringing around $8; celluloid rings made in Japan in the 1930s, now valued at about $6; boxed bath sets ($5 to $6); doll carriages made of wicker and now valued at around $75 or a bit more; and a variety of books and booklets, such as *Shirley Temple's Favorite Poems, Shirley Temple's Favorite Songs,* and *Little Princess*, which have recently fetched $6 to $7 each.

There are collectors of Shirley Temple memorabilia all over the country, and typical of them is Miss Joann Janzen, of 1721 Park Place, Wichita, Kan. She has been collecting objects related to the former child movie star for years, and on her address labels the phrase "Shirley Temple Collector" even precedes her own name.

Miss Janzen has a wide variety of dolls, including paper dolls; a large collection of Shirley Temple books, including some published in foreign countries; Shirley Temple embroidery sets; pattern books with the star's photograph on the covers; cereal bowls, plates, pitchers, and mugs; crayon coloring books; bisque figures; song books; sheet music; placards and posters; and numerous other objects. In addition, Miss Janzen also collects paper dolls of other celebrities that have been published during the past four decades.

Few films have endeared themselves to the American public over a period of so many years as did *The Wizard of Oz,* a fantastically appealing 1939 movie version of L. Frank Baum's book, *The Wonderful Wizard of Oz.* Starred in the role of Dorothy was a young singer who had been christened Frances Gumm but who, when she entered film making at the age of 11, changed her name to Judy Garland. Her rendition in that picture of the song *Over the Rainbow* not only captivated those who heard it originally but still enchants those who watch the picture's television reruns.

Judy Garland had earlier teamed with Mickey Rooney in making the popular *Andy Hardy* series and other films; and she was one of the relatively few child stars who continued and expanded her singing career in maturity. Few popular singers in recent times, in fact, have encountered the acclaim that greeted her whenever and wherever she appeared, until her career and her life were tragically ended.

Soon after the production of *The Wizard of Oz,* Judy Garland dolls were placed on the market, passing immediately into the possession of thousands of small girls. Today they are selling to adult collectors at prices far above those brought originally, proving conclusively that it does not take a century or more for a collectible object to appreciate sharply in value. The dolls, made with jointed arms and legs and human hair wigs, ranged from 14 to 18 inches high and retailed at $6 to $9, clothed.

Dolls also were produced at the same time in the likeness of another child star whose career in the movies began simultaneously with Judy Garland's. Her name: Deanna Durbin. These dolls were being marketed in the early 1940s with composition bodies, jointed arms and legs, and human hair wigs. Made in heights from 15 to 21 inches, they were sold with an autographed picture of the star at $4.50 to $9. Some have recently been offered at $65.

Appearing briefly in the movies in the 1930s was a diminutive young lady with a vivacious face and an accent that did little to further her career as a speaking actress but hindered it not one whit as a champion ice skater. She was Sonja Henie, and Olympic medals attested her prowess on the ice. Dolls marketed under the trade name of Sonia were patented in 1938 by the Ideal Novelty & Toy Co., of Long Island City, N. Y. In the early 1940s dolls looking very much like Sonja Henie were being sold under the name Queen of the Ice at $6. The dolls were dressed in skating outfits with costumes available in various colors and featured movable heads, arms, and legs. They stood 18 inches tall. They are now valued at about $35.

Gene Autry, to whom fans accorded the title "King of the Cowboys," could not only pilot horses but also planes. He served for three years at the outset of World War II as a copilot of the Air Transport Command's huge transport planes in the Pacific Theater of Operations. Then, following his honorable discharge, Gene went into action entertaining troops overseas.

Autry was a star in several of the top entertainment media — the movies, radio, recordings, and the rodeo, in which he also had financial holdings. He sang in his films, and his recordings for Columbia Records became best-sellers of the day. His likeness, accompanied by that of his horse, Champion, graced the lobbies of theatres all over the country.

Autry's career flowered after he was invited to appear on Rudy Vallee's radio show in Hollywood in 1936. The name of his home, Melody Ranch, became almost as well known as that of the Presidents of the United States.

It was inevitable that Gene Autry dolls should be marketed. But Gene Autry's multitudinous fans were not content with dolls alone; a wide variety of other objects that bore the singing cowboy's name were marketed. These included wallets, which will now bring a couple of dollars or more; tin membership insignia for those joining his fan club; books; toy pistols (worth up to $55); and other things. The Gene Autry dolls are now selling for about $25, a Gene Autry Muros Swiss watch at $125.

Equally as famous as Gene Autry was "Hopalong Cassidy," a character created in a novel of that name in 1910 by Clarence E. Mulford. The masculinely handsome Bill Boyd began starring in the *Hopalong Cassidy* movie series in 1934, and by 1946 he could look back on more than three score of them. Boyd obviously knew a good thing when he saw it: He acquired the rights to the character from the author toward the end of the 1940s and was given the role in a radio series. Subsequently the National Broadcasting Co. acquired television rights.

During those years in which Hopalong's antics were witnessed and cheered by millions, literally dozens of Hopalong Cassidy objects were created and marketed. These naturally included dolls, among them a rubber one 20½ inches tall that has commanded as much as $60 on today's booming market for character objects — a fancy price indeed for a rubber toy.

Other collectible "Hoppy" items included wrist watches that will bring $20 to $60 or more; magazines now worth $2 to $2.50 a copy; lunch pails that are bringing $5 or more; jackknives currently selling at $6; advertising buttons worth about $1.50; colored pocket photo badges worth $5; cap pistols selling at a minimum of $5; an advertising breakfast milk glass, recently offered at $12.50; picture mugs; bicycles; shirts; and complete cowboy outfits.

A third extremely popular and highly durable cowboy was and is Roy Rogers, who may not be quite as inseparable from his horse

Trigger as he is from his wife, Dale Evans, and their children — but is almost so.

Rogers' entertainment career somewhat parallels that of Gene Autry. He starred in numerous western movies, made recordings, appeared on radio, and has recently been appearing as a guest star, along with Dale Evans, on television shows.

Watches bearing likenesses of and named after popular screen stars of the 1930s and 1940s, ranging from Bill Boyd to Mickey Mouse, are among today's prime collectible character objects. They bring exceptionally high prices by comparison with their original cost. Roy Rogers was no exception. An Ingraham Roy Rogers wrist watch will now bring as much as $75. Roy Rogers watches also were made by Bradley Time Corporation. A Rogers Ingraham alarm clock is worth $50 to $75.

Other Roy Rogers collectibles, with their current values include, among other things: metal deputy badges ($2.50); cameras ($6–$10); 6-inch-high copper banks in the shape of a boot ($12.50–$15); neckerchiefs ($7.50–$15), and a variety of pins and buttons at $3.50 to $5.

The Lone Ranger was produced both as motion picture serials and radio serials. The program was created by George W. Trendle on radio station WZYZ, Detroit. Lee Powell played the role in the movies and Brace Beamer originally on radio. Lone Ranger watches were made by New Haven and also by Everbrite Watch Company. In 1940, Sears, Roebuck was selling the New Haven lapel watches in a five-sided style, with black enamel case and a 30-hour movement for only $1.39. The Lone Ranger was pictured on his equally famous horse and from his lips issued, in cartoon style, the famous cry "Hi-Yo, Silver!" at the top of the dial. It came complete with an artificial leather lapel guard. The New Haven watches also came with a strap to which a leather holster, containing a miniature pistol, was attached. The holster was lettered "Lone Ranger."

The dial of an Everbrite wrist watch pictured the Lone Ranger astride his horse in color. This retailed for $2.95 in 1940 and was referred to in advertisements as the Hi-Yo, Silver! watch. These watches are now valued at as much as $60 to $85.

Again, a diversity of other Lone Ranger character objects are now being collected, and prices are on the rise. Some of these, with approximate current values, are: ceramic toothbrush holder, $35; advertising buttons, $2–$2.50; Lone Ranger Safety Club brass star-badge, $5–$6; windup toy with Lone Ranger on Silver, $10–$15; pedometer, $12.50–$25; metal toy pistol of 1938, $5–$7.50; ring in the shape of a six-shooter (radio premium), $25–$35; Lone Rangers Club of America pin, $2.50; first aid kit (1938), complete, $12.50–$15; Lone Ranger game, issued by Parker Brothers in 1938, $12.50–$20; hairbrush, $6; and books, such as *The Lone Ranger Traps the Smugglers* (1941) and *The Lone Ranger and the Mystery Ranch* (1938), sell for about $4.

In some instances the personalities themselves headed or were stockholders in companies that marketed products bearing their names or likenesses; in other cases the objects were created and marketed by commercial firms that paid a royalty to the celebrity or to the copyright holder of titles for the use of their names.

Jimmy Durante, star of stage, screen, nightclubs, radio, and television, a comedian beloved by millions, often fascinated audiences by his mispronunciation of words or the coining of words not likely to be found in any dictionary. One of these was "umbriago," and so in late 1945 the Umbriago Corporation of New York City patented Umbriago doll heads. Shortly thereafter these composition-head Umbriago finger dolls, dressed in a hat, coat and baggy trousers, were on the market. The Joseph Hagn Company (now American Interstate Corporation), wholesale distributors of Chicago, sold these 12-inch finger dolls in 1946 at $7.20 a dozen, boxed.

Although the movie career of Tom Mix dates back as far as that of William S. Hart, numerous objects bearing his name were issued during the 1930s, before he met his accidental death in 1940. Despite his background, which included service as a sheriff, Texas Ranger, and soldier of fortune, Tom Mix became a movie cowboy with a flair. The all-white costumes he donned for public appearances became a trademark, and he is reputed to have spent lavishly the fortune he earned in pictures. He was a screen idol of his day and acted all his scenes, regardless of the danger involved. In those days the names of movie cowboys' horses were as well known as those of the stars themselves, and Tony will likely be remembered as long as is Mix.

Ralston Purina Company, which sponsored a Tom Mix radio series, issued a number of premiums now being collected. These included a Straight Shooters' cloth membership patch, pins picturing Tom and Tony, books, such as *Trail of the Terrible* (1935), and a booklet, *Life of Tom Mix and the Ralston Straight Shooters' Manual*. The last-named, issued in 1933, contained a listing of Ralston's Straight Shooter premiums, and it will take about $50 to buy a copy now. Ingersoll created a Tom Mix pocket watch that originally sold for about a dollar; it is now exceedingly scarce and has been offered for sale at $600, or about the top price at which the rarest Mickey Mouse watches have sold.

Other Tom Mix collectibles include a siren ring ($30); a Straight Shooters' "genuine gold ore sample" ($10); a metal magnifying glass and compass ($25–$35); a picture pocket knife ($25); a "Valorous Medal and Ribbon Bar," 1940s (the medal glowed in the dark) ($45); various badges and pins that will bring $6 or $7; a Straight Shooters' I.D. bracelet, $25; and a Ralston premium knife, $18.50.

In addition, there were various Tom Mix toys and Tom Mix clothes; a dozen issues of a comic book offered for a box top by Ralston; a six-shooter (given for a Ralston box top); a signal arrowhead with a combination compass, magnifying glass and siren; spurs; a cat's eye ring that glowed in the dark; a rocket parachute; a pocket knife; a sheriff's badge; a flashlight; several telegraph sets; and some of the *Big Little Books* that will be discussed in the chapter entitled "What We Read."

Tom Mix himself did not appear on the Ralston-sponsored radio series, but the title role was taken by a series of actors, including Artells Dickson, Russell Thorson, Jack Holden, and "Curley" Bradley. Ralston's St. Louis advertising agency, Gardner Advertising Company, created the show for its client in 1933.

The many members of the Tom Mix Straight Shooters accepted a pledge that was somewhat similar to the Boy Scout oath except that they also promised to eat Ralston cereal regularly!

Among the most popular pictures of all times was *Gone with the Wind,* based on the best-selling novel by Margaret Mitchell, the diminutive Atlanta author, and starring Clark Gable, Vivien Leigh, Leslie Howard, and other screen notables. So what could be more appropriate than a Gone with the Wind doll? One was trademarked in 1937 by Valerie McMahan, of Washington, D. C. A search of merchandise catalogs of the period, however, has thus far failed to bring any of these dolls to light, nor have I seen any or come across advertisements for any during recent years. Madame Alexander did create a Scarlett O'Hara doll, named after the heroine of the book and movie. One of these in vinyl, 12 inches tall, has recently been advertised at $15 and a 14-inch composition doll has been offered for $25. And Scarlett-O and Rhett puffholders, originally available in 1940, are now worth much more than the original $1.50.

Other movie stars with dolls named after them include Jane Withers (a 13½-inch-tall composition doll is now valued at about

$22.50–$25); Oliver Hardy (a rubber doll whose hat lifts, $15); Margaret O'Brien; and Carmen Miranda. A 16½-inch cloth body doll named after Miss Miranda was offered for sale not long ago at the rather astonishing price of $175.

Paper dolls were also issued in the likenesses of Sonja Henie, Deanna Durbin, Claudette Colbert, Carmen Miranda, Alice Faye, and Jeannette MacDonald, among others. And of course dolls issued in the images of such animated cartoon immortals as Mickey Mouse, Donald Duck, et al., were turned out by the thousands, but these are considered in a subsequent chapter discussing Walt Disney characters.

As the 1930s began, the motion pictures were presenting both established stars of the silent film days and new talent, of which there was no shortage. There was, however, a shortage of rats in Hollywood for use in pictures — a situation that sent their prices soaring to $2 each. The shortage of cockroaches was not as severe: They were selling at only a dollar.

Films that were attracting packed houses in 1930 included: *New York Nights* with Norma Talmadge and Gilbert Roland; *Lilies of the Field,* starring the beauteous Corinne Griffith; *Untamed,* with the girl who had changed her name from Lucille LeSueur and who was to continue a long reign in pictures — Joan Crawford; Norma Shearer and Robert Montgomery in *Their Own Desire;* Janet Gaynor and Charles Farrell in *Sunny Side Up; The Marriage Playground,* with Fredric March and Mary Brian; George Arliss in *Disraeli; They Had to See Paris,* starring the inimitable Will Rogers; a musical extravaganza, *Gold Diggers of Broadway;* and Maurice Chevalier and Jeannette MacDonald in *The Love Parade.*

As the 1930s progressed, notable films were turned out almost by the carload to climax with the presentation of the Academy Award in 1939 to *Gone with the Wind.* Other outstanding motion pictures of the decade that will bring back memories to many included Ronald Colman of the incomparable voice in *A Tale of Two Cities,* based on the novel by Charles Dickens; Metro-Goldwyn-Mayer's *Anna Karenina,* which starred the great Garbo and Fredric March; *Romeo and Juliet* with Leslie Howard and Norma Shearer in the title roles, and also starring John Barrymore; the two-million-dollar *Mutiny on the Bounty* with long-to-be-remembered portrayals by Charles Laughton and Clark Gable; and Norma Shearer, Fredric March and Charles Laughton in *The Barretts of Wimpole Street.*

But those provide only a starter, and they recall only a few of the names that were emblazoned on theater marquees in those years. So many other names come to mind: Carole Lombard, Ginger Rogers, Ava Gardner, Ingrid Bergman, Joan Blondell, Ann Sothern, Robert Taylor, John Garfield, Van Johnson — and so many others who by a word or a gesture could bring laughter or tears.

In addition to the dolls and other character objects thus far discussed, there are numerous other collectibles pertaining to the films of the 1930s and 1940s, including lobby posters and placards of all sizes, many of which are now utilized to decorate rumpus rooms or dens. The prices are still low for most posters, but they are likely to rise in the coming years as the supply ebbs and demand mounts. Prices for average posters will generally range from about $1 to $10, depending upon scarcity, desirability (often based on the picture or stars advertised), size, and colors used in printing. Many lobby posters in color from the 1930s are now being offered at $1.50 each. But a 26x40-inch sheet poster depicting Melvyn Douglas and Lionel Atwill in *Vampire Bat* is valued at $10, and a 22x28-inch poster showing a closeup of Bing Crosby in *The Road to Hollywood* (his solo "Road" performance) is tagged at $7.50. Numerous Western picture posters are available at $3 to $5. Scarce horror and adventure posters will bring a few dollars more. But a 26x40 poster showing Harold Lloyd in *Movie Crazy*, produced in 1940, together with a set of eight 11x14-inch lobby cards, is priced at $27.

Souvenir programs of top movies may be sleepers today. Even *Gone with the Wind* programs rarely bring more than $3.50. However, a 23-page souvenir booklet of Warner Brothers' *Show of Shows*, produced in the late 1930s and one of the first color films, is advertised at $20.

Other things to watch for: stills (glossy prints) of the stars, particularly autographed ones; reels of animated cartoons — not only those by Disney but by others, including Max Fleischer; replicas of animated cartoon characters made in a wide variety of materials (see the chapter on Walt Disney creations); and scrapbooks containing clippings of pictures and stories relating to the movies.

The character of motion pictures has changed since the impact of television began about 1949, and the picture houses themselves are undergoing sharp changes. The small screens gave way to the huge screens, and now the miniature screens are making their advent as are the pocket theatres, and the so-called "art" theatres and adult movie houses. Movie stars are turning to television, and new stars that no one had heard of a week ago are emerging today.

But even with the emergence of these bright new stars and the changing character of the medium, the memories of those who were old enough to attend the movies in the 1930s and 1940s will long retain the impression made by such extraordinarily popular pictures as *King Kong,* produced in 1933 and starring the beautiful Fay Wray, Robert Armstrong and Bruce Cabot. Nearly three decades after its first appearance on the screen, *King Kong* is still a favorite of the television reruns.

And even today there are imitations of Warner Oland in the title role of the extremely popular *Charlie Chan* series. After Oland's death, the title role was given to Sidney Toler. Charlie's "Number One" son was played by a star quite popular today, Keye Luke. (Oland, who was of Scandinavian descent, will also be recalled for his starring role as Dr. Fu Manchu.)

Nor is Charlie Chaplin neglected by the current crop of mimics. His last popular film, *The Great Dictator,* starring Chaplin as Hitler and comedian Jack Oakie as Mussolini, proved that even in times of national emergency we can maintain our sense of balance and of humor.

Numerous actors who first appeared on the stage or in the movies rose to greater heights via radio and television, and some of these will be discussed in the pages that follow.

And, although we are devoting a separate chapter to Walt Disney, the other pioneer animated cartoon geniuses should not be neglected. Notable among these was Max Fleischer, among whose productions was *Betty Boop.* This vivacious young lady subsequently was molded into a television star. A popular novelty is a Betty Boop doll. These were made in composition, wood, and of plaster-of-paris and will now bring $10 to $20 each. Many collectors, however, are not aware that a Betty Boop watch also was made. Manufactured by Ingraham as a stem-wind pocket-type watch, the dial featured an illustration of Betty in color with animated arms that pointed to the time. This watch was sold exclusively by Montgomery Ward in 1934 at a cost of only 98 cents. The asking price of one of these now (they are scarce) is $300! And the jointed wooden Betty Boop doll will bring $50. Another novelty was a Betty Boop Ukelele, featuring the Fleischer characters Betty, Bimbo, and Koko. Made in 1935 and also sold for 98 cents, this is now valued at $30 to $35. A Betty Boop windup toy will bring about $50.

Before leaving the movies, you may want to know that there are W.C. Fields souvenir iced tea spoons available at about $6.50. And regardless of whether Mickey Rooney ever undertook painting or not, *His Own Paint Book* now brings $3. It dates from about 1940.

We have come a long way in entertainment via the airwaves since Dr. Lee De Forest made the first modern broadcast of a human voice by radio in 1907. And the strides made since pioneer station KDKA went on the air with regular broadcasts in Pittsburgh in 1921 have revolutionized the industry.

It was the daytime serial that made the first tremendous impact upon radio audiences and, consequently, upon radio advertisers. In the 1930s and 1940s there were no other programs that could sell merchandise with the effectiveness of the serials. The majority of the daily episodes of serials in those years were 15 minutes long; and many stations carried as many as twenty 15-minute segments daily.

Those serials were the source of scores of collectible objects today — items lumped together as radio premiums. Sponsors of the serials offered articles ranging from pocket knives to radio decoders, from flashlights to secret compartment rings. Listeners received these premiums for sending in boxtops or wrappers from the merchandise the sponsors vended. The premiums were designed for the small fry on the absolutely correct theory that they would use their persuasive powers to induce their parents to buy the merchandise needed as the source of the boxtops or wrappers. How successful the theory was is evidenced by the fact that the radio serials continued as the top sellers of goods throughout the 1940s.

Adventure, mystery, and horror serials were interspersed with the tearjerkers we know affectionately as soap operas. Many of the old-time radio listeners today will recall such programs as *Lorenzo Jones, Stella Dallas, Romance of Helen Trent, Alias Jimmy Valentine, Second Husband, John's Other Wife, Betty and Bob, Just Plain Bill* and *David Harum.* All of these, and a good many more, were produced under the aegis of the advertising agency that became the major buyer of air time by late in 1939 — Blacker, Sample & Hummert, Inc.

But other agencies were producing similar shows and also investing heavily in radio time. In 1929, two comedians known previously as "Sam 'n' Henry" changed their names to "Amos 'n' Andy" on a show broadcast over WMAQ in Chicago. They were Freeman Gosden and Charles Correll. That their debut in their new show was a success is reflected by the fact that Pepsodent promptly bought it to sell toothpaste and it was broadcast via the National Broadcasting Company network, of which Niles Trammel, who had been reared in Marietta, Ga., was then president. *Amos 'n' Andy* became one of the most successful radio shows of all time and enjoyed one of the longest continuous runs in history.

The show was so popular that numerous articles, primarily toys or items in the category of trivia, were created and named after the show's principals. Such trivial things as a chalk ashtray originally sold many years ago will now bring $15 on the collectors' market. A windup Fresh Air taxicab commands $37.50 or more.

One of the big-time sellers of merchandise was Little Orphan Annie, created originally by Harold Gray, an Illinois cartoonist, as a comic strip. (The name may have come from a poem written by James Whitcomb Riley in 1885 under the title *Little Orphant Annie.*) This appealing little tyke, with her dog Sandy, experienced many harrowing adventures over many years while her Daddy Warbucks was away on all sorts of missions. The *Little Orphan Annie* radio program appealed to old and young alike, but especially to the Wander Co. (now Sandoz-Wander, Inc.), Chicago manufacturers (under a Swiss license) of Ovaltine, which sponsored the show.

In 1931, Ovaltine was advertising a variety of mugs intended for use in drinking that concoction, and featuring illustrations in color of such characters as Uncle Wiggily and Grandpa Goosey-Gander. The mugs were made of Sebring pottery and were offered, together with a three-day-trial package of Ovaltine, for 25 cents. Before long, the company began offering mugs with a likeness of Orphan Annie and Sandy. By 1934, the company was offering to Ovaltine users a free "Shake-up" mug to shake up cold Ovaltine as a summer drink, provided they sent in an aluminum seal found under the lids of Ovaltine cans. These mugs depicted Orphan Annie carrying on a conversation with Sandy about the merits of the drink and beginning with the exclamation she so frequently used, "Leapin' Lizards!" In turn, Sandy was shown uttering his favorite (and only) word, "Arf."

The illustrations and sayings on the mugs were changed annually, except that Sandy's reply was constantly "Arf," and the company began asking not only the foil seal but 10 cents for handling and postage. In addition, mugs made from Beetleware — an artificial china-like material — for serving hot Ovaltine were offered, and the Annie and Sandy poses on these, too, were changed with the years. These foil-plus-10-cents mugs are now bringing $7 to $15 each.

Numerous Orphan Annie items appeared in rapid succession. The current choice item is the New Haven nonjewel wrist watch with its 30-hour movement, chromium case, and leather strap. In 1934, the Joseph Hagn Company was offering an Orphan Annie watch for $2.65, and in 1939 they were selling for only $2.98. It's now worth about $135.

An Orphan Annie miniature electric stove that actually operated was among the other choice objects produced and named after the touslehaired waif. This will bring around $25 today. Other collectible Orphan Annie items of the 1930s and 1940s, together with their approximate values, include: the Ovaltine radio decoders issued in 1935 through 1939, $20–$25; radio identification bracelet, $8.50; china sugar bowl, $9–$10; ceramic salt and pepper set, $15; Secret Society badge, $20–$25; Annie and Sandy hanging vase, $17.50–$20; brass decoder badge, $10–$20; a black-and-yellow Sandy windup toy, $55; and a ceramic tea set, $20.

The scripts for the radio shows in the 1930s were written by Ovaltine's Chicago advertising agency. In 1940, Ovaltine took on the sponsorship of the *Captain Midnight* show, and *Little Orphan Annie* found a new sponsor — Quaker Puffed Wheat Sparkies. Among the Quaker Orphan Annie premiums was a pair of fabulous pilot's wings with a pilot light and a cockpit.

Charlie McCarthy, for all his wisecracking, proved to be a lucrative offspring for the ventriloquist Edgar Bergen, since the pair (and subsequently another offspring, Mortimer Snerd), elicited ovations wherever they appeared — on radio, in the movies, in nightclubs, and, finally, on television. Several Charlie McCarthy collectible objects are around today. Silverplated souvenir teaspoons appeared in 1939 and will currently bring $3.75 to $5. A 1938 Charlie McCarthy radio game called "Topper" has recently been advertised at $25 and a 31-inch-tall dressed dummy at $20. Composition figures of this high-hatted little man are now worth $15 to $20, and a 1939 Mortimer Snerd tin windup toy has an asking price of $15 nowadays. The choicest item, however, is the Charlie McCarthy one-day alarm clock with a likeness of Charlie's face enameled in colors across the dial. The case was made of die-cast metal, and the clock sold in 1940 for $2.50. It is likely to bring closer to $150 today. (There was also a somewhat cheaper model in 1940 being sold at just $1.86.) Charlie McCarthy, Inc., New York City, obtained a trademark for a Charlie McCarthy doll in August, 1937, and in the following year one for a Mortimer Snerd doll was granted to Edgar J. Bergen of Hollywood. The dolls will sell now from about $27.50 to $40; and Charlie McCarthy hand puppets will bring $20 to $40. A Mortimer Snerd puppet with a composition head and movable hands and feet is now selling at approximately $25. A Marx toy windup car with Charlie brings $35 to $85.

As was the case with so many characters that began as comic strips or comic books, *Superman* also wound up as a radio serial. *Superman* was created by Jerome Siegel and Joe Schuster and first saw the light of publication in the magazine *Action Comics* in 1938. Hundreds of thousands of readers and spectators through the years have watched the newspaper reporter Clark Kent change swiftly into his Superman raiment and perform feats of sheer incredibility.

So popular was the radio series, which began in 1945, that throngs of youngsters joined the Supermen Club of America and wore pins to attest their distinction. Naturally these are collectible, and, although originally offered as a radio premium, are fetching up to $20 each, in celluloid yet! *Superman* was a major hit in the comic books, which will be discussed in the chapter dealing with reading habits of the two decades. The original radio Superman was Bud Collyer, the well-known radio and television personality.

The first of the comic strips to introduce violence was *Dick Tracy,* created by Chester Gould in the *Chicago Tribune* in 1931. This beak-nosed detective who, by luck or pluck, pursued more criminals and villains through the years to prison or grave than has the FBI, reached such heights of popularity that he graduated to the movies (Republic Pictures, 1937), and to radio, and also the comic book. Matt Crowley played the role on radio.

There are dozens of Dick Tracy collectibles now, most of them in the gadget category. Naturally there is a Dick Tracy wrist watch, and it was first offered commercially around 1934 at $2.65. The New Haven Watch Co. was still producing them with a colored dial and a chromium-finished case in the 1940s with a suggested retail price of $2.95. The earlier models are now worth around $125 to $150 and the later ones only slightly less. A Marx toy, Dick Tracy Official Squad Car, friction-operated, is now selling at about $20.

Other Dick Tracy gadgets have climbed to rather formidable price heights, and among them are: metal siren pistol made in the 1940s, $45; Secret Service flashlight, also a product of the 1940s, $20; Secret Service badge, $5 (though it has been offered as high as $25); membership pin in the Secret Service Patrol (1930s), $10–$12; Dick Tracy Detective pin, $4–$15; Dick Tracy Crimestopper, featuring a pocket knife and a fold-out clue detector and whistle, $15–$25; and police radio, as much as $25. Also produced were Dick Tracy secret compartment rings, Crimestoppers suspender clasps and belt set with a red enameled buckle in the shape of a detective star, lettered "Courteous-Alert-Efficient-Dick Tracy Detective Agency" (1934). The belt was of cowhide and sold for less than a dollar.

Once again we overlap fields with *Captain Midnight,* one of the favorite fictional characters bearing the title "Captain." This indomitable hero, created by Robert M. Burtt and Willfred G. Moore, appeared both as a comic book and a radio "personality," and you will encounter him again in the chapter dealing with comic strips and books.

Various gadgets associated with *Captain Midnight* appeared in the early 1940s. Ovaltine, which had done so handsomely with its Orphan Annie mugs, came out with a Beetleware Captain Midnight mug, whose current value is in the neighborhood of $15. A two-piece shake-up mug issued in 1947, is valued at about $25. A 1941 radio premium metal decoder has had an asking price as high as $55, and a 1945 decoder, $25. Other Captain Midnight collectibles include: a secret compartment ring, for which as much as $40 has been asked; a membership medal in the 1940 Flight Patrol, $15; and a secret coin, $13–$15. Coveted collectibles are the Code-o-Graph devices issued annually.

Skippy, originally created as a comic strip by the versatile Percy Crosby, who also authored such books as *Skippy* (1925), *Skippy: A Novel* (1929), *Skippy Rambles* (1932), and *Always Belittlin'* (1933), was another graduate to radio in the 1930s. The *Skippy* program led to the creation of what has been characterized as the first "great" secret society concocted via radio. One of this society's SSSS membership pins, made of celluloid, will now cost you about $15.

Jack Armstrong, the All-American Boy graduated from radio to movie serials, the latter produced by Columbia Pictures. The radio premiums stem from the 1930s and early 1940s and include a Sky Ranger plane — with a cardboard fuselage and aluminum wings and tail — that is now worth about $35, and a flashlight, for which as much as $30 to $40 has been asked. However, in the opinion of many collectors of radio premiums, the plane should be of greater value than the flashlight. There is also a pedometer, worth $15. This radio show was sponsored by Wheaties.

Buck Rogers was another character of great versatility — comic strips, comic books, radio, and the movies. The movie, made in 1939, starred the rugged Buster Crabbe. The comic books featuring him will be discussed later, but there is a great variety of Buck Rogers trivia around for the collector, and some of these, which looked ahead to an era beyond the time of their creation, are highly valued. For examples, the 1934 12-inch-long Rocket Ship, a windup toy, has a price tag in some dealers' shops reading $75 to $95. The same price has been asked for a 1937 set of Monorail Space Ships in the original boxes, and a single one of the Space Ships can bring more than one-third of that figure. The Buck Rogers Helium Water Pistol's price now ranges from $50 to $75, and the Atomic Pistol has about the same value. A Buck Rogers 25th Century button will easily fetch $10 and the Solar Scout Badge has recently been priced as high as $40 by at least one dealer. A Ray Gun is priced at $25. Mind you, we are not certain whether there have been takers at some of the maximum prices asked, but, if not, there undoubtedly will be. The first sponsor of the radio show was Kellogg's Rice Krispies. Cocomalt sponsored it later.

Other radio serials that must be accorded brief mention include the following:

The Shadow also appeared as a newspaper strip and was later made into a motion picture by Columbia Pictures, starring Victor Jory (1940). At one time Orson Welles played the radio role of The Shadow, otherwise known as Lamont Cranston. Premiums stemmed from this show too.

Crime Busters, a series created by Phillips H. Lord, who, incidentally, also played the title role in radio's *Seth Parker* programs. Hickok, Inc., manufactured Crime Busters belts. Also produced as a result of this show were such items as toy automobiles, toy machine guns, neckties, playsuits and sweatshirts, and, of course, a comic book. Royalties on the sale of all such objects accrued to the show's creator.

The *Frank Buck* show starred the noted big game trapper and motion picture producer who wrote (with Edward Anthony) *Bring 'Em Back Alive* and other books, all with co-authors. A Good Luck Coin from his radio show of the early 1930s is valued at $25–$30, and it isn't even legal tender.

Howie Wing was produced in the 1930s. Five or six dollars will get you a metal Howie Wing Cadet membership pin.

A celluloid membership pin from the *Pretty Kitty Kelly* radio show originally offered as a premium will bring $5 to $8.

A Good Luck coin from the *Red Ryder* show of the 1940s is valued at around $10.

Can you remember *Howdy Doody* in the episode entitled *The*

Magical Forest? In Howdy's image a puppet was created and his likeness and name appeared on souvenir spoons of plated silver and children's plastic sun glasses.

Flash Gordon, created by Alex Raymond in the 1930s, was a feature of the comic pages, the comic books, and radio. A space compass bearing the name of this intrepid adventurer is now valued at $20, and a 1948 phonograph record with Flash illustrated on its face has risen in value to $20. A two-way telephone also lies in wait for those lucky enough to encounter it tucked away somewhere in basement or attic ($18).

Terry and the Pirates, originally created by Milton Caniff in 1934 and made into a movie by Columbia Pictures in 1940, also appeared as a radio series. A record pressed in 1948 with a Terry illustration on the label is now valued at about $20. More about Terry in the chapter on comic strips and books.

Sky King premiums included a Signascope, a device with a band that glowed in the dark for sending signals at night, a mirror that could be used to flash signals in the daytime, and a secret code; a ring with a band of plastic that glowed at night; and a combination magnifying glass and whistle, housed in a secret compartment, could be used for signaling.

Several *Tom Corbett, Space Cadet* premiums have been offered.

And, although they apparently offered no premiums, two extremely popular series should also be mentioned. One was *Gangbusters,* created in 1935 by Phillips H. Lord, originally based upon FBI files and later on police files. This was a noisy and violent show with a wide following. Mr. Lord also created the series *Mr. District Attorney* (1939). The other popular series was *The Thin Man,* starring Les Damon and Claudia Morgan as the radio Nick and Nora Charles (William Powell and Myrna Loy played those roles in the movie versions).

There were so many other situation and comedy radio programs of the period that it is impossible to list them all here. One of the more durable was *The Goldbergs,* which starred Gertrude Berg and originated about 1930. The big nighttime stars were Jack Benny, born Benjamin Kubelsky, who began his radio career in 1932 and rapidly became Public Entertainer No. 1; Fred Allen, born John F. Sullivan, noted for his quick wit and his "feud" with Jack Benny; Bob Hope, who, his fans trust, will go on forever; and Eddie Cantor, one of several stars who introduced much new talent on their shows.

And who remembers those days who does not also recall Joe Penner, the onetime burlesque comic who made the bigtime in radio and made famous the lines "Wanna buy a duck?" and "Oh, you na-a-asty man!", *Lum and Abner* (Norris Goff and Chester Lauch); *The Great Gildersleeve* (originally Hal Peary) and the show on which he started, *Fibber McGee and Molly* (Marian and Jim Jordan); *Myrt and Marge* (Mrs. Myrtle Vail Damerel and Mrs. Peter Fick); George Burns and Gracie Allen, who subsequently went into television; *Easy Aces,* with Goodman and Jane Ace; the *Sinclair Minstrels; Blondie; Nick Carter; Inner Sanctum;* and *Stoopnagle and Budd?*

Radio newscasters of those days included several who will be long remembered, among them Boake Carter, Gabriel Heatter, H. V. Kaltenborn, Edward R. Murrow, Lowell Thomas, Bob Trout, Walter Winchell, and the sportscasters Graham McNamee, Bill Stern, Bill Munday, and Ted Husing.

The *Major Bowes Amateur Hour* of the 1930s, first sponsored on the networks by Chase and Sanborn coffee and later by Chrysler Corp., made famous the line uttered on each show by the Major himself, "Around and around she goes, and where she stops, nobody knows."

Most durable of the vocalists was Kate Smith, who made *When The Moon Comes Over the Mountain* better known than the National Anthem and whose greeting "Hello, Everybody!" still brings television audiences to smart attention.

Some of the noted pioneer radio announcers are still around, too, among them Ben Grauer of NBC, who served as announcer for Walter Winchell and who has been doing the New York Times Square New Year's Eve broadcast for the Johnny Carson television show for the past several years; and Milton J. Cross, who announced most of the classical music shows and is still heard on the Metropolitan Opera radio broadcasts on Saturday afternoons.

Many oldtimers will recall the popular musical programs of the thirties — the *Philco Hour,* Wayne King's Orchestra, Walter Damrosch's G.E. Orchestra, Guy Lombardo and His Royal Canadians, Ted Weems's Orchestra, the *Voice of Firestone*, Phil Spitalny's Orchestra, and Ben Bernie, remembered for his opening lines: "Yowsah, yowsah, yowsah, ladies and gentlemen . . . It's a lonesome old town. . . . This is Ben Bernie and all the lads." Bernie, incidentally, carried on a popular "feud" with Walter Winchell, paralleling the Benny–Allen feud.

And there were Phil Baker, Arthur Godfrey, Olsen and Johnson,

Ma Perkins, Vic and Sade, Pepper Young's Family . . . these and so many more.

And Orson Welles. . . .

No one who heard his broadcast *The War of the Worlds* on the night of October 30, 1938, is ever likely to forget it. Based on the novel by H. G. Wells, the broadcast originated as a *Mercury Theater on the Air* program over the Columbia Broadcasting System network, and featured Welles describing in that sonorous and perfectly marvelous voice an invasion of the world by enemy forces from Mars. Somehow the broadcast became incredibly credible, and a large part of the Eastern seaboard was thrown into panic. It was a dramatization that was all too realistic. As a newspaper reporter in those days, I well remember the panic in the city in which I was working. One family residing a few houses down the street from me jumped into their car and fled. Fled? Where to? They simply drove, and finally they realized the nightmare wasn't real, and they returned home, weary, chagrined, and passionately furious.

One newspaper quoted Welles the following day as saying he didn't know what he was doing, and CBS made a public apology. But *The War of the Worlds* will unquestionably remain longer in the minds of those who heard it than any other program — and it made Welles famous.

The original show, incidentally, is now available both on tape and as a two-record phonograph album. Numerous other original shows of the 1930s and 1940s also are available on tape at prices ranging from about $7 to $15 a reel. They include many that we have mentioned in this survey.

Chuck Schaden, executive editor of the Chicago northwest side Press Newspaper Group, has a regular Saturday afternoon show on Radio Station WLTD, Evanston, reminiscing about the "golden age" of radio and broadcasting rare old shows. The three-hour-long program is entitled *Those Were the Days* and has a host of listeners. He also has a tape collection of more than 3,000 individual radio programs dating from 1930. He has interviewed many early radio stars on his show. Schaden operates a business called The Hall Closet, which swaps old-time radio tapes with other collectors or will tape shows for collectors at a small cost. His business address is Trio Enterprises, Inc., 4941 North Milwaukee, Chicago.

The legitimate theater in the 1930s was afflicted by the same malady that had struck the populace in general — a lack of money. The number of theatergoers dwindled because the price of admission was more urgently needed for bread and butter, and most of the "angels" had flown off to hiding places until the ill winds could blow over. Besides, the price of admission to the movies was much cheaper.

Nevertheless, there evolved during the thirties some noble experiments, among which was the Federal Theater program — a project stemming out of the Works Progress Administration. One of its major objectives was to provide employment for theatrical workers by producing plays whose admission charges were small. The program lasted for about four years but, as was the case with so many New Deal programs, was lambasted within and outside Congress until funds for it were finally stopped in 1939.

Another development of the thirties was the Group Theatre, founded by Harold Clurman, Cheryl Crawford and Lee Strasberg. The Group attracted many distinguished actors and playwrights, and one of its notable achievements lay in introducing to the public the work of Clifford Odets, a Philadelphian, four of whose plays were presented during the single year 1935. They were *Awake and Sing, Till the Day I Die, Paradise Lost,* and *Waiting for Lefty.* Odets went on to further successes later in the decade.

Elmer Rice's *Street Scene* won the Pulitzer Prize in 1929 and Marc Connelly's long-to-be-remembered *The Green Pastures* in 1930. The latter was based on Roark Bradford's best-seller *Ol' Man Adam and His Chillun,* featured an all-Negro cast, and ran for five years. Other Pulitzer Prize-winners during the thirties were: *Alison's House,* by Susan Glaspell, 1931; the fabulous musical, *Of Thee I Sing,* by George S. Kaufman, Morrie Ryskind, and Ira Gershwin, 1932; *Both Your Houses,* by Maxwell Anderson, 1933; *Men in White,* by Sidney Kingsley, 1934; *The Old Maid,* by Zoe Akins, 1935; *Idiot's Delight,* by Robert E. Sherwood, 1936; *You Can't Take It With You,* by George S. Kaufman and Moss Hart, 1937; *Our Town,* by Thornton Wilder, 1938; *Abe Lincoln in Illinois,* also by Robert E. Sherwood, 1939, and in 1940 the award went to the rising William Saroyan for his *The Time of Your Life.*

These were not the only outstanding or delightful or amusing plays of the period. Eugene O'Neill's *Ah, Wilderness* was a distinguished comedy of 1933, following by two years his tragic play *Mourning Becomes Electra.* Lillian Hellman's best-remembered play was *The Children's Hour,* produced in 1934, although the same playwright's *The Little Foxes* (1939) also made a major impact on theatergoers.

The adaptation of Clarence Day's best-selling *Life with Father* by Russel Crouse and Howard Lindsay first appeared on the stage in 1939, and some critics thought it might run forever. It almost did. The historical dramas of Maxwell Anderson, additional contributions from the highly successful team of Kaufman and Hart, as well as those from Robert E. Sherwood, and a delightful comedy, *The Male Animal,* by James Thurber and Elliott Nugent, added to the brightness of the theater during the decade.

Musical comedies began coming of age in the thirties, notably with the presentation of *Porgy and Bess* in 1935, based on the original novel by DuBose Heyward, with music by the incomparable George Gershwin. Other highly-successful musicals were created by the team of Richard Rodgers and Lorenz Hart, by Cole Porter, and others. This type of production was climaxed with the presentation of Rodgers and Hammerstein's *Oklahoma!* in 1943.

A number of promising newcomers appeared on the stage during the 1930s, many of whom went on to much greater achievements later. Some of them subsequently found more rewarding movie careers. They included Bob Hope, Katharine Hepburn, Fred MacMurray, Henry Fonda, George Murphy, Ethel Merman, John Garfield, Jimmy Stewart, José Ferrer, Margaret Sullavan, Montgomery Clift, Orson Welles, Imogene Coca, Mary Martin, Joseph Cotten, and many others. And there were yeoman performances by those who already had become stalwarts of the stage, such as Helen Hayes, Eva LeGallienne, Leslie Howard, Gertrude Lawrence, Alfred Lunt and Lynn Fontanne, Dame Judith Anderson, Josephine Hull, Katharine Cornell, Jane Cowl, George M. Cohan, and Tallulah Bankhead.

The primary collectibles from the theater of the two decades include autographed photos of the stars, programs, lobby posters and placards, and, when they are occasionally offered for sale, typescripts of the plays or original scores. Some collectors amass admission tickets and clippings of reviews.

Vaudeville had seen its best days on the stage and moved over to radio and, later, television. Burlesque thrived for a while but eventually was driven off the stage in many areas, especially New York City, by those who termed it indecent.

For many there was not much to sing about in the early thirties; nevertheless music burst out all over. The symphony remained popular and was brought, via radio, into hundreds of thousands of homes whose occupants otherwise might never have heard the brilliant sound of talented musicians playing under the direction of distinguished conductors. Dancing was an extremely popular pastime, and dance bands were in their heyday throughout the 1930s and 1940s. But the big development was "swing." Its greatest exponent was Benny Goodman, crowned by an adulating public as undisputed "King of Swing." Swing was dance music, and more. It was hot jazz, and more. From it evolved the jitterbug, whose ranks increased as the years wore on. From it, too, evolved the nondancing dancer — the individual who came to dance but remained merely to listen. Swing's addicts, aside from the musicians themselves, were the jitterbugs and the teenage girls who blossomed out as the bobbysoxers. Under the influence of swing, the small bands grew larger, and other names in addition to Goodman became bywords among the younger set — Duke Ellington, Fletcher Henderson, Cab Calloway, Jimmy and Tommy Dorsey, Hal Kemp, Glen Gray and the Casa Loma Band, Count Basie, Bob Crosby, Artie Shaw, Gene Krupa, and Louis Armstrong. All of them didn't play swing all the time, but swing was the thing. Traditional jazz took a back seat, at least temporarily.

Other bands popular during the period included those of Kay Kyser, Guy Lombardo, Sammy Kaye, Fred Waring, Ben Bernie, Horace Heidt, Wayne King, Ted Weems, Paul Whiteman, Bennie Moten, Jack Teagarden, Xavier Cugat, Glenn Miller, Ozzie Nelson, Rudy Vallee, Larry Clinton, Phil Spitalny, Ted Lewis, and Eddie Duchin.

New dances emerged, too, such as the Big Apple, the Shag, and the Lindy Hop.

In addition to the thousands who heard these and other bands on radio, more thousands listened to them on the juke box, which began its career at a nickel a record — but the price has subsequently kept pace with that of shoes and bacon. The juke box became one of our national institutions, and today the early ones — along with the early slot gambling devices and a miscellany of other vending contrivances — are being sought by a growing band of collectors, and at increasing prices.

There were a host of popular singers of the day, some of whom we have already mentioned. Rudy Vallee set the pace, won admiration and a fortune, and went on to Hollywood to establish a radio program on which much new talent was first introduced. He also appeared in a few movies.

Incidentally, when Vallee had a show emanating from the Hollywood Cabaret Restaurant in New York City, wooden clappers lettered "Rudy Vallee and the World's Most Amazing Floor Show" were distributed to members of the audience. It goes without saying that these are collectible.

A young singer who set out on his own in 1929 and was a smash hit by 1931 was one of the most durable of all crooners. He was the "Old Groaner," Bing Crosby. Bing made musical history with his renditions of *I Surrender, Dear, Sunday, Monday and Always,* and, later, *White Christmas.* He embarked upon motion pictures and before the mid-1940s was the top box office attraction. He also was among the top runners in radio. Crosby won an Oscar for his role as Father O'Malley in the film *Going My Way,* and he costarred with Bob Hope in trivial but nevertheless delightful comedies on the screen.

Major Edward Bowes's radio *Amateur Hour* gave Frank Sinatra his break. After his appearance on the show, he was given a contract for a tour with "The Hoboken Four." In 1939, Sinatra joined the band of Harry James, then changed to Tommy Dorsey's orchestra and also began making records. He set out on his own in 1942 and was among the first of the crooners to cause riots among the bobbysoxers. Sinatra starred on the *Lucky Strike Hit Parade* on CBS.

Some fabulous songs appeared in the 1930s and 1940s, and some zany ones, too. A phenomenon among the latter was *Mairzy Doats,* created in 1942 by Jerry Livingston, Milton Drake, and Al Hoffman and published a couple of years thereafter by Robbins Music Corporation. It immediately became a top hit, and the meaning of the lyrics may still remain obscured for a few who just didn't keep pace with the times.

Sad songs were tied to events of the day. Among these were *Lindy Junior,* which stemmed from the kidnaping of the Lindbergh baby and appeared as sheet music in 1932 from Paradise Song Studios with a picture of the baby on the cover. Its value as a collector's item is now $15. In the same category was one called *Hauptmann Paid with His Life Today,* published in 1936 by Mrs. Ima Ruth Board of Texas. When a copy can be found, it's now valued at $35.

Many popular song hits of those days derived from Broadway musicals or motion pictures for which they were originally written by such talented folk as the Gershwin brothers, Rodgers and Hart, Cole Porter, Irving Berlin, and Jerome Kern.

Among the Gershwin brothers' popular hits were *I Got Rhythm, Embraceable You,* and *I Got Plenty of Nuttin'.* The team of Rodgers and Hart contributed a slew of songs that at one time were on almost everyone's lips. They included *Love Me Tonight. There's a Small*

Hotel, and *The Lady Is a Tramp.* From Irving Berlin came *Isn't It a Lovely Day?* and Cole Porter turned out such hits as *Night and Day, I Get a Kick Out of You, Begin the Beguine,* and *I've Got You Under My Skin.*

I Found a Million Dollar Baby, by Billy Rose was a major musical outcropping in 1931 and continued popular for years. So was *Life Is Just a Bowl of Cherries,* first heard in the *Scandals* show produced by George White. *Smoke Gets in Your Eyes* came from the musical *Roberta* and was composed by Jerome Kern, who also turned out *All the Things You Are* from the musical *Very Warm for May.*

Wacky songs flourished. Among those best remembered today, in addition to *Mairzy Doats,* are *The Music Goes Round and Round, A Tisket, a Tasket, Flat Foot Floogie, Three Little Fishes,* and *Dipsy Doodle.*

And who, once having heard them, will forget *Three Little Words, Bye, Bye Blues, Night and Day, Goodnight, Sweetheart, Did You Ever See a Dream Walking?, Lazybones, Pennies from Heaven, Goody! Goody!, Rosalie, Cocktails for Two, Paris in the Spring, You're an Old Smoothie, Red Sails in the Sunset, Thanks for the Memory, I'm an Old Cowhand, That Old Feeling,* and *I'll Never Smile Again?*

There were dozens of others, many of which still crop up on radio and television these days.

Although the production of sheet music was diminishing rapidly by the 1930s, many pieces with photographic covers of the singers are being collected, even though their values at present are small, ranging generally from a half dollar to about $2.

Phonograph records of the early 1930s, along with those of preceding decades, are attracting some collectors, and desirable ones will bring from a dollar to $2 or $3, some quite scarce ones a bit more. Many records, however, are still available at less than a dollar. Conceivably, some of these could prove a good investment now, since they are likely to be more avidly collected in the years ahead.

The traveling circus is fading from the scene today, but some of the big shows were still around in the thirties. Some truly fascinating relics and mementos of the early circus are preserved in the Circus Hall of Fame, founded in Sarasota, Fla. Among these are some traveling equipment, including the largest bandwagon ever constructed — the Two Hemispheres Band Chariot made for Barnum & Bailey in 1902 at a cost of $40,000, which was considerable for those days. The Ringling brothers bought Barnum & Bailey's

Greatest Show on Earth in 1907. When the last of the brothers, John died in 1936, seven of the Ringling circuses were still in operation.

Among the most collectible circus items from the 1930s and early 1940s are lithographed posters, and choice ones are worth $40 to $50, although smaller ones of lesser interest can still be found for $10 or so. Circus handbills are worth several dollars each, and other paper collectibles relating to the circus include route cards and full-page newspaper advertisements.

Of course many tangible objects relating to the circus are of value. Among them are all types of rolling stock, circus props, carved figureheads from wagons (which are in a class similar to those of ship figureheads), autographed photographs of performers, and toy circus replicas, particularly those produced by the firm founded by A. Schoenhut.

Calliopes with automatic note keyboards in operating condition will bring $2,000 or more. Circus collectors also are interested in replicas in miniature of circus bands, animals, performers, and so on, a good many of which were created some years ago by Colonel Freddie Daw, founder of the Circus Hobby Hall, Coral Gables, Fla. There is also a Circus Fans Association of America.

Those interested in circus rolling stock will find a most informative chapter on the builders and carvers of circus wagons in Frederick Fried's thoroughly-researched book, *Artists in Wood* (New York: Clarkson N. Potter, Inc./Publisher, 1970).

Despite the fact that entertainment, including music, by way of radio had diverted many from the phonograph, the latter instruments were still turned out in profusion in the early 1930s, and recordings continued to multiply like taxes.

Ornate console phonographs were available at under $100, some for less than $50. The American Wholesale Corp. Division of Butler Brothers of Baltimore offered a 1930 console Mastercraft phonograph with walnut chassis at just $32 wholesale, and a much larger model with a two-spring motor for $50.

Montgomery Ward in 1931 advertised portable Melophonic phonographs at only $8.95 to $22.95 for a two-spring motor affair with a fabricoid covering and copper trim. The following year, Sears featured a $5.98 portable model and a console at $25. Ward offered 1934 portables at just $6.75 and $9.95.

But electric record players and combination radio-phonographs were rapidly supplanting the bulkier console model phonos. In the late 1930s, Wholesale Radio Service Co. had electric players to play records through any radio without connections for $11.95 and $14.75.

By 1940, one was hard-pressed to find a console phonograph alone anywhere, but the combinations had a blossoming beauty.

At the outset of the 1930s 78-rpm records were being made by carloads and were usually divided into such categories as popular dance music, classical, popular songs, instrumental selections, old favorites, comedy songs and talks, sacred songs, hill country music and mountain ballads, and Negro spirituals. Those produced by the older established companies were predominant; the proliferation of record-pressers had not begun.

In addition to recordings by the well-known orchestras, bands, and noted vocalists of the day, at the outset of the thirties, one encountered recordings by "Singin' Sam," Chick Bullock, Chubby Parker, the Cumberland Ridge Runners, the "Arkansas Woodchopper," "Tom and Don," Hank Keene, Bradley Kincaid, and the Pickard Family. How many of you recall any of those names?

In 1933, a very young and a very small fellow recorded *Billy Richardson's Last Ride* and *Berry Picking Time* to the accompaniment of a guitar. His name should be more familiar: It was George Gobel.

Among the more popular recording stars whose names also will strike a chord with many readers were Ruth Etting, Morton Downey, Gene Austin, Red Foley, Jimmy Rodgers, the Vagabonds, and Gene Arnold. The Carter Family was turning out sentimental and sacred songs with the speed of a steam piston, but nobody was turning out more songs than Gene Autry.

Comedy songs and dialogues were being recorded in 1930, but they appealed chiefly to Grandpa. They bore such titillating titles as *Uncle Si at the Village Barber Shop, Rufus Green Takes a Trip, Pass Around the Bottle,* and *Hi and Sy and the Fence Line.*

Popular dance tunes in the same year included *Carolina Moon, Weary River, Carry Me Back to Connemara, Dancing with Tears in My Eyes, Moonlight on the Colorado* (no, not on the Wabash, Ermintrude), *Sweetheart of All My Dreams,* and *Sleeping Beauty Waltz.*

Who could ask for more entertainment than that provided for those of us who lived through the palpitating days of the thirties and the convulsive ones of the forties? We have not covered it all but perhaps what we have covered will generate that warm glow of nostalgia for some; and perhaps there may even be those who will say, "If I had my life to live over again, I'd want it to include those desperate, dear, incredible days."

Top: Freeman Gosden and Charles Correll, radio's Amos 'n' Andy. Below: Idol of the radio public, Rudy Vallee was also a genius at discovering new talent. (*Courtesy National Broadcasting Co.*)

Top: Popular singer Kate Smith, in the heyday of her radio show. (*Courtesy CBS Radio Network.*) Below: Ed Wynn, "The Perfect Fool," who made the transition from radio to television with delightful ease. (*Courtesy National Broadcasting Co.*)

Perennial favorite Bob Hope is shown (top) with Jerry Colonna. Below: Jack Benny and Fred Allen used their radio "feud" as a running gag. This photo was taken in March 1937. (*Courtesy National Broadcasting Co.*)

Top: Jim and Marian Jordan ("Fibber McGee and Molly") with Edgar Bergen and Charlie McCarthy in 1941. (*Courtesy National Broadcasting Co.*) **Below Left:** An Edgar Bergen's Charlie McCarthy puppet. **Below Right:** Charlie McCarthy card game, 1932. (*Courtesy Ted Hake, Philadelphia.*)

Top Left: Shirley Temple movie poster. (*Collection of Joanne Janzen.*) Top Right: This Betty Boop Watch, originally offered by Montgomery Ward for only 98 cents, has soared to a value of $300. It was exclusive with Ward in 1934. Below Right: Movie poster collectors will pay top dollar for choice items, such as this Anna Q. Nilsson display from the thirties. (*Photo by James D. Howard, Atlanta, Ga.*)

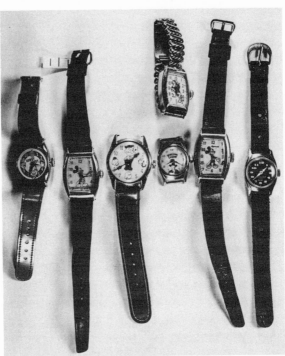

Top: The Lone Ranger toy figure brings high prices today. **Below:** Collectible character watches. **From Left:** Howdy Doody, Mickey Mouse, Popeye, Lone Ranger (above) and Hopalong Cassidy (below), another Mickey Mouse, and Zorro. (*Courtesy Ted Hake, Philadelphia.*)

Left: Dolls (reading across) of Judy Garland, Sonja Henie, Queen of the Ice, Deanna Durbin, Shirley Temple and Orphan Annie. **Top Right:** Orphan Annie and Dick Tracy wrist watches as advertised in 1940. **Second Row Right:** Jointed Popeye, Orphan Annie, and Comical Mouse figures, and Popeye Walking toy of early thirties. **Third Row Left:** When wound, these Amos 'n' Andy Marx Toys shuffled along; their arms shook, and their eyes moved up and down. Their original wholesale price was $12 a pair. Shown below is an Amos 'n' Andy window display, featuring the Madame Queen Beauty Parlor, Lodge room, patent office, Great Home Bank and Fresh Air Taxi Co. office. This color lithographed display measured 30 inches long. **Third Row Right:** Original $2.50 Charlie McCarthy Alarm clock of 1940. **Below Right:** This Amos 'n' Andy mechanical taxicab, when wound, operated eccentrically—starting, stopping, and rattling. Its box container represented the Fresh Air Taxicab Co. office. Montgomery Ward's price in 1931 for this was just 48 cents. It has recently been offered as a collector's item for $45 to $165!

Top: Lone Ranger Hi-Yo Silver watch by Everbrite Watch Co. at left; the New Haven lapel Lone Ranger watch with holster and pistol at right. Below Left: Radio Cruiser was modeled after a square rigger and was equipped with a built-in speaker. It measures 19½ inches long and 16½ inches high. Below Right: These puff holders of 1940 were called "Scarlett-o" and "Rhett" and had glass ball faces.

Top: Joanne Janzen, Witchita, Kansas, surrounded by some of her extensive collection of Shirley Temple memorabilia. Below: 40-inch Shirley Temple paper dolls from the Janzen collection.

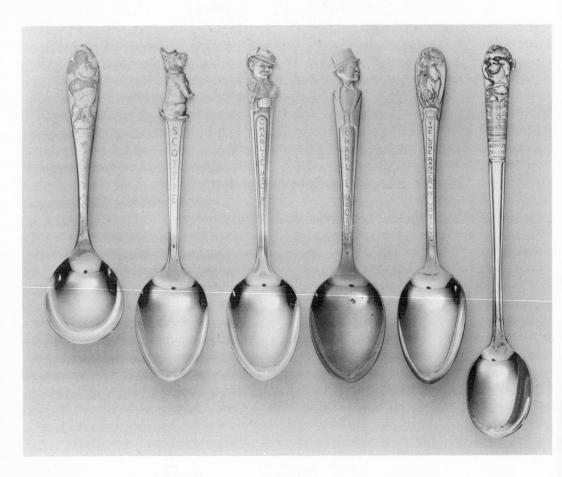

Comic characters and movie stars were popular subjects for silverplated souvenir spoons. From left: Mickey Mouse, Scottie, Charlie McCarthy, another Charlie, the Lone Ranger, and Howdy Doody. (*Courtesy International Silver Co. Historical Library.*)

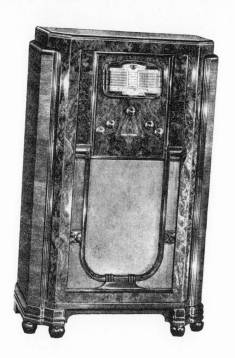

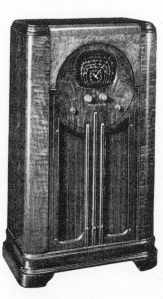

Top Left: 1936 Stromberg-Carlson Acoustical Labyrinth radio sold for $275. **Top Right:** Mastercraft phonograph (1930) had two doors, spaces for record albums, and cost only about $50. **Below:** 1933 Philco radio, 1936 American Bosch, 1936 Grunow.

Autographed complimentary copy of "Deep Night," with words by Rudy Vallee and music by Charlie Henderson. (© 1929 by Ager, Yellen & Bornstein, Inc.)

Complimentary four-page song sheet from the motion picture *The Cat and The Fiddle*, distributed as a souvenir by Loew's Theatres, 1931. The music was composed by Jerome Kern and Otto Harbach and was copyrighted by Jerome Kern, 1931, and published by T. B. Harms Co., N.Y.

4 WHAT WE READ

THE trouble with books in the thirties and forties was that one could read and understand them. There was no mumbo-jumbo, no explicit delineation of sex acts, and darned few four-letter words.

We read *Anthony Adverse, Gone with the Wind, Collier's, The Saturday Evening Post, Photoplay,* and a lot of comic books. Those seeking titillation could find a copy of *Film Fun* at the corner newsstand, and the serious-minded could turn to the *Literary Digest* or *Fortune.* Almost everyone read the funnies, and "See you in the funny papers" became a popular expression.

Dale Carnegie told us how to win friends and influence people in 1936, and so many persons read his advice that there were hardly any enemies left — on this side of the Atlantic. Ernest Hemingway gave us adventure galore, and Erle Stanley Gardner turned out "whodunits" by the ream for those who wanted to relax.

Even though hardbound books in the thirties were priced at $2 to $2.50 and literacy had reached the point where a great many persons could read and wanted to when greater excitement was not at hand, cash to invest in anything except necessities was the problem. This gave rise to the phenomenon of the privately-operated lending library and the development of book clubs that offered subscribers popular fiction and nonfiction at reduced rates. Those who wanted to read Charles Morgan's best-selling novel *The Fountain* in 1932 or James Hilton's enchanting *Lost Horizon* in 1935 but were loath to shell out $2 to $2.50 could, if they read rapidly, read either book on loan from a private lending library at a charge of just 10 cents. That was the going fee for borrowing books that were returned within three days.

Chains of such libraries sprang up around the country, many of them housed in bookshops, including, among others, The Intimate Bookshop, operated during the 1930s by the author of the book you are now reading. The latter was a successful venture until I began taking home the best books in my establishment and failed to return them. Thus — alas! — I consigned myself to the category of the candy store operator who ate up all his profits.

Among the major novelists of the 1930s were Thomas Wolfe, whose *Look Homeward, Angel* of 1929 was followed by the equally poignant *You Can't Go Home Again* in 1935, and by other books following his untimely death in 1938; Ernest Hemingway with his *Death in the Afternoon, The Green Hills of Arica,* and *To Have and Have Not;* John Steinbeck with *The Pastures of Heaven, To a God Unknown, Tortilla Flat, In Dubious Battle, Of Mice and Men,* and *The Grapes of Wrath* (the last-named having won the Pulitzer Prize in 1940); William Faulkner with his novels of decadence, among them *As I Lay Dying, Sanctuary, Absalom! Absalom!, Pylon,* and *The Wild Palms;* William Saroyan, who wrote *The Daring Young Man on the Flying Trapeze, and Other Stories* in 1936 and followed this with *Inhale, Exhale, Love Here Is My Hat,* and *The Trouble with Tigers;* Marjorie Kinnan Rawlings, whose *The Yearling* won the 1939 Pulitzer Prize; Pearl S. Buck, who took that prize in 1933 with *The Good Earth;* and James T. Farrell, whose Studs Lonigan series began in 1932 with *Young Lonigan: A Boyhood in Chicago Streets.* To the list might be added Hervey Allen, whose *Anthony Adverse* was as enormously popular as it was long. And, although she was not a major novelist, having produced only one novel in her lifetime, we can no more neglect Margaret Mitchell than readers neglected her *Gone with the Wind* in 1936 and the years following. The book took Pulitzer Prize honors in 1937 and, as noted earlier, was fashioned into an almost equally successful motion picture.

F. Scott Fitzgerald, whose earlier novels had been smash hits in the 1920s, saw his fortunes on the wane in the 1930s except for the publicaton of *Tender Is the Night* and *Taps at Reveille,* but there was a revival of interest in his work in the 1940s with the posthumous publication of *The Last Tycoon.* Thousands read Walter D. Edmonds's *Drums Along the Mohawk* in 1936, Kenneth Roberts's

Northwest Passage in 1937, and J. P. Marquand's *The Late George Apley* in the same year.

Among the more popular writers, many of whose stories appeared in magazines as well as book form, were Temple Bailey, Sophie Kerr, Fannie Hurst, Margaret Culkin Banning, Willa Cather, Faith Baldwin, Sinclair Lewis, Ursula Parrott, Edison Marshall, Helen Topping Miller, Kathleen Norris, Edna Ferber, Mary Roberts Rinehart, Vicki Baum, Frances Parkinson Keyes, Dorothy Canfield Fisher, and Booth Tarkington.

Many long-established magazines flourished during the two decades, among them *The Saturday Evening Post, Woman's Home Companion, Literary Digest* (until it broke its neck stumbling over a political poll), *Ladies' Home Journal, Collier's Weekly, Liberty, Delineator,* and others, but the big splash of the thirties was made by Henry R. Luce, the founder of *Time* in 1923 and *Fortune* in 1930, who, in 1936, acquired the old humorous monthly *Life* and converted it into a weekly news-and-feature pictorial. The new *Life* mingled cheesecake with social and economic pictorial essays and chopped through the gobbledygook of scientific phraseology to make such things as the splitting of the atom comprehensible to the lay reader.

It was *Life* that generated the passion for picture magazines. A multitude of them appeared but only a few, notably *Look,* withstood the test of time (until 1971) and the scrutiny of increasingly critical readers.

Numerous pulp magazines had a large following among the hoi polloi, particularly those dealing with pseudo-science, the incredible, and matters ghastly. A few of these were *Horror, Terror, Weird, Spider, G-8, Astounding,* and *Strange.*

A host of "little magazines" were created during the two decades, many of these devoted to ventures in "experimental" writing, others to exposés. Those whose names may be best remembered include *Pagany; Contempo* (one entire issue of which was devoted to work by and about William Faulkner and which is now valued at in excess of $100 a copy); *Story,* edited by Whit Burnett and Martha Foley and concerned exclusively with the short story; *The American Spectator,* a literary newspaper edited by George Jean Nathan and other distinguished writers; *Partisan Review,* a bimonthly devoted to revolutionary literature and probably tops among the left-wing publications; and *The Southern Review,* an outstanding literary quarterly founded in 1935 at Louisiana State University.

In the late 1930s and through the 1940s many writers began dealing more openly with sex, though not nearly so openly as it is dealt with today. (Now, sex seems to have become an obsession with the masses and the four-letter word is a basic ingredient of most bestsellers.) The movie magazines, particularly those featuring considerable cheesecake, developed a wide following. There were many of these, the front-runners including *Screen Guide, Screenland, Motion Picture Classic, Modern Screen, Silver Screen, Movie Stars Parade, Movies, Movieland, Movie Story,* and *Photoplay.*

While the first editions of several of the major authors mentioned earlier will fetch high prices on today's out-of-print book market and while some of the scarcer magazines listed are worth fairly substantial sums, it is the comic book that has become the prime phenomenon on the collectors' market today.

Although often treated as a separate category, the "Big Little Books" belong with the comics. These small books measuring about three inches square and a couple of inches thick were published during the 1930s by Whitman Publishing Company and featured a combination of text and continuous illustration. The right-hand pages of these books contained panels of strip drawings and the accompanying text was printed on the left-hand pages. In "Big Little Book" format were published perhaps the majority of the most popular comic strips of the decade until the series' waning years.

The books were devoted to the adventures of such characters and personalities as Dick Tracy, Red Ryder, Popeye, Tailspin Tommy, Flash Gordon, Orphan Annie, Gene Autry, Roy Rogers, Terry and the Pirates, Mickey Mouse, Tarzan, Jungle Jim, The Phantom, Captain Midnight, Secret Agent X-9, Tim McCoy, Smilin' Jack, Captain Easy, Shirley Temple, Ken Maynard, Jackie Cooper, and many others.

These books will generally bring from $4 to $8.50 on the market now, although a few are of greater value. The latter include the *Flash Gordon* books, which have been offered recently for $18 each; the *Buck Rogers* series, for which $15 each is being asked, and *Terry and the Pirates,* valued at around $10.

It was the big brother of the "Big Little Books" — the full-blown comic book — that did the miniature ones in, late in the thirties. And comic books were the outgrowth of comic strips, which date back to the late 19th century, and have been read avidly since.

Among the best-known of the pioneer comic strip creators is R. F. Outcault, whose notorious *Yellow Kid* was created in 1896 in the old

New York *World.* Outcault is better known today, however, for his
Buster Brown strip, which first appeared in 1902 and which led to
a whole passel, as they are wont to say in the hinterlands, of collectible objects. A year after the *Yellow Kid* had first appeared, Rudolph
Dirks created *The Katzenjammer Kids* for the Hearst newspapers.
Subsequently, Dirks and Hearst were involved in a legal controversy
as a result of which the latter was accorded the legal right to the title
of *The Katzenjammer Kids* and Dirks was granted the right to use
his original characters but not under their original title. This resulted in the employment of another artist, H. H. Knerr, to carry on *The
Katzenjammer Kids,* but Dirks continued his own strip under the
title *The Captain and the Kids.*

Other pioneers in the comic strip field included F. B. Opper, who
fathered *Happy Hooligan* and *Alphonse and Gaston,* both in 1902;
Carl E. Schultze, whose *Foxy Grandpa* appeared in the New York
Herald in 1900; "Bud" (Harry C.) Fisher, who created the always-to-
be-remembered *Mutt and Jeff* in 1907 in the San Francisco *Chroni-
cle;* Charles W. Kahles, whose *Hairbreadth Harry* was originated in
1906 in the Philadelphia *Press;* Cliff Sterrett with his *Polly and Her
Pals* (New York *Journal*), which began about 1912; George Mc-
Manus, whose *Bringing Up Father,* starring Maggie and Jiggs, first
saw the light of day in 1913 in the New York *American;* Winsor
McCay with his *Little Nemo in Slumberland,* and Sydney Smith
with *The Gumps.*

The true devotee of the comic strip will also remember such
names as Rube Goldberg (*Boob McNutt* and others); Frank Willard
(*Moon Mullins*); Jimmy Murphy (*Toots and Casper*); Edgar Martin
(*Boots and Her Buddies*); Harold Gray (*Little Orphan Annie,* later
to become merely *Orphan Annie*); Walter Berndt (*Smitty*); Ad
Carter (*Just Kids*); Merrill Blosser (*Freckles and His Friends*); Russ
Westover (*Tillie the Toiler*); Percy Crosby (*Skippy*); R. M. Brinker-
hoff (*Little Mary Mixup*); Martin V. Branner (*Winnie Winkle*); Paul
Robinson (*Etta Kett*); Charlie Plumb and Bill Conselman (*Ella Cin-
ders*); Larry Whitington, followed by Ernie Bushmiller (*Fritzi Ritz*);
Harry Tuthill (*The Bungle Family*); Billy De Beck (*Barney Google,*
whose title, after De Beck's death, was changed to *Snuffy Smith* and
was then drawn by Fred Lasswell); and Elzie Segar (*Thimble
Theatre,* which later became *Popeye*).

Books have been written about both the comic strip and the comic
book, and I do not intend to delineate in detail the history of either
but rather to point out that the comic book came into being in the

1930s, grew to maturity in the 1940s, and that the possessor of a slew of either the strips or the early books may be better off financially than those who own merely savings certificates or stocks and bonds.

An impressive array of new comic strips appeared in the 1930s and 1940s. Among these were *Flash Gordon* and *Jungle Jim*, both by Alex Raymond; *Alley Oop* by V. T. Hamlin; *Pete the Tramp* by C. D. Russell; *Blondie* by Chic Young; *Smilin' Jack* by Zack Mosley; *Joe Palooka* by "Ham" (Hammond E.) Fisher; *Li'l Abner* by Al Capp (who had started out as an assistant to Fisher); *Smokey Stover* by Bill Holman; *Abbie 'n Slats* by Raeburn Van Buren; *Mandrake the Magician* by Lee Falk and Phil Davis, who also in 1936 created *The Phantom*; *Dick Tracy* by Chester Gould; *Steve Canyon* by Milton Caniff; *Wash Tubbs, Captain Easy,* and *Buz Sawyer,* all by Roy Crane; *Terry and the Pirates* by Milton Caniff (who subsequently relinquished it to George Wunder); *Pogo* by Walt Kelly; *Barnaby* by Crockett Johnson; *Brick Bradford* by Clarence Gray; *Superman* by Jerry Siegel and Joe Shuster; and others, this list by no means being inclusive.

One of the most popular strips, *Buck Rogers in the Twenty-Fifth Century,* first appeared in 1929, executed by Phil Nowlan and Dick Calkins. The strip spawned a radio show of the same name, with the script written by Jack Johnstone, in 1932; later *Buck Rogers* appeared as a comic book.

As we have pointed out in the chapter on entertainment, a number of comic books were adapted to radio and also to the movies; and a number of movie stars also had their own radio programs or programs named after them or the characters they played, and these also became the subjects of comic books.

A typical example is Popeye, who was as amusing in animated cartoons on movie screens as he was in the newspaper comic pages. Elzie Segar created Popeye, along with his girl friend, Olive Oyl, the mendacious Mr. Wimpy, and other bodacious characters in 1919, and the strip was syndicated by King Features, after appearing in the Hearst papers, under the original title, as mentioned, of *Thimble Theatre.* The *Popeye* animated cartoons were the product of Max Fleischer. Popeye also has reached many thousands via television. Since 1939, the comic strip has been carried on by various other writers and artists.

Popeye collectibles began appearing in the late 1920s when a Popeye Daily Dime Bank made its way to the marketplaces. It's now worth $15 or more. Since Popeye was invariably drawn with a corncob pipe stuck in the corner of his mouth, it was natural that sooner or later a Popeye Pipe Toss game would appear, and it did, in 1935. Its value is about $25 now in mint condition in the original box. The Popeye wristwatch, made by New Haven, was being offered in the 1930s at $4.40. It had a chromium-plated case with a drawing of Popeye in color on the dial. If you have one and would rather have $125 cash, that's about what it will bring.

There are numerous other Popeye collectibles. A wooden jointed figure of him 1 foot tall is valued at around $30, and smaller rubber figures of Popeye, Olive Oyl, and Wimpy are worth $12.50 each. A 1944 composition figure of Popeye is worth a couple of dollars less. Other Popeye collectibles and their approximate values as of this writing include: a mechanical bank, Popeye Knockout Bank, featuring Popeye and his opponent, Joe Socko, $42.50; a Kazoo in the shape of a pipe, $5; Popeye the Pilot, a Marx toy, $75; Popeye pencil sharpener, $12; a ring, $10; puzzle, $2.50; pocket knife, $15; a Chein keywind toy, Popeye in Barrel, $25 to $60; and a Popeye-with-suitcases windup, $27.50.

It might be appropriate to point out at this time that a fellow named M. C. Gaines is generally credited with being the outstanding pioneer of comic books, if not the "father" of them. During the 1930s several businesses utilized comic books, which were primarily reprints of some of the strips, as premiums. (Subsequently a number of companies, well known in the premium field, issued their own comic books. For example, General Mills' Wheaties issued a Jack Armstrong comic, a giveaway in 1949 and now valued at $15 to $20. *Terry and the Pirates* also was issued as a premium color comic book in 1938 and its value is currently about $10.)

Famous Funnies, issued in 1933, is usually credited with being the first of the modern-day comic books even though the reprints of comic strips bound in book form had actually appeared as early as 1908, when, according to Professor Jerry G. Bails in his *The Guidebook to Comics Fandom* (Glendale, Cal.: Bill Spicer, 1965), Cupples & Leon issued in booklet form reprints of the *Buster Brown* strips. Professor Bails says *Famous Funnies* was offered for sale through chain stores, and a year later Eastern Color Printing Company began issuing it on a regular basis. Its retail price was a dime. In either 1935 or 1936 (authorities differ on the exact year), M. C. Gaines produced a book called *Popular Comics,* published by George Delacorte. Those interested in the activities of Gaines as a pioneer in this field will find an excellent chapter about them by Ted White in the book *All in Color for a Dime,* edited by Dick Lupoff and Don Thompson (New Rochelle, N. Y.: Arlington House, 1970), a volume highly recommended to the buff.

In 1936, *Tip Top Comics* was published by United Features Syndicate. *King Comics* was published by David McKay Company, and King Features, one of the major syndicates handling comic strips, began leasing rights to reprint its strips. *New Fun Comics,* which had appeared in 1935, presented original material rather than reprints, and *Detective Comics,* first published in 1937, concentrated on a single plot. The proliferation had begun.

The adventure strip and comic books devoted to individual stories in each issue were prime developments of the late 1930s. *Ace* comics appeared in 1937, *Action* in 1938, and *Batman* in 1939. By the end of the decade several dozen comic books were being published on a regular basis, some as monthlies and others as quarterlies. They truly flourished in the decade that followed. It is not our purpose to list them all here but rather to mention a few of the highlights about this field and to discuss some of the objects stemming from the comic book (and comic strip) characters that are now collectible in their own right.

The first *Superman* adventures appeared in *Action Comics* in 1938, and in 1939 the comic strip was syndicated by McClure. The following year Superman became a radio hero and in 1942 a movie cartoon hero. Subsequently, the comic book was published by National Periodical Publications, Inc., and few comic book-and-strip characters have been more popular than this one created by Jerry Siegel and Joe Shuster. A rather detailed history of this fictitious character and his adventures appears in *All in Color for a Dime.*

If you think rare books that have appreciated 100 percent in the past half century are good investments, then think again about *Superman.* The first issue of *Action Comics* containing his adventures has soared from its original price of a dime to $300 — if you can find one. The first issue of the quarterly *Superman* comic book will have about the same price tag today. The 1939 issues of the magazine, however, drop to about $5 each. Most readers will not have to be told that Superman later appeared in "live" movies with George Reeves in the starring role and was graduated from there to the Broadway stage as a musical. *Superman* had a lot of imitators, but none was quite so successful.

A popular organization among the youngsters at the outset of the 1940s was one called Supermen Club of America. Membership cost a dime, and the money also paid for a membership certificate. There also are Superman buttons; dime banks ($12); rings ($50), and secret codes, currently collectible.

Batman, drawn by Robert Kane, an artist from the Bronx, first appeared in *Detective Comics* in 1939 and in the following year had a magazine all his own. It was not until four years later that he made it to the newspaper comic strips, but only for three years, after which he reappeared in comic book form. (Batman and his sidekick Robin made the grade in television in the 1960s, and numerous Batman collectible objects stem from that period.)

The first issue of *Batman* is worth only a third of what the first issue of *Action Comics* commands — but $100 for an erstwhile 10-cent magazine isn't bad.

Milton Caniff, a prolific artist, created *Terry and the Pirates* as a comic strip first appearing in the Chicago *Tribune.* The hero, Terry Lee, experienced a series of intriguing adventures in the Orient, many of them revolving around or involving two female characters known as Burma and the Dragon Lady. Another character was Pat Ryan, who, along with Burma, was Terry's friend. There are some but not a great many premiums from the radio show of this name, as mentioned in the chapter on entertainment. They included, however, a Pirate Gold Detector Ring. None of these has as yet, however, detected Blackbeard's hoard. A picture-record will bring $20 today.

Captain Marvel made his debut in *Whiz Comics* and subsequently (1941) in *Captain Marvel Adventures,* published by Fawcett, and in *Marvel Family Comics.* The drawings were by C. C. Beck, and, as was the case with so many other comic book heroes, *Captain Marvel* also ended up as a movie serial made by Republic Pictures. There was also a book entitled *Captain Marvel, Jr.,* published by Fawcett, beginning in the fall of 1942.

It is surprising how many "Captains" there were among the comic book heroes. The titles of other books give their identity: *Captain America, Captain Battle, Jr., Captain Fearless, Captain Fight, Captain Easy,* and *Captain Midnight.*

If many comic book heroes (and heroines) ended up in the movies, at least one character started out as a movie serial and ended up as a comic book. This was *Jungle Girl,* filmed by Republic Pictures.

A variety of new comic books were stimulated by World War II, and most of the narratives were linked to the war. These included: *Boy Commandos, Girl Commandos, Captain America, Spy Smasher, Thrilling Comics, Star Spangled Comics, Speed Comics,*

Spy Smasher (later the subject of movie serials by Republic Pictures), *Atomic Bomb, Bomber, Fighting Yank, Miss America, Our Flag, Rangers of Freedom, Stars and Stripes, Uncle Sam, Victory,* and *War Victory Adventures.* The list is not complete but it represents a good sampling of the titles.

Although most comic book leading characters were male, there were also a few females, and even though the vast majority of the books were devoted primarily to lusty adventure, one of the major comic book publishers, Fiction House, did issue a series in which a large part of the attention was devoted to titillating females.

Capitalizing upon the success and wide appeal of mystery novels, there were a number of mystery comics, too. *Marvel Mystery Comics,* which began publication in 1939, was an early one. Popular, also, were comics featuring detectives. One named just that — *Detective Comics* — first appeared in 1937, a year after the appearance of *Detective Picture Stories.* There was also *Detective Eye,* first published in 1940 and apparently lasting only a couple of issues.

The scope of the comic books may be indicated by a few titles: *Amazing Man, Black Terror, Blue Beetle, Bulletman, Catman, Cyclone, Dollman, Fantastic, Human Torch, Planet, Samson, Sky Blazers, Slam Bang, Smash, Startling, Supersnipe, Tough Kid Squad, Weird,* and *Wonder Woman.*

Why do adults collect comic books? Not long ago, the Associated Press quoted Bill Blackbeard, founder-director of the San Francisco Academy of Comic Art (the world's largest private collection) as saying that the comics are of considerable cultural significance, and that the comic strip itself is a "wholly indigenous American art form." (The collection of which he is director, incidentally, is valued at somewhere between $200,000 and $300,000.)

Professor Wm. Eugene Atkinson of the Department of History at Texas Christian University, Fort Worth, is one of the adult collectors of comic books — with a method in his seeming madness.

"As a professor of American history," he told this writer, "I have been interested in the political uses of the comic strips and the movie cartoons. Such comics as *Little Orphan Annie, Terry and the Pirates, Pogo,* and *Dick Tracy* have revealed changing political attitudes on the part of their creators.

"During the early 1930s," Professor Atkinson added, "the early movie cartoons seemed to have a direct connection with the attitude of the nation regarding the Depression; and in the early 1940s the propaganda explicit in such movie shorts is quite startling."

Professor Atkinson admits that his professorial colleagues give him a hard time for spending his lunch hour watching cartoons on the Fort Worth television stations, but he plans to prepare an article for a scholarly journal on the politics of popular cartoons.

And speaking of the attention devoted by scholars to the comics, there is a deadly serious, yet perfectly delightful and informative quarterly magazine devoted to comic books, comic strips, and animated cartoons. Entitled *Funnyworld,* it is published by Mike Barrier in Little Rock, Ark., and is slanted entirely toward adult readers and students in this field. Publisher Barrier calls it an "amateur" magazine, but it outclasses many commercial ones.

Adults collect comic art for various reasons, not the least among which is the charming nostalgia the hobby generates. It helps enable some to recapture in part the wonderful and often breathless days of their youth. Some collect it because it is a popular art and a peculiarly American one. And, of course, there are some who collect it because they figure there's a potential profit in it. They're right, but they might be scorned by the "true" collector.

Several years ago an organization of these collectors was formed — The Academy of Comic-Book Fans and Collectors. Among its functions were the publication of a newsletter, conducting an annual awards poll, and maintaining a library of fan magazines.

Since we brought the subject up, just what are comic books worth? Value depends upon a variety of factors, among which is condition. Only books in mint or virtually pristine condition bring top prices. Those that are severely damaged, badly soiled, or have missing pages are worthless from the collector's standpoint.

Rarity is another factor, as is age. We have mentioned a couple of top prices. Perhaps a sampling of prices recently asked for certain issues would be of interest. One major outlet lists these:

Adventure #41 (1939), $50; *All-Star* #2 (1940), $90; *Boy Commandos* #3 (1943), $12; *Flash* #1 (1940), $200; *Comic Cavalcade* #1 (1942), $20; *World's Finest* #2 (1942), $30; *Batman* #4 (1941), $35; *Detective* #64 (in which the *Boy Commandos* were originated), $20; *Mad* #1 (1952), $40; *Mickey Mouse Magazine,* Vol. 1, No. 1 (1935), $135; and *Thunda* #1, $55.

If those prices seem extraordinarily high, you should know that each of the magazines listed above was really "something special": It was a first issue, or a first issue in which a new character later to become famous was introduced, or it contained outstanding artwork.

There are still many — actually thousands — of comic books to be found in a price range of $1 to $10. The trouble is, of course, that dedicated collectors are after the scarce ones. In view of the fact that so many magazines were issued, it would seem on the surface that their very abundance would serve to hold prices down — but in truth there is not the abundance one would suspect. Hundreds of thousands of these magazines were donated to the scrap paper drives during World War II by owners who never suspected they would be worth more than their cover price. All of which goes to show how great it would be to have hindsight ahead of time.

Comic book collectors also seek original sketches drawn for fans by the artists. Pencil sketches about 8x10 inches will usually bring $5 up, ink sketches more.

Before getting away from prices, some of the choice movie fan magazines of the 1930s will bring as much as $10, though many are cheaper. Certain issues of general magazines featuring top movie stars or comic book characters also will bring $5 to $10. (The August 1950 issue of *Look* containing four pages about Hopalong Cassidy has an asking price of $15.) Some of the earlier science fiction magazines will fetch $5 to $20 or so, and the early radio and television magazines are climbing in value. Even newspaper comic strip pages are being collected now.

One's heart goes out to the small apartment dwellers who suddenly become addicted to comic book and other magazine collecting: What does one do when all the pantry shelves in the kitchen, the space under the beds, and the clothes closets are filled?

Although not everyone would agree, comic art *is* art. The Chaffee Art Gallery in Rutland, Vt., featured an exhibit of comic art in 1971. Loaned by W. Thomson Fagan, a dedicated Rutland collector, it included original comic art from the pens of Outcault, Walt Kelly, Al Capp, Will Eisner and others.

Book and magazine collectors have been around for centuries, of course, but it would be difficult to find a more dedicated one than Herb Bridges, of Sharpsburg, Georgia. Some years ago, Mr. Bridges, then a very young man, began collecting all the editions of *Gone with the Wind* he could find. Thirteen entirely different editions of this book have been published in the United States, and there is a copy of each in the Bridges collection. The book has been translated into 26 different languages and published in 36 countries. Mr. Bridges has managed to assemble every one of these editions except the one published in Cuba.

His collection today totals approximately 300 volumes of this one book, plus numerous mementos of the book, the motion picture based upon it, and mementos of the author herself. The collection has been exhibited in various parts of the country.

The first edition of this book must have a May 1936 copyright date, and it is worth $60 or more on today's market. Autographed or inscribed, it will bring more.

Top: A handful of the editions of *Gone with the Wind* in the collection of Herb Bridges, Sharpsburg, Ga. Below: The first edition of Margaret Mitchell's *Gone with the Wind* with the May 1936 copyright notice, currently valued at $60 or more. (*Courtesy Herb Bridges.*)

Top: Little Orphan Annie cards. **Below:** Little Orphan Annie card game. (*Courtesy Ted Hake, Phila.*)

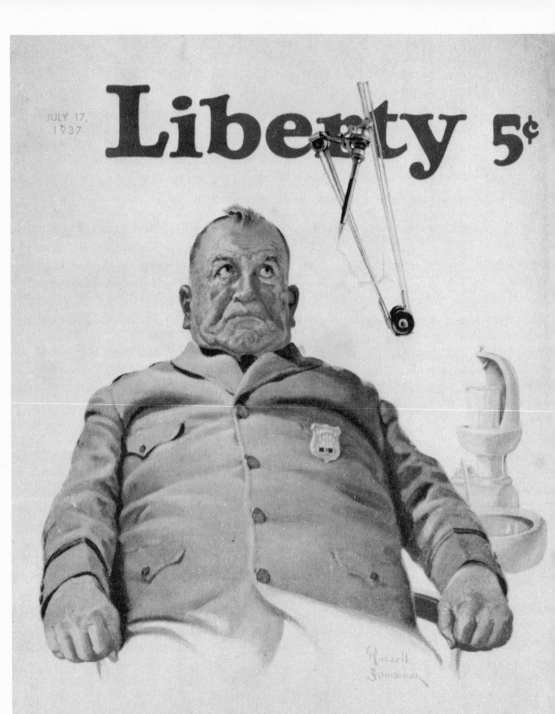

Store placards such as this showing the issue of July 17, 1937, promoted *Liberty* magazine.

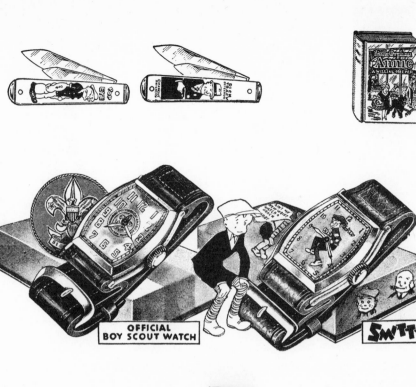

Top Left: These Dick Tracy and Popeye jackknives were sold in the forties. They were 3 inches long, had two blades, and mounted on cardboard display pieces. **Top Right:** Big Little Book, *Little Orphan Annie, A Willing Helper*, sold for less than 50¢ in 1932. **Center:** Montgomery Ward sold New Haven's Smitty watch in 1934 for $3.67, complete with leather watch. Alongside, an official Boy Scout watch. **Below Left:** This Marx B.O. Plenty windup toy is now worth around $25. **Below right:** "Bringing Up Father" by George McManus was one of 12 comic books published by Cupple and Leon in 1930.

These were among the most popular comic books of the thirties and forties. (*Courtesy Tom Fagan, Rutland, Vt.*)

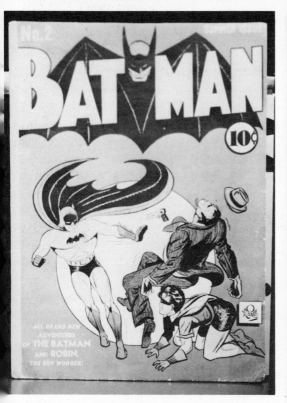

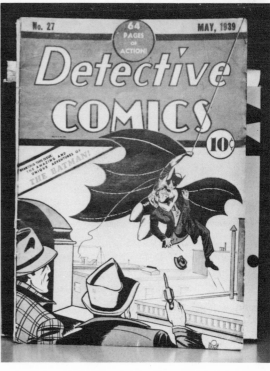

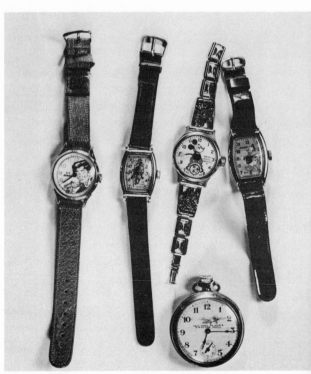

Top: Highly collectible jointed Superman figure. (*Courtesy Ted Hake, Phila.*) Below Center: Popeye wrist watch made by the New Haven Watch Co. now brings about $125 on the collectors' market. Bottom: Character watches are among most sought-after and highest priced collectibles of the thirties. From Left: Li'l Abner, the Lone Ranger, Mickey Mouse, Donald Duck, and (below) watch commemorating New York to Paris flight. (*Courtesy Ted Hake, Phila.*)

5 DRESS AND ACCESSORIES

STOCKS and bonds were not the only things that went down with the onset of the Great Depression. So did women's dresses. The knee-high skirts of the Jazz Age had dropped by the early thirties to a very few inches above shoe tops. (Conversely, with the advent of good times, they went back up again.)

Women not only wore their skirts longer; they wore their hair longer. As short skirts went out of favor, so did the bobbed hair of the twenties. And women again began wearing corsets, whether they needed them or not. Certainly a good many did.

The big impact on women's fashions in the thirties was made by a combination of movie stars and dress designers. The latter even began to give names to their creations, many of which appeared with a profusion of frills. Dieting for a flatter stomach had not yet become a fad, so the ladies held their middles in through a combination of the corset and tighter-fitting garments. By the mid-thirties cotton as a material for undergarments lost favor to silk and rayon.

Shoes, generally, were sensible: there was enough room at the front for toes to spread out, and, although high heels were available, lower ones were favored for daytime wear. Women's hats were small and snug-fitting. The 1933–34 Sears, Roebuck catalog offered the "Jester's Cap," created in Paris. It exuded a pleasant impudence. The Sears version was hand-draped in rayon-faced velvet with a pleated cockade of ribbon at the side. Turbans appeared everywhere. They imparted a carefree appearance at a time when few people indeed were actually free from care. And the French beret surged into popularity. Sears heralded it as offered at the "lowest price in America for genuine all wool French Berets." The price? Three for a dollar! If one didn't like France, she could get a Belgian beret. (College males had been wearing berets a few years earlier.)

Ribbed stockings were popular for a while, but as time went on stockings became extremely sheer. That flat chest was outmoded — wherever this was possible — and the ladies became curvaceous. In the judgment of the males of the era, this was all to the good. Even the lines of hips began to show, thanks to the tighter-fitting garments.

There were not nearly so many changes in the style of men's clothing except that trouser legs were considerably more than ample, widening to cuffs that were just about the length of the shoe. In the early thirties, the two-button coat predominated, and every well-dressed male wore a vest. Somewhat later vests went out of style along with stiff collars. Men's jackets with belted backs came in but spats went out. The extremely wide tie was much in evidence by 1930.

Hollywood's glamor was catching, and one upshot was the burgeoning of the beauty parlor, which at the outset specialized in hairdos, particularly the "permanent" wave. And while there have been beauty adjuncts since the time man's memory runneth not to the contrary, these began to multiply in the 1930s. So did a variety of dress accessories, thereby creating for the present generation a multitude of interesting, conversation-provoking, and, though by no means antique, even collectible objects. These may have little or no appeal to those whose concern is with loftier trifles, but they do hold a certain fascination for those in whose breasts stirs some curiosity about the fads, the antics, and the way of life of their recent forebears.

These things ranged from compacts, makeup boxes, and handbags to atomizers, powderettes, and ceramic bath salts novelties. The commercial spirit of Art Deco mingled curiously with what was vaguely called "modernism" — a mingling into which we shall delve in greater detail later — was reflected in the compacts of the period, which flowed from the assembly lines in a never-ceasing stream. Those with chromium finishes and enamel fronts were to be seen everywhere. There appeared in profusion enameled designs of tendrillike curlicues, baskets of flowers, dogs, and birds.

The redoubtable and aggressive firm of Evans was a leader in the field of stylish new compacts, turning out some lively cases with cloisonné work and others with chain-attached lipstick with stone settings in the ends. The lipsticks served as a carrying handle. The Elgin-American Manufacturing Company was another top producer of striking vanity cases. There were black enamel cases with designs in gold, red, and white; cases with white and black designs on turquoise blue enamel; and cases of black and gold designs on white enamel. There were double compacts and triple compacts that combined cigarette cases with the necessaries for milady's complexion. The Girey Company made a Kamra-Pak vanity in the shape of a camera. There were oval compacts, square compacts, oblong compacts, and those in the shape of a heart.

The Klix compact opened with a gentle squeeze. Within the range of the hoi polloi were compacts plated with gold or of silver. Evans made a compact with a spiderweb design complete with jeweled spider. There was one with a long swinging handle, and there were compacts with sweethearts in shaded enamel silhouette on the exterior of the case.

At the outbreak of war, compacts appeared with military motifs such as the American eagle and stars and stripes. There were also boxed compact and neck chain and locket ensembles. There were other ensembles, such as compacts with bracelets and those with matching combs. There was a Marathon Foto-Pak compact with a locket-type cover in which there was space for two small photographs. There were leather vanities, including one type of lambskin with top and bottom of the case zippered together. And there were Lucite compacts, one resembling a well-cooked flapjack, both in shape and finish.

These concise descriptions provide merely a starter. Apparently no one as yet collects compacts, and you could be the first in your townhouse to start the ball rolling.

Novelty makeup boxes constitute another potential field of pioneering collecting. In its 1936 catalog, the Harry Greenwold, Wallenstein-Mayer Company, of Cincinnati offered a 5-inch beauty makeup box in the shape of a silverplated coach — quite a resplendent affair. The same wholesale firm illustrated another with a silverplated figure of a greyhound atop the case and still another with the figure of a seated German shepherd dog. There was even one graced with a miniature silverplated buck, head held high in the air. Less expensive ones were made of Britannia metal.

Puff novelties also abounded. Some were made in the form of dolls and inverted hats. Ceramic figures in animal shapes that once held bath salts should be highly collectible by now. One of these was called Krazy Kat; another was in the form of a dog that might well have been called Krazy Dawg, but wasn't. Still another was the figure of a policeman 8 inches tall. The head was the stopper.

About 1930 fancy glass jars were designed to serve as talcum powder containers. Some were produced in colored and frosted glass and were packed with scented talc and a puff.

Another unexplored field is that of novelty whiskbrushes and powder brushes. The latter were made with porcelain figure tops, including dolls and animals. The 1940 catalog of Joseph Hagn Company illustrated a whiskbroom with a pressed fiber Scotty dog as its holder when not in use. It also offered a feather duster with a porcelain doll top. These were popular for several years. For the males there was a whiskbroom–tie rack combination. The tie rack was in the shape of a horseshoe, and the brush hung from the top center. There were also a variety of novelty containers for military brushes.

Commercial Art Deco jewelry boxes of plated silver and other materials were being made as late as the end of the 1930s. A choice one, decorated with a kneeling female nude finial, boasted individual velvet-lined swinging trays with automatic locks. It wholesaled for $18 in 1936. One of this type was recently offered by an antiques dealer for only $24.50. An oval semi-porcelain jewel or trinket box with a kneeling nude on the cover was offered by Montgomery Ward in a 1932 sale catalog at just 39 cents. The same catalog presented a powder jar of ceramic graced with a seated partially-clad female for 45 cents.

Atomizers and perfume bottles constitute a rich field for the glass collector willing to content herself or himself with productions of the thirties and forties. But make no mistake about it: Some pippins were turned out during these years, and they are discussed in more detail in the chapter on glass.

Also collectible are novelty hat stands, some of which were made with colored felt dressed doll heads at the base. Most of these were originally quite inexpensive.

Such costume accessories as brooches, pendants, pins, and buckles have adorned the female figure through the centuries to lend additional glitter to woman's natural charms. The two decades upon which our attention is focused are no exception. Jewelry of artificial and semiprecious stones abounded, much of it heavy and reminiscent of primitive cultures. There were familiar names in the field of high fashion: Van Cleef, Chanel, Cartier, Arpels, and others. But there were far more who catered to those in the market for bagatelles and, the times being what they were, the only affordable nonessentials for the majority of ladies in the early thirties were indeed bagatelles. Many of these accessories were marked with the stamp of commercial Art Deco diluted by an admixture of novelty for which a sudden penchant had developed.

For those who could not afford or were reluctant to invest in the costlier jewels in the early thirties, pendants with small diamonds were available at prices of $18 up. For the housewife who wanted to splurge a little, a filigree pendant of 14-karat gold adorned with four diamonds was available at just $52. Necklaces with pearls and onyx on 16-inch strands were being offered at $20. Saucy brooches with rhinestones and other imitations of precious stones were plentiful, many of them featuring a favorite Art Deco-Modernism motif — a female figure accompanied by an oversized dog. There were novelty brooches in the form of roosters, horses, fish, lovebirds, parrots, innumerable breeds of dogs (including the collie and the bullpup), peacocks, and butterflies.

Greeting the onset of the 1940s were novel forms of coat and lapel pins with coral, pearl clusters, garnets, and other stones, including one in the shape of a flying duck. There were silver bracelets with sailing ships and doves; saucy lapel watches (Clinton made one depicting a dolphin leaping happily over a tiny watch case in the shape of a ship's wheel in 10-karat gold and with seven jewels that sold at $29.50); rings that reflected the influence at least of Art Deco (including a wedding band boldly lettered in cutout gold "I Love You Truly" and capped with a band of orange blossoms); commercial Art Deco lockets; novelty earrings, and charms that ran the gamut of designers' imaginations.

Novelty chains featuring fairy tale characters and animals, and novelty necklaces and pins were made for the children. In addition, immediately after the outbreak of World War II a great variety of military costume accessories were produced. They will be considered in the chapter entitled "The Impact of War."

The mesh handbag was in style in the early forties with gold mesh favored. And for evening wear there were beaded bags and black velvet ones studded with stones or seed pearls. A large number of imported embroidered bags sported designs in a streamlined version of Art Deco.

The impact traditionally made by Parisian fashions upon style in this country was not quite so great in the thirties as it had been theretofore, due to some extent to the aura of glamor exuding from Hollywood. True, the dictates of such designers as Schiaparelli and Poiret were gospel to many in the ranks of the gentry, but a greater impact upon the masses was made by the styles that graced the svelte figures of the glamor ladies of the silver screen. Copies of dresses worn by the stars popped up all over, including the shops in the hinterlands.

Other authorities have dealt at some length with the dress of this period, and we do not propose to do so here. Suffice it to say that the dress and accessories of the two decades veered toward greater informality than before. Pompousness was becoming passé, and girls were deciding to be girls again.

Watch by Cartier with jade chimera, gold and platinum pendant, lapel brooch watch with rubies, diamonds, onyx and black, signed, *c.* 1923. (*Courtesy Minneapolis Institute of Arts, anonymous loan.*)

Top: Striking Art Deco pin set with 99 diamonds and 10 cabachon sapphires placed in the centers of the floral patterns of varicolored natural mother-of-pearl. Even the flowers are geometrically stylized in a popular Art Deco floral pattern. The back of this pin repeats the design and is etched into the platinum. (*Courtesy Mrs. Theodore Davidov, Bethesda, Md.*) Below: Art Deco bracelet with four strands of emerald beads, yellow gold, and diamond clasp, *c.* 1935, exhibited at the Finch College Museum of Art's Art Deco 1971 exhibition. (*Courtesy Hartmen Galleries, Inc.*)

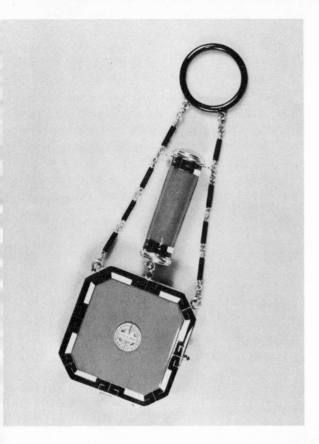

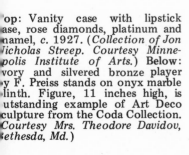

Top: Vanity case with lipstick case, rose diamonds, platinum and enamel, c. 1927. (*Collection of Jon Nicholas Streep. Courtesy Minneapolis Institute of Arts.*) Below: Ivory and silvered bronze player by F. Preiss stands on onyx marble plinth. Figure, 11 inches high, is outstanding example of Art Deco sculpture from the Coda Collection. (*Courtesy Mrs. Theodore Davidov, Bethesda, Md.*)

Top Left: Nautical Pendant watch by Clinton, early forties. (*Bennett Brothers, Inc.*) **Top Right:** A sentimental favorite—sterling friendship rings from the forties. **Below Left:** Early thirties chromium-plated hand mirror by Evans reflects Art Deco in its engine-turned stripes, French enamel color contrast. **Below Right:** "I Love You Truly" wedding ring of the early forties.

Top Left: Wooden military comb and brush set containers, 1942. **Top Right:** Gold mesh bag. **Second Row Left:** In early thirties caps were popular headgear for both men and boys. **Second Row Right:** Art Deco leather pocketbook, 1930. **Below:** Paris Fashion Shoes (top); Connie Styles Creations (below).

Left: This all-wool French beret (at top) was sold by Sears, Roebuck at three for a dollar in 1933. Below is the Jester's Cap, featured by Sears the same year. Right: As the thirties opened, this was the fashionable length for dresses.

REGULAR SIZES

Left: Wool coat with "wolf-dyed" Manchurian dog fur collar and cuffs and rayon and cotton lining was offered in 1934 by Montgomery Ward at $9.98! Right: Baggy pants with cuffs that extended almost the entire length of the shoe were featured in the Sears, Roebuck 1933-1934 catalog.

Art Deco designs were featured in these compacts of the thirties and forties.

Novelty costume pins and brooches of the forties. (*Courtesy Americana Interstate Corp.*)

CERAMICS

ALTHOUGH certain forms of ceramics were poorly adaptable to Art Deco, some — notably figurines — with Art Deco influence did appear during the two decades that hold our attention here. A large percentage of these were produced abroad, particularly in France and Bohemia. In addition, numerous other types of highly collectible ceramics were produced in the 1930s and 1940s, some of them from potteries established during these decades and others stemming from factories that had been in existence for years and some of which ceased operations before 1950.

Among the scarcest collectible pottery from this period were pieces made in a tiny hamlet in Moore County, North Carolina. The community was named, appropriately, Jugtown, situated between Asheboro and Seagrove. Rather crude utilitarian pottery had been produced in Jugtown for decades, whence the hamlet obtained its name. Prior to the 1930s, most production consisted of such things as flower pots, jardinieres, crocks, and jugs, the last-named in considerable favor with North Carolina bootleggers.

Early in the 1930s, when working on a newspaper in High Point, N. C., I heard of interesting experiments with ceramics being undertaken in Jugtown by a husband-and-wife artist team, Jacques and Juliana Busbee, who had moved there in an effort to revive an industry that was on the wane. So I paid them a visit — a fruitful one — and remained to purchase a stock of their wares, primarily pitchers and beer mugs, which I intended to offer for sale in a bookstore I owned as an adjunct to my newspapering. I had already discovered, the hard way, that while many of the residents of my own community could read, few of them took the time to do so. However, a great many of them indeed drank beer. I still have the best of the books that were in my stock at that time, having removed them to my home for reading purposes and safekeeping, but unfortunately I managed to dispose of the pitchers and mugs made under the supervision of the Busbees. For Jugtown pottery today is high on the ceramic collectors' list, and the prices of choice pieces seem extraordinarily high.

The Busbees had begun their venture in Jugtown during World War I and had managed to latch on to a remarkable young man named Ben Owen, who actually made the ware with the guidance and under the supervision of Mr. and Mrs. Busbee. The products featured simple, early shapes and forms but with a variety of intriguing glazes. The ware was stamped "Jugtown Pottery" from early in the 1920s until late in the 1940s, and during the latter part of the 1920s some of it began to reflect the influence of Chinese pottery. More of it, incidentally, was sold in New York than was sold in North Carolina.

Although the Busbees were artists, they also were practical. They knew that in order to sell the pottery, they had to promote it; and they inspired a number of articles in magazines and newspapers around the country, including one by me in the newspaper by which I was employed. As a result, the very name "Jugtown Pottery" took on an aura of glamor — an aura that has increased in intensity with the years.

Jacques Busbee continued directing the operations at his pottery until his death in 1947, and Mrs. Busbee and Ben Owen carried on for some years thereafter. The pottery ceased operations in 1959 but was taken over by other management in 1960. Today, Ben Owen is still making fine pottery, stamping his wares "Ben Owen Master Potter," and justifiably so.

The decorative pieces with fine glazes today find a ready market wherever they turn up, but they are hard to find. Prices of the pieces still available took a spurt after Jean Crawford wrote a book about the pottery, *Jugtown Pottery, History and Design* (Winston-Salem, N. C.: John F. Blair, Publisher, 1964).

Other types of art pottery were being produced during the period, including some by distinguished potteries that were soon to cease their operations. Among these were wares of the famous Rookwood Pottery, whose end came in 1967 but which had changed hands in 1959 and had been transferred from Cincinnati to Starkville, Miss.; Weller Pottery, which was located in Zanesville, Ohio, and had been in production from the 1870s until 1948; and Roseville Pottery Company, also located in Ohio and operating from 1898 to 1954. All of these potteries were advertising their wares and were creating new lines in the 1930s and 1940s.

Both Rookwood and Roseville ran advertising in some of the major women's periodicals. In 1940, Roseville offered its new White Rose line in an advertisement in *Woman's Home Companion,* and in 1941 it carried a series of advertisements promoting its Bushberry line. This pottery was embossed "Roseville U.S.A.," beginning in the 1930s. Several other lines were introduced in the 1930s, including Monticello, Laurel, Primrose, Orian, Topeco, Tourmaline, and Velmoss. Roseville pieces will generally range in price today from a very few dollars to around $50. However, exceptionally desirable and scarce pieces will bring more. All the earlier pieces of Roseville had a matte glaze, but a glossy glaze was introduced toward the end of the company's existence.

In 1930, Rookwood Pottery was emphasizing its textures, commenting in an advertisement that year: "Today at Rookwood, textures remains a paramount aim; color and form following in close harmony." It also boasted its kinship to fine old Chinese wares, offering in the same year "Rookwood in the spirit of Han pottery" with a "terra verte" matte glaze with brown decorations. A choice production in the spring of 1930 was a 14-inch-high ovoid vase titled "The Antelope Rider" and with a form described as "born of the same impulse as the rock-scratchings in prehistoric caves." The colors were described by the company as "old ivory, filched from the shoulders of marching black men . . . burnt orange, wrung from the flesh of sun-scorched fruits . . . deep black, dipped from the midnight waters of the Congo." The vase was priced at that time at $100 and was being sold, as were its other wares, through such outlets as Tiffany and Company in New York City, Kayser and Allman in Philadelphia, Hutzler Brothers in Baltimore, and Marshall Field and Company in Chicago.

In the early 1930s, J. D. Wareham was serving as president of Rookwood Pottery, having come up through the ranks; but the company faced severe financial problems from which it failed to recover.

Rookwood was never cheap pottery, and outstanding pieces today will sell to a ready market at excellent prices; some have brought $200 to $300 and more. It was, however, produced in great abundance through the years, and a great deal of it is still around and available.

Weller introduced a number of new patterns in the 1930s and 1940s, although the company, with so many others, was hurt by the Depression. In an effort to maintain business volume, the company turned to the production of beer mugs around 1933 or 1934 and, according to Lucile Henzke in her excellent book *American Art Pottery* (Camden, N.J.: Thomas Nelson, Inc., 1970), sold these in great profusion. Among the late patterns were Comet, Crystalline, Darsie, Delsa, Floral, Dorland, Flemish, Juneau, Ivoris, Mi-Flo, and Manhattan, together with some others whose names now are known only to experienced collectors of this ware.

Many Weller and Roseville lines bear a striking resemblance, but the choicer and scarcer pieces of Weller will bring higher prices — up to $300 or more and are therefore comparable with those of some of the fine Rookwood pieces. The patterns of the 1930s and 1940s are generally available at much smaller sums, and many are being advertised for under $30.

Haviland china has been collected for several decades. The Haviland factories were established in Limoges, France. In the late 19th century two Haviland factories were created, one operated by Charles Haviland, and the other by Theodore Haviland. In 1936, when William David Haviland was at the helm of the Theodore Haviland company, this company began the manufacture of china in the United States as well as in Limoges, and its products were being widely advertised and sold. Haviland has always been top-quality porcelain and has been widely collected in table services in numerous patterns. Much of that turned out in this country in the late 1930s and the 1940s now brings prices above the original retail prices, although it was relatively expensive when first made. In 1940, for example, a 94-piece set of Theodore Haviland Chalfonte pattern was advertised at $140.65, and a 94-piece set of the Troy pattern at $130.65. The Theodore Haviland American Varenne pattern, with a garland of red roses and yellow and green pastel shades, was a hit of 1942 and sold at $129.10 for a 94-piece setting. The Veronica and Rosalinde patterns also were being made in this country that year. Haviland, of course, is still being made, and there is a steady demand for both current and earlier patterns. The demand for discontinued patterns, in fact, is so great that several "matching services" firms, companies that specialize in locating discontinued pattern pieces to enable collectors to complete their sets, are doing a thriving business.

Turned out in tremendous quantities throughout the two decades, as it still is today, was Noritake china, made since shortly after the opening of this century at the Noritake factory in Nagoya, Japan. The factory is operated now under the name Nippon Toki Kaisha. The wares, many patterns quite attractive, have poured into this country, and early and discontinued patterns are being collected, chief among them being one known as Azalea. Noritake was fashioned into complete dinner services and such other utilitarian objects as vases and bowls. This china is being exported to 80 countries, attesting its popularity.

A particularly attractive pattern made in the early 1940s was Dresdlina. This featured American Beauty roses and garden flowers in delicate colorings of rose, violet, and green. A service of Dresdlina for 12 was offered in 1940 at a price of $81.35. Nerissa was another popular pattern of the same period. It had a conventional border decoration in neutral color with an ivory background and white enameled flowers. The Royce pattern was an imitation of bone china decoration with a conventional border of delicate blue on an ivory background with small clusters of flowers. Handles were decorated with coin gold. Other patterns of the forties included Carmela, Senta, Barbizon, Savoia, and Gavotte.

Noritake also produced numerous vases, hand-decorated with 22-karat gold and in a medley of shapes.

Individual Noritake dishes, bowls, plates, platters, cups and saucers, and cream and sugar sets will now bring from around $3 to $15 each.

Nippon china is also now being collected, and much of this was manufactured in the 1930s and 1940s. The term "Nippon" is presently used to refer generally to porcelains made in various small Japanese factories, most of them late last century or in the present one. These pieces bore various names and often incorporated in their markings the word "Nippon." Some were marked "hand painted" and others bear a depiction of a rising sun. Some Noritake also was marked "Nippon." All sorts of small decorative objects appeared in the 1930s and early 1940s, and these are collectible although not of great value. The bulk of the 1930–1949 production consisted of gift items, such as vases, figural cream and sugar sets, novelty pitchers, teapots, bonbon dishes, cookie jars, and the like.

Items which sold in the 1930s for 50 cents or under will often bring $4 to $20 or more now. Chocolate pots are currently worth $8 to $20, jam jars $10 to $15, and pitchers $8 to $25. Nippon dinner sets were available in the early 1940s in various floral patterns outlined in gold, and services for 12 were selling for around $55.

Collectors have watched prices of Royal Bayreuth china multiply three or four times in the past few years and have noted prices of $50 to $85 on a Sunbonnet Babies plate, $135 for a single Tapestry pattern matchholder, and $40 or so for a small trinket box. But they may be surprised to know that Montgomery Ward was offering 33-piece Royal Bayreuth dinner services for $28.75 in 1932!

Numerous other Bavarian factories were sending porcelain by the shipload into the United States at this period, some of it made especially for American-headquartered importing firms that had established plants in Bavaria and in Austria. Names familiar to collectors include Karlsbad, a name used by both Heinrichs, a New York importing firm, and the firm of Thun; H & Co., also the trademark of Heinrichs; and Edelstein. These potteries produced pleasant, well-made, and, often, handsomely decorated table services to retail at quite low prices, but individual pieces now command prices considerably above those at which they were originally retailed.

Ward was offering Thun Karlsbad dinner services for six at just $15.65 and Heinrichs services for six at just a couple of dollars more in 1932. Two years later, Ward had a 32-piece dinner set of Heinrichs china decorated with garlands of pink roses for only $10.95.

Within recent months collectors have been expressing interest in porcelain marked "Black Knight," although little seems to be known about this china. It was being made for Graham & Zenger, Inc., of New York City. To promote the ware, the firm offered for 25 cents a booklet entitled *The Gracious Art of Dining,* written by Mrs. John Alexander King, of the staff of *Delineator* magazine. The china was sold by such establishments as Ovington's in New York City, John Wanamaker in Philadelphia, and R. H. Stearns Company in Boston.

In 1930, the company apparently sponsored publication of an exceptionally handsome book, *Color Follows Color as Course Follows Course,* written by Helen Ufford and William F. Bruning and copyrighted by the latter. It contained a gallery of patterns of Black Knight china in full color and is now a collector's item itself but is apparently quite scarce.

Much other fine porcelain and art pottery from the period is also available today, including new designs by Wedgwood and Royal Doulton, of England; lovely pieces of American-made Lenox china; interesting art-type pottery made by John Frank at the Frankoma Pottery, which he established in 1933 at Sapulpa, Okla.; pottery with exceptionally fine glazes manufactured by the Zane Pottery until 1941 in Zanesville, Ohio; and wares produced by numerous other firms.

Earthenware service pieces designed and made in Norway with simple, clean lines and decorations had their influence on earthenware production in the United States. The pieces were extremely functional and uncluttered. Porsgrunds Porselaensfabrik turned out some delightful wares of this type designed by Nora Gulbrandsen in the 1930s. Interesting modern designs also were created by Thorbjørn Feyling and Anker Olsen for Egersunds Fayancefabriks Co. A/S and by Ragnar Grimsrud for Graverens Teglverk A/S, Stavanger.

Individual modern earthenwares were designed and made by Karl and Marit Teigen, Lili Scheel, Maja Refsum, Lillemor Aars, and William Knutzen, all of Oslo. Arne Jørgensen created for Gann's Potteri & Teglverk, Sandes, an extremely interesting tea set with a yellow-gray glaze, part-lustreless, and with copper-colored edges, and the same company marketed another tea set designed by Magne Stueland that was half-lustreless with a pale yellow-gray glaze and black bands.

The Art Deco influence on pottery was limited largely to decorative adjuncts. The Joseph Hagn Co. offered in 1942 an Art Deco three-piece majolica console set. A full female figure adorned the centerpiece, and female busts graced the two urns that completed the set. The same company presented a cow creamer in the form of a black, tan, and white cow seated on its haunches and wearing a ludicrous expression that reflected perfectly the penchant for frivolous decoration that dominated the thirties. But the mood was evidenced particularly in an extensive array of figures and figurines that ranged from dancers to sailor girls and equestriennes. These were made both in ceramics and a combination of plaster and composition and were designed for use on the mantel or table.

Among the better figures in the Art Deco mode were a group of faience ones offered by Paul A. Straub & Co., Inc., of New York City. Most of these were of dancers, skillfully modeled and many but not all of them mounted on oval bases. Reds, greens, and blues were the predominating colors. These retailed at prices of from a few dollars for small figures to around $50 for the large ones. The figures were made in Europe and were described as "on the Vienna order." All pieces were decorated under the glaze, and any of them would enhance a collection of Art Deco ceramics.

Although virtually nothing has been written about them thus far, Vernonware china dinner sets were designed by the distinguished artist, the late Rockwell Kent, for Vernon Kilns, Los Angeles, in 1940, and these pieces certainly will become increasingly collectible. For these pieces Kent did a series of 30 drawings, picturing scenes and activities in the United States of those days, ranging from cotton-picking scenes in the Carolinas to the New York skyline.

Finally, although it may not be generally know, Community Plate, longtime makers of plated silver wares, created a line of Community china in 1939, its first three patterns being Deauville, Grosvenor, and Noblesse. The patterns were crafted in "modern" shapes, and a service for eight, consisting of 67 pieces, was priced at $69.50.

Pottery and porcelain trifles made in Occupied Japan are beginning to be avidly collected but are discussed in detail in the chapter on "The Impact of War."

Top: Plate of Longwy faien signed, c. 1926, from Lillian N sau, Ltd. New York. (Courte Minn. Institute of Arts.) Belo Ceramic blue-gray water pitch c. 1930. (Collection of Harv Feinstein. Courtesy Finch Colle Museum of Art.)

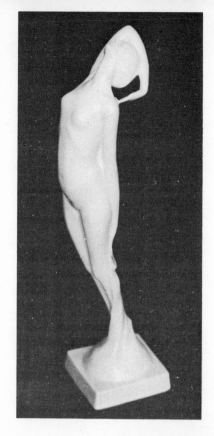

Top Left: Bisque figure by A. Bohm, *c. 1920. (Collection of Stanley Insler. Courtesy Minneapolis Institute of Arts.)* **Top Right:** Zane Pottery vase, made by the Zane Pottery Co., Zanesville, Ohio, which began under this name in 1921 and continued until 1941 when the name was changed to Gonder Ceramic Arts. (*Author's collection. Photo by J. D. (Don) Howard, Atlanta.*) **Below:** Art Deco geometric vase, French, enamel on copper, multilayered and multicolored, signed C. Faure. (*Courtesy National Antiques Show, Madison Square Garden.*)

Top Left: Rookwood vase showing the Chinese Han pottery influence, 1930. **Top Center:** Roseville pottery of 1930. **Top Right:** Blue ewer-vase made by Van Briggle Pottery in Colorado Springs, Colo., 1937. (*Author's collection.*) **Center Left:** Planter in unusually attractive form made by Roseville Pottery Co., Zanesville, O., probably late thirties or early forties. (*Author's collection.*) **Center Right:** 1930 Roseville pieces, embossed "Roseville" on bottom. **Below Left:** Royal Bayreuth tray decorated in blue, pink, green, magenta, and gold; 10 inches long. **Below Right:** Jugtown miniature vase (3¾ inches high) in magenta and blue-green, made by Jugtown Pottery, Jugtown, N.C. (*Author's collection. Photos by J. D. (Don) Howard, Atlanta.*)

Top Left: The attractive and elaborate Aurora pattern in Lenox china, introduced in 1936, and now collectible. (*Courtesy Lenox, Inc.*) **Top Right:** Lenox's Rutledge pattern, introduced in 1939. (*Courtesy Lenox, Inc.*) **Center:** Lenox's Rhodora pattern in a plate, cup and saucer, 1939. **Below Center:** Plate, cup and saucer in Lenox's 1939 Rhodora Pattern. **Below:** Montgomery Ward in 1934 was offering such prime collectibles as this 32-piece set of Chantilly pattern in Royal Bayreuth china for $26.95 (left). Note the inset trademark of the Heinrichs Bavarian china (right).

Top Left: This Wedgwood tea set in a limited edition of 3,000 sets commemorated the visit to America of Great Britain's King George VI and Queen Elizabeth in 1939. **Top Right:** Wedgwood commemorative Longfellow tea plate in Queensware. There were two Longfellow scenes, and the plates retailed in 1939 at $12 for a set of 12. They were sold in this country by Jones McDuffee, of Boston. **Center:** Noritake's Dresdlina pattern of the thirties featured hand-painted floral sprays on a pure white body. (*Courtesy Americana Interstate Corp.*) **Below:** Community Plate, a veteran producer of silverplated wares, went into production of Community China at the beginning of the thirties. This is its Deauville pattern.

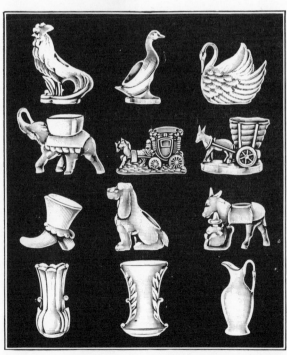

Top Left: Van Camp Sea Food Company's California pottery Tuna Baker and Salad Server and its ceramic entree plate of the early forties. (*Courtesy Van Camp Sea Food Co., Division Ralston Purina Co., St. Louis Mo.*) Top Right: Hand-painted decorative Nippon wares of 1930, as offered by the American Wholesale Corp. Division of Butler Brothers. Below: Handmade Sevilla Art pottery was produced by Sevilla in the Blue Ridge mountains in the early forties.

Collectible ceramics. **Top:** Novelties of 1930 came filled with bath salts. **Center:** twine holders of the early forties were offered by Americana Interstate Corp., formerly Joseph Hagn Co. **Below:** Cookie jars and Brown Fox jug of 1940.

Top: Group of "Made in Occupied Japan" figurines. These trifles have attracted numerous collectors. (*Author's collection. Photo by J. D. (Don) Howard, Atlanta.*) Below: Cheap Japanese ceramic ware such as this was offered during the thirties as Satsuma. Many buy it today believing that it is old.

GLASS

ALTHOUGH collectors of that broad category generally lumped together as "art glass" look upon the last two decades of the 19th century and the opening years of the present one as the exciting years of glassmaking, the 1930s and 1940s, in their own way, were really no less exciting, and they are growing more exciting as the years add perspective.

It seems virtually certain that much glass now being collected and attributed to the late 19th century was actually made during the thirties and forties. Certainly, from my own experience, more than a trifling amount of the glass being offered by some dealers and represented as having been produced in the 1880s or 1890s was in fact made during the third and fourth decades of this century. It is not difficult for the beginning collector or the inexperienced dealer to go astray with relation to dates, and not solely because of the 20th-century reproductions: Many types of glass being blown late in the 19th century were still being blown in the 1930s and 1940s. This is especially true of certain Bohemian types and Venetian wares. But the two decades under consideration also witnessed the production of new types of glass — new, that is, from the standpoint of form and decoration.

Swedish and Norwegian glass had their influence upon glass production elsewhere, particularly with relation to shape. In the 1930s "modern" glass was being manufactured in Norway by Hadeland

Glassverk and designed by Sverre Pettersen, who also designed a number of distinguished engraved pieces that bear kinship to those produced after 1930 by the Corning Glass Works in our own country.

As with architecture and furniture, functionalism provided a keynote for much of the glass production of the late 1920s and the 1930s. Unadorned transparent glass in simple forms emerged. Functionalism in glass design came to its fullest fruition in Sweden during and after 1930, especially in the work of Edward Hald and Simon Gate at Orrefors. In Holland, new designs and techniques were pioneered by Cornelis de Lorm and by A. D. Copier at the Unica Studio of the Royal Dutch Glass Works at Leerdam.

The influence of Maurice Marinot, the French painter-turned-glassmaker, was important in the 1930s, when he began blowing his own glass, utilizing a tremendous variety of techniques in its decoration. He favored geometrical patterns and utilized air bubbles successfully as ornamentation. Massive structures were his forte. To find Marinot glass today outside of collections would be a considerable feat.

During the thirties Crystalleries de Baccarat in France turned out some fascinating tablewares designed by Georges Chevalier, and also a variety of intriguing perfume bottles or flasks. It was their form, not decoration, that gave them distinction, and they are much sought today.

Also in France, the Daum brothers of Nancy, Auguste and Antonin, abandoned the cameo glass they had been producing for many years under the stimulus of that produced by the great French artisan Emile Gallé and turned instead to the types of glass that Marinot had made. In the 1940s, the Daum factory made clear crystal pieces in abstract shapes that can claim a kinship with certain examples of abstract painting. Some of their glass was sold by Wanamaker's in this country.

Another Frenchman, Jean Luce, also designed "modern style" glass, some of it cut and engraved. His type of cutting imparted great brilliance to his objects.

Another master French craftsman, René Lalique, specialized in molded glass, most of it clear or frosted, and some pieces were produced in abstract forms. However, Lalique is better known for his "sculptured" pieces with birds, insects, fish, and female figures in relief. Since 1945, when René Lalique died, the factory he founded has been carried on by his son Marc. Lalique made numerous perfume flasks, which still excite considerable collector interest. In the

1930s, Lalique crafted a large amount of decorative table glass adapted to the gay mood of those years.

In the United States, the Steuben Division of the Corning Glass Works at Corning, New York, produced decorated and other types of art glass under the guiding genius of Frederick Carder. After Mr. Carder's retirement in 1934, Steuben turned to "modern" glass. These later pieces were made of heavy transparent crystal in striking designs created by J. M. Gates, Sidney Waugh, and other noted glass designers and artists. Some of the magnificent engraved pieces are reminiscent, as commented earlier, of some of the work done at Orrefors but by the use of the copper wheel, Steuben craftsmen carried the art of engraving far beyond what had been achieved before and brought it to new heights of artistry. Steuben glass today is in many of the world's finest collections, and a number of examples are presented in the book *A Selection of Engraved Crystal by Steuben,* copyrighted by Steuben Glass and published in 1961.

Modern types of glass were also made during the 1930s by many established American firms: Bryce Brothers, of Mt. Pleasant, Pa., which, with its predecessor companies, had been operating since 1850 and which became a part of the United States Glass Co. combine in the early 1890s but had established another factory under its own name in 1896; Cambridge Glass Co., which had begun production in Cambridge, Ohio at the outset of this century and continued until 1958; the Fostoria Glass Co., of Moundsville, W. Va., which has been in existence since 1887; the A.H. Heisey Glass Co., established in 1893 in Newark, Ohio, and operating until 1958 when its molds and name were acquired by Imperial Glass Co.; the Libbey Glass Co., of Toledo, Ohio, an outgrowth of the New England Glass Co., which made some distinguished glass in the 1930s under the direction of A. Douglas Nash; the Pairpoint Glass Corp., New Bedford, Mass., a successor to the Mt. Washington Glass Co.: and others.

Later in this chapter, we'll discuss quite briefly some of the productions of the companies mentioned above, but at this point it's appropriate to emphasize that, at least from a mass collecting standpoint, the so-called "Depression glass" has emerged from the 1930s as something of a current phenomenon. This glass is still so inexpensive that anyone can afford to collect it, and, although the supplies are diminishing, it remains relatively plentiful.

This molded and mold-etched glass was manufactured in complete dinner services by several glasshouses during the depression years to cater to those who preferred not to eat from cans and grocers' packages but could not afford fine china. In the 1930s there were hordes of families in this category. The glass was sold in what were then the five-and-ten-cent stores (they've long since been graduated to a level of greater affluence), and by a number of chain stores.

Its producers included the Hazel-Atlas, Macbeth-Evans, Hocking, Federal, Imperial, Jeannette, Westmoreland, and McKee glass companies and a few others.

The pieces were made primarily in solid colors of pink, green, yellow, and amber, as well as in clear glass, black, and an opalescent white. There were some pieces in red and in blue. They featured a wide variety of mold-etched designs, many of which are reflected in the pattern names themselves, such as Ring, Raindrops, Ribbon, Thistle, Sunflower, Thumbprint, Strawberry, and so on. Others were endowed with fancier names, such as Queen Mary, Windsor, Royal Lace, Madrid, and Florentine.

One favorite among today's collectors is the pattern known as American Sweetheart, made by the Macbeth-Evans Glass Company in various colors, including the opalescent white that was called Monax, and also in an ivory shade known by the trade name Cremax.

Some patterns were identified only by numbers. Collectors have been giving the numbered patterns — and certain others whose original names have become obscured by time — names of their own. A pioneer in the field of identifying and researching Depression glass was Mrs. Hazel Marie Weatherman of Springfield, Mo., whose book, *A Guidebook to Colored Glassware of the 1920's and 1930's,* published in 1969, was so popular that the author issued a revised and expanded edition in 1970 under the title *Colored Glassware of the Depression Era.* Another pioneer in the field was Sandra McPhee Stout, whose 1970 book is entitled *Depression Glass in Color;* it presents in color more than 400 pieces in 80 patterns.

I searched back through numerous trade catalogs of the 1930s and found an abundance of Depression glass illustrated, with original pattern names given. The fact that the American Wholesale Division of Butler Brothers was offering patterns of this type of glass named Optic Ring and Colonial Block in its 1930 catalogs indicates clearly that production actually began earlier than that year. Westmoreland Glass Company's English Hobnail pattern, which had been made in the 1920s, was offered in the 1931–1932 Montgomery Ward catalog at $4.44 for an 18-piece set. This pattern was relatively expensive. In a 1932 sales catalog the same company offered a Cameo pattern 16-piece luncheon set in clear glass for only $1.

Even hardware wholesaling firms offered this glass, the Belknap Hardware & Manufacturing Co. of Louisville, Ky., tendering 12-dozen pieces of pink Mayfair in 1937 at a wholesale price of $37.80. Footed sherbets were $1.29 a dozen; tumblers, $1.08 a dozen; and luncheon plates, $2.52 a dozen.

Macbeth-Evans's American Sweetheart in rose-tinted color was offered by Ward in 1934 at just 95 cents for 15 pieces. (A dinner plate alone in this pattern will cost you $3.50 or more today on the collectors' market, and a cereal bowl will bring $2.75.) As late as 1940, a service for four in the Homespun pattern in Wild Rose (pink), made by Jeannette Glass Co., was available for only $1.58.

Although Depression glass is still fairly abundant, it may not be as simple a task as one would think to assemble a complete dinner set in certain patterns. Many families discarded their Depression glass when better times returned, and, of course, large quantities were broken through the years. Undoubtedly, however, much of this glass is still stashed away both out of sight and out of mind in many homes.

Prices of patterns will now vary a good bit. A pink creamer and sugar set in the Miss American pattern is now worth around $12, but the set in clear glass in the Manhattan pattern is valued at only about one-fourth that amount. Butter dishes are among the more expensive pieces today: A covered butter in green in the Madrid pattern is valued at around $18, approximately the same as one in the Adam or Lovebirds pattern. An American Sweetheart juice pitcher and six glasses is now tagged $150. A Royal Lace cookie jar now has a price tag of about $10, above the value of one in the Open Rose patterns. Luncheon plates generally start at about $2.50, and some cost several dollars more. An American Sweetheart Monax lazy susan is $75.

All this glass has no great elegance, but don't try to argue its merits with a collector. Since the hunt for it has really just begun in earnest, the prices unquestionably are going to get higher.

Much opalescent Hobnail glass is thought by some collectors (and dealers as well) to be older than it is. This glass was being produced in the 1930s and 1940s by the Duncan and Miller Glass Co. of Washington, Pa., the Fenton Art Glass Co. of Williamstown, W. Va., and others. Forms included numerous small vases, compotes, cups and saucers, plates, candleholders, tumblers, and bowls. In 1944, the

Joseph Hagn Co. offered twelve 23-piece breakfast or luncheon sets (a total of 276 pieces) of Moonstone Hobnail glass for $18.60. Cup and saucer sets and small plates have recently been traded at prices of $3 or $4 each.

The Akro Agate glass now being collected was made between 1932 and 1951 by the Akro Agate Co. in Clarksburg, W. Va. Identifying this ware — made chiefly in the form of miniature planters, children's tea sets, small vases and the like, as well as marbles — is the depiction of a crow flying through a capital letter "A" on the bottom of the objects. Akro Agate is marbled glass, sometimes called slag glass. Small Akro Agate ashtrays will now fetch $3 or $4, miniature flower pots from $3 to $6, and miniature cups and saucers about $6. They were selling for around 95 cents a dozen in the 1940s.

Figural glass candy containers were produced for many years prior to the decades with which we are concerned, but it may surprise some to know that these little figural containers also were being made in the 1930s to hold, as did their predecessors, small, hard, pill-shaped pieces of candy. Some of those produced in the thirties were made of clear glass, others of colored glass, ruby in particular.

It was quite logical, in view of the interest in the exploits of the *Graf Zeppelin* and other unusual aircraft of the period, that one of the candy containers offered in 1930 should have been in the shape of a zeppelin, 6 inches long. Another was in the shape of a limousine with the body painted green and the top black, and still another in the likeness of a touring car.

Other forms of these containers made in the thirties included telephones, lanterns, wheelbarrows, fire trucks, locomotives, dolls' nursing bottles, Santa Clauses, pistols, and propeller aircraft. Montgomery Ward in 1932 offered for 57 cents an assortment of five containers filled with candy. Some of these containers today are valued at from $3.50 to around $30.

The A. H. Heisey Glass Co. specialized in high-quality glasswares throughout its existence from 1895 until 1958. Heisey glass has been widely collected for several years. Heisey was advertising its fine crystal wares in the 1930s and 1940s in women's magazines. In 1934, a Heisey cut crystal compote in a Floral Leaf and Lettuce pattern with a gold-plated metal cupid figural baluster and metal base was being offered at a wholesale price of only $1.75. The company advertised its combination crystal epergne candlesticks, featuring a one-piece vase with flanking candlesticks in 1939. In 1940, the firm advertised footed tumblers with Ticonderoga cutting at $8; a goblet with Chauteau cutting at $2.25; a cocktail icer and liner with Daisy cutting at $2.25, and an etched Torte plate at $4. Heisey's Crystolite table service was offered in 1941 and had actually been made a few years earlier, as was table crystal in its Orchid etched pattern.

Clear crystal was preferred to color after 1930, although some colored glass continued to be made. Although the Crystolite line was offered in its 1956 catalog, and some collectors think it belongs to this period, the advertisements of 1941 clearly reveal that it was produced more than a decade earlier. Not all Heisey glass is marked, but most of it can be identified by the company's trademark of an "H" within a diamond either in the glass or on a paper label. In many instances, of course, the labels have been lost.

Among the other Heisey patterns of the thirties and forties well worth collecting are Lariat, Old Sandwich, Queen Anne, Waffle Keg, and Warwick, though this is by no means an inclusive list. The Queen Anne pattern was produced in pastel shades called Alexandrite and Sahara.

Several good books dealing with Heisey glass are available. Nearly all of the company's original glass is worth collecting, and prices have been increasing during the past few years.

Among the 19th-century American glasshouses still continuing production is the Fostoria Glass Co., established in Fostoria, Ohio in late 1887 and moved in 1891 to Moundsville, W. Va., where it still continues operations in a plant covering more than eight acres. As was the case with many other glasshouses, Fostoria had made a considerable amount of colored glass prior to the onset of the Depression in 1929. By the mid-1920s, in fact, about 90 percent of the company's production was in colored glass. The trend was rapidly reversed in the 1930s and by 1938, only 10 percent of total production was colored glass.

All of the company's glass is handmade, and during the Depression years production veered toward simple, unadorned crystal. Much interest reawakened in its plain geometric American pattern that had originally been introduced after the turn of the century.

During World War II, and in the years immediately following, Fostoria concentrated on simple shapes and simple cuttings but with the emphasis still on glass of high quality.

An extensive program of advertising in leading magazines launched in 1924 was continued through the 1930s and 1940s. In 1931 the company was making a pattern called Wisteria, which became quite popular. Its cut rock crystal in formal shapes predominated in 1932 and was made in objects ranging from iced appetizer sets to candlesticks in several patterns with prices of stemware starting at $1 and going up to about $1.50.

In mid-1930 the company introduced its Bubble Balls, clear and colored spheres with an opening in the top so that the balls could be filled with water and ivy or single weighted flowers such as roses inserted for decorating tables, shelves, or mantels. The Regency pattern in the company's Westchester shape was introduced in 1935 also and was adapted admirably for complementing the emphasis on function in architecture, furniture, and other adjuncts of the homes of those days. Delicately etched glassware was popular in the late 1930s, and in 1939 the Colonial Mirror line was introduced, featuring a Colonial period conception etched on crystal. More elaborate etchings in patterns called Buttercup, Navarre, Willowmere, and Chintz appeared early in the 1940s. Most of the patterns issued during the 1930s and 1940s are collectible and represent top craftsmanship.

Many collectors are currently interested in glass made by the Cambridge Glass Company, founded in Cambridge, Ohio in 1901 by Arthur J. Bennett. The company continued in operation until 1958, although it had closed for a while in 1954. This company produced numerous types of glass in the thirties and forties that are now eagerly sought. The articles are identified by the trademark of a "c" in a triangle or by black and gold paper labels with the firm's emblem. The opaque colored glass most sought now by many collectors was introduced in the 1920s and production of some of this was continued into the thirties. Perhaps the most popular of all Cambridge opaque wares are its Crown Tuscan pieces, which are flesh pink. During the years of the Depression, Cambridge continued to turn out quality glass instead of lowering quality as did some glasshouses. After the factory closed, the molds were acquired by Imperial Glass Co.

Collectible glass also was turned out by the Pairpoint Corporation, successor in 1894 to the noted Mt. Washington Glass Works, of New Bedford, Mass., and by the Gunderson Glass Works, which was organized in New Bedford in 1939 after Pairpoint had closed down as a result of losses, due in large measure to Japanese competition. Gunderson made a Peach Blow glass that resembled that of Mt. Washington but was thicker. Gunderson also reproduced Mt. Washington's Burmese. Both of these reproductions now sell at high prices. Another Gunderson creation, Camellia, shaded from rose to plum in color, also interests collectors.

Bohemian glass, which earlier had played havoc with certain American art glass wares because it was cheaper both in quality and price, continued to pour into the United States in the 1930s and was retailed by some of the chain establishments, including Montgomery Ward. In 1931, for example, Ward was offering a Bohemian iced tea set — a large pitcher and six glasses with dandelion yellow and Chinese red splashes on a green ground (flashed glass) — for just $2.98. The pitcher alone has been found in antiques shops currently priced at $25 or more. Ward also offered another Bohemian iced tea set with blue glass threading over a base of rose color. The price for the complete set: $3.25. A year later the price was lowered to only $1.98.

The following year, Montgomery Ward offered at 79 cents each Bohemian Spatter glass footed vases of the type now bringing $15 to $20; blue hobnail tumblers sold for 39 cents; and handled baskets in pastel pink glass with a blue cobweb design in the glass were offered at 29 cents.

Paul A. Straub & Co. of New York City offered in the 1930s a great variety of Bohemian glass at what will now seem extraordinarily low prices. Eight inch diameter engraved crystal ivy or bubble balls were tendered at $30 a dozen, wholesale. Cut glass decanters that reproduced old English and Irish designs were carried in stock in 50 patterns. Quart sizes of these that now sell for $40 to $55 were wholesaling at just $4.50. Bohemian crystal 9 inch diameter fruit bowls with Egermann engraving (named after Friedrich Egermann, the noted Bohemian glassmaker who died in 1864) wholesaled for $3.25 and similar violet or pansy vases at $6 a dozen.

Straub offered hand-painted cordial sets consisting of an attractive bottle and eight glasses at $1.85 a set in its wholesale catalog. Hand-painted tumbleups of crystal (then termed "night sets") were available at $12 a dozen, and gemel crystal oil bottles were wholesaling at $9 a dozen.

Venetian glass remained popular during the early 1930s and was offered in tremendous variety from latticino goblets to sea-blue aquaria imprisoning glass mermaids. Incidentally, tropical fish, including goldfish, were extremely popular "pets" during the thirties, and to lend verve to the sun parlor or the living room, producers crafted a diversity of novel aquaria. From Japan came a bowl with a fabulous water garden — an ideal home for guppies — and another in the form of a Japanese temple jar, complete with teakwood stand and pierced cover. For those who liked the idea but wanted to shun the burden of feeding live fish, there were bowls with fish of colored glass illumined by a light hidden in the mirrored base. Another creation of 1932 was a glass table aquarium decorated with a garden of geometric forms in crystal with jewellike glass fish swimming among cubes, spheres, and a glass obelisk.

The collector who thumbs through the 1930 catalog of the American Wholesale Division of Butler Brothers may gnash his teeth in anguish over the Czechoslovakian spangled and spatter glass pieces for which he may now be paying $15 to $35 each but which were then selling at 60 cents a throw. They included vases, rose bowls, pitchers, baskets, handled mugs, and other objects. These were distributed in assortments of 60 pieces per case, which means that a full case could have been purchased for about the price of many individual pieces now.

The collector who wants to have a field day with the glass of the thirties and forties, however, may well wish to turn his attention to perfume and cologne bottles. These were made in wondrous variety, ranging in form and quality from the ridiculous to the sublime. The production of these containers was so vast that we will be able to hit only a few of the high spots.

Inexpensive perfume packaged in glass bottles in the shape of animals and birds was imported in the 1930s. The bottles were of colored glass and wholesaled, filled, for less than 80 cents a dozen. There were numerous types of decorated glass atomizers, many of them enameled in colors, some gold-plated, and others with glass containers mounted on metal bases. Some were made in Art Deco form, and these are going to be eagerly sought.

Straub was selling Bohemian cut crystal perfume bottles in "modern" shapes at $7.80 a dozen, wholesale. Many interesting bottles were created for Lucien Lelong perfumes during the middle and late thirties. This company's Indiscreet perfume was retailing in sinuous drapery-fold bottles with bowtie stoppers in 1938 at prices ranging from $5 to $60. Lelong also offered that year a miniature illuminated Christmas tree, decked with 11 small bottles of perfume, for $10. The company's Castle featured four turret bottles around the corners of a glass castle, each containing a Lelong fragrance.

Novelty containers were rampant. Hagn offered Czarina, the Great Parfum, created by Carol in the form of two wolfhounds, each with a one-ounce bottle of perfume tied about its neck. St. Moritz perfume offered a miniature dog kennel with a sliding entrance, inside of which two miniature St. Bernard dogs carried tiny glass vials of perfume around their necks. Cardinal presented perfumes housed inside three miniature book-shaped bottles on a gilt stand under the name Three Novels of Charm.

Tap cologne came in a tiny glass barrel with a polished brass spigot and mounted on a brass stand. Golf Bag perfumes came in — what else? — a replica of a golf bag made of Scotch plaid silk and with a hobnail brass collar and base. The three perfume bottles it contained were in the shape of golf clubs. The Perfume Caravan was a replica of a covered wagon with perfume housed in its water jugs and with duffel bags filled with sachet. Karoff's Imperial Bath Cocktail was an after-bath cologne in a champagne bottle with a bucket base of copper. Lecog's Cologne Clipper was in the shape of a sailboat on whose deck stood three bottles of toilet water. Barette was a miniature bar with three glass containers representing a champagne bottle, goblet, and cocktail shaker. A beveled mirror stood behind the bar and a polished brass footrail in front.

Containers in the shapes of apples made in two sections housed bottles of Apple perfume. Another container was made in the form of a miniature cruet stand of metal with three bottles of perfume. There was a plaster elephant with a glass bottle of perfume attached to its trunk. It came in colors, including pink.

Of course there were musical perfume atomizers — containers with musical movements fitted in their bases. The Horn of Plenty perfume bottle was in the shape of a glass cornucopia 11 inches long. Swedish-type glass perfume bottles boasted charmingly-contrived animals and birds atop ball stoppers. Yesteryear perfume came inside a glass model of a Victorian lady housed under a glass dome. There were perfume lamps that would burn perfume for 24 hours; they would also burn oil. There were three-piece vanity sets with glass perfume bottles flanking a matching powder jar, and four-piece sets that included a tray. Royal Dabs came out in the early 1940s with gold-finished jeweled filigree bottles set with tiny rubies, emeralds, or sapphires. Tic-Toc perfume by Babs Creations, Inc., came in a glass replica of an 18th century clock housed under a glass dome or bell jar. What-Not perfumes offered three bottles on a hammered brass hanging whatnot stand measuring 5¾ inches tall. Wrisley made matched opalescent hobnail glass sets containing cologne, bath crystals, and dusting powder in 1942.

Perfume Hi-Light was a miniature floor lamp with perfume bottle light bulbs. Love Seat was a sachet cushion hiding two bottles of perfume and with its seat doubling as a jewel case. There was also a Sa-Chaise Lounge, which was a replica of just what its name indicates. The Grandfather Clock was also just that, with a bottle of perfume for the dial. The bottle could be replaced with a real watch to serve as a permanent timepiece.

And there were fragrance bottles in the form of miniature telephones, beds, radios, and an array of other objects, believable and incredible.

During the late 1930s and early 1940s Corning Glass also presented some inexpensive glassware, including its Classic Ivex ware with a geometric floral design in color on each piece of ivory-colored glass, and Chinex that resembled semi-porcelain in an ivory color with an embossed floral pattern.

In 1940, Montgomery Ward offered the Valkyrie line, a Swedish modern glass, with goblets, sherbets, and cocktail glasses at 24 cents each. And the collector of those charming colorplates from the old *Godey's Lady's Book* will be interested in Godey stemware, featuring Godey-type prints fired on the glass. This came in blues, greens, and various pastel shades with gold bands and an enameled dot border around the prints.

This chapter does not purport to cover all the intriguing glass produced during the 1930 to 1950 decades, but I hope that it has given some indication of the fascinating variety that will appeal to many collectors.

Top: Vase by Charder, blue and purple with cut geometric design; signed, c. 1930. From Barry and Audrey Friedman Antiques. (*Courtesy Minneapolis Institute of Arts.*) Below: Two lavender glass vases showing two extreme facets of Art Deco and an Art Deco steel cigarette box with glass flowers on top. (*Collection of Maurice D. Blum and John J. Greer. Photo by Marlin E. Fenical.*)

Top: One of a set of glass dishes 9 inches in diameter, unsigned but in the Lalique manner. (*Collection of Maurice D. Blum and John J. Greer. Photo by Marlin E. Fenical.*) **Center Left:** Cobalt blue hand-carved vase, 16 inches high, signed R. Lalique, France—apparently an early piece. The glass is more than an inch thick. (*From the Blum & Greer Art Deco collection. Photo by Marlin E. Fenical.*) **Center Right:** Crown Tuscan tray made by Cambridge Glass Co., Cambridge, Ohio. This ware is sought by an increasing number of collectors. (*Author's collection. Photo by J. D. (Don) Howard, Atlanta.*) **Below:** A new line of opalescent glass vases introduced by Paul A. Straub & Co., Inc., in the thirties.

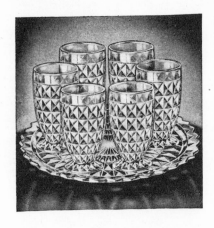

Top: Depression glass, Windsor pattern, from the thirties (left) and forties (right). **Below Left:** Depression glass, Homespun pattern, Wild Rose color, 1940. **Below Right:** Fostoria Glass Bubble-Balls of 1935 displayed single flowers. The stems were weighted so they would sink to the bottom of the water-filled globe. (*Courtesy Fostoria Glass Co.*)

Top: Bohemian glass specialties were offered in the thirties by Paul A. Straub & Co., Inc., New York City. Twin oil bottles are shown on top and hand-decorated night sets below. Below: Corning's Chinex glass as offered by Montgomery Ward, 1940.

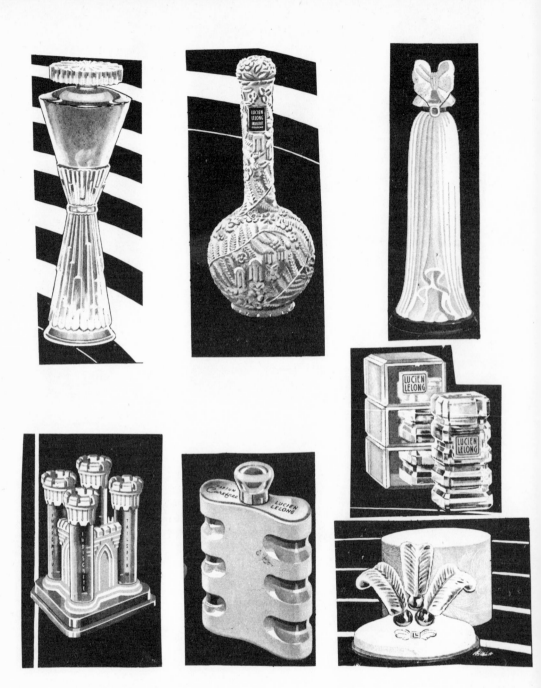

"Modern" Lucien Lelong perfume bottles of the thirties and early forties. (*Courtesy Lucien Lelong Corp.*)

Top Left: Highly attractive Bohemian crystal glass with Egermann engraving as offered in the thirties by Paul A. Straub & Co., Inc. Top Right: Valkyrie Swedish "modern" glass of 1940. (*Courtesy Montgomery Ward.*) Below: Striking glass creations by Royal Dabs of the early forties featured perfume bottles and atomizers set with stones and encased in filigree.

Top: Glass boudoir sets of the early forties. At left is a six-piece set, consisting of two torchieres (lamps) with crystal bases (top) and molded glass perfume bottles and powder jar (below). At top right are three crystal perfume bottles and, below, crystal bottles and mirror tray. (*Courtesy Americana Interstate Corp.*) Center Left: Tiffin glass of 1930 came in rose, green, gold, and blue. Pieces were identified by a paper label. Center Right: Cardinal Perfume's "Three Novels of Charm" perfume set with three glass book-like bottles on gilt stand sold for only $1.40 in thirties. Below Left: Heisey vase with Ticonderoga cutting, 1940. Below Right: Akro Agate Horn of Plenty.

Top: Heisey Crystolite, by A. H. Heisey & Co., Newark, Ohio. Below: Fostoria Glass Colonial Mirror pattern of etched crystal appeared in 1939.

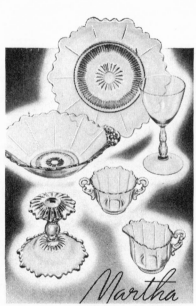

Top: Animal perfume sets of late thirties. Center: Figural glass candy containers were offered in 1930. Below: The Cambridge (Ohio) Glass Company's Martha Pattern of handmade glass was sold in 1939.

THE HOME AND ITS FURNISHINGS

THE prefabricated home of today stems largely from the preoccupation with functionalism in the late 1920s and the 1930s. According to the doctrine of functionalism, the form of objects and the materials of which they were made should be dictated primarily by the uses to which they were to be put.

Functionalism had its effect upon architecture and upon furnishings alike. In the 1930s there were references to the functional style and the modern style and also the "futuristic" style, and the terms were often being used interchangeably so that there was some confusion as to their precise meanings. Since styles are often called "modern" at their inception, the word frequently becomes relatively meaningless. But "modernistic" did have its application to a specific style in the thirties and was used to designate one that represented a rather radical departure from the characteristics of preceding styles and that emphasized what we now refer to as "streamlining."

The functional style was almost the antithesis of the ornately decorative styles, including Art Nouveau, that had preceded it. William Morris and the Arts and Crafts Movement anticipated the functional style. Morris had decreed: "Have nothing in your house that you do not know to be useful or believe to be beautiful." Yet there was a sharp difference between the aesthetic theories of Morris and of the major styles that were to follow. Morris abhorred the machine; the theorists of Art Nouveau accepted it; and those of functionalism embraced it.

The connoisseur of antiques deplores the machine, eschewing for the most part the products of the "machine age" that began at the close of the first quarter of the 19th century. Our own lawmakers had stipulated until only a few years ago that antiques, from the legal viewpoint at least, did not include objects made after 1830. Yet there were those early in this century who believed that the machine and artistic expression were not necessarily alien to one another. They included several figures associated with the Art Nouveau movement, among them the American architect, Louis Sullivan. During and after World War I the machine came into its own. And with the machine came functionalism and a rebellion against ornamentation.

The concepts of functionalism were first nurtured abroad, notably in Germany and the Scandinavian countries. Today we associate the emergence of functionalism intimately with the great Bauhaus school — originally established at Weimar and subsequently moved to Dessau and then Berlin — and with its founder, Walter Gropius. This school embraced the machine as an essential ingredient of modern living. Its purpose was to teach design for machine execution. Yet the Bauhaus by no means "invented" functionalism; its goals had been anticipated earlier by the German Werkbund, which as early as 1907 accepted the machine and set about devising techniques for controlling it to man's benefit.

Among the major exponents of functionalism, and certainly one of the more vocal, was Charles Edouard Jeanneret, far better known by the name Le Corbusier, a Swiss-born architect who worked largely in France. He and his associates were leading exponents of the alliance between the craftsman and the machine, and their concern was with objects that would serve specifically the purpose for which they were intended. They viewed ornamentation as of little value and, in many cases, detrimental. They selected their materials for the characteristics that would permit them to function most fully in the capacities for which they were designed.

As a result of the concern with functionalism, new materials were adopted and, before long, were in widespread use. Foremost among these were metals in tubular form. Le Corbusier created numerous objects of furniture made of chromium-plated tubular steel, and often combined steel and leather for comfort as well as function. But Le Corbusier was not the first to work with tubular steel. A member of the Bauhaus, Marcel Breur, had designed some striking tubular metal chairs in the mid-1920s to which the term "modern" or "modernistic" could appropriately be applied, even though tubular metal had been utilized for this purpose a dozen years earlier. Such chairs and other tubular metal furniture were made in some profusion in the latter part of the 1920s and in the 1930s, many of them by the Austrian firm of Thonet, whose founder, Michael Thonet, had first devised the bent-wood chair. In the 20th century, this business was carried on by the founder's sons.

In 1930 René Herbst founded in France an organization known as *Union des Artistes Modernes,* whose members were both artists and artisans concerned intimately with the dominance of form and the pursuit of materials they could use to create new forms dominated by function.

Michael Thonet's influence extended itself in the 1930s with the utilization of bent plywood for functional furniture forms. Finland took an early lead in this field, the firm of Artek producing laminated wood chairs designed by Alvar Aalto, who also combined bent plywood with tubular metal to create some intriguing new forms. The pioneering Marcel Breur also plunged into the use of plywood and created some chairs of exceptional strength. A noted designer in the same field in Sweden was Bruno Mathsson.

As one might guess, this preoccupation with function could lead to extremes — and did. The curvilinear gave way to the rectilinear and the geometric form, and, in some extreme aspects, reflected the influence of Cubism.

In some instances, too, emphasis on function led to a sort of antiseptic austerity that, carried to extremes, could be grim and forbidding. Yet the principal practitioners of functionalism found ways to relieve this severity. They managed to create an atmosphere — or at least an illusion — of spaciousness by reversing the practice of the Victorians and not overcrowding any room. And, although Le Corbusier and his disciples favored walls clad only in prophylactic white paint, others imparted verve by the use of blockprinted wallpapers.

There was, in the 1930s, a curious mingling of the old and the new. Built-ins of all kinds became the rage, and the use of decorative adjuncts in the Art Deco style mocked the sternness to which functionalism had given rise. While functional furniture had its impact and, in fact, took over many homes, it yielded in many others to traditional forms that managed to make certain concessions to the "modern" style.

The use of structural steel, concrete, and glass made heavy inroads in the thirties, because with their use major economies could be effected — a prime consideration in an era in which the Depression was rampant. The use of such materials was a boon to prefabrication and led eventually to the prefabricated homes of today, but in the thirties they were adapted to the prefabrication of such things as bathrooms and parts of kitchens. Mass production methods held down costs and helped enable the less affluent to reside in respectable if not sumptuous dwelling places. Elegance gave way to simplicity, though not to insipidity, and already the luxurious buildings of the past, including the movie palaces and the ornately-decorated office edifices, were on their way to becoming relics.

In attempting to achieve harmony inside the home, interior decorators of the thirties and early forties avoided the use of heavy colors in draperies and related these colors to those of the walls or the rug. Blond finishes for furniture were preferred, and those who couldn't afford new blond furniture were advised to bleach their dark pieces such as those made of mahogany or walnut. A combination of white and gold was popular for numerous pieces.

The Century of Progress Exposition in Chicago in 1933 featured the "modernistic" in design and had its influence upon decorators and designers alike. The magazine *Good Housekeeping* constructed as its exhibit a "Stran-Steel" house with the cooperation of several producers of building materials, furniture, and accessories. It featured tubular steel terrace furniture, and many rectangular pieces of furniture adapted to function.

Swedish "modern" furniture began to wield great influence and was a smash hit at the 1939 New York World's Fair. Informality was becoming the keynote of modern living, and a passion for Ranch houses developed. The erstwhile austerity that had accompanied functionalism began rapidly dissipating. The Swedish designers managed to combine both simplicity and attractiveness while never losing sight of function. The Swedes supplemented the built-ins with a variety of systems that could be built up unit by unit — then, if desired, modified or changed.

Tubular steel was joined shortly by steel wire plated with chrome, and American designers began eyeing the furniture of both Sweden and of Norway, where there had been extensive use of steel and iron in furniture production and where cost, durability, and comfort had been prime considerations of designers and manufacturers alike. The Norwegians favored light tones and utilized considerable quantities of leather in natural colors on upholstered pieces. A great deal of light oak was used, and pine, when utilized, was treated with lye.

Another development of the period was unit and multipurpose furniture, although some unit furniture had been created as far back as the latter part of the 19th century. Unit storage furniture for offices preceded its adoption in the home.

Even by the end of the thirties the "modern" style was exceedingly difficult to define, so many branches had the tree grown. One writer, Mary Davis Gillies, then associate editor of *McCall's* magazine, wrote a book called *Popular Home Decoration* (Wm. H. Wise & Co., Inc.) in which she advised her readers to steer clear of modern furniture if they were unable to distinguish good design from that which was merely bizarre.

A glance through the magazines of the 1930s and 1940s devoted to home decoration and furnishing reveals that the "modern" furniture winning greatest acceptance was plain and unadorned, avoided jagged edges, and combined comfort with maximum utility.

Although a considerable quantity of furniture of this type was manufactured in Grand Rapids and smaller quantities in North Carolina, an outstanding producer was the Herman Miller Furniture Co. of Zeeland, Mich., which utilized the services of such talented artists and architects as George Nelson, Charles Eames, Isamu Noguchi, and Paul Lazlo.

Much of the furniture by these designers is shown in a handsome hardbound book, *The Herman Miller Collection,* issued by the company in 1948. Miller in 1937 discontinued production of period reproductions because its designer, Gilbert Rohde, convinced the company that such imitations of the old traditional designs were "insincere aesthetically." In the book, the designer George Nelson wrote that the company's goal was "a permanent collection designed to meet fully the requirements for modern living."

It is interesting to note that individuals trained in *architecture* designed the bulk of the Miller furniture. This was done on the premise that the process of design is related both to the structures in which the furniture is used and to the people who use it, Nelson noted. Nelson himself was trained as an architect and at one time was on the staff of *The Architectural Forum.*

Miller placed emphasis on multipurpose design, because this was of prime advantage in an increasingly mobile society in which versatility of furniture was desirable. As an example, Miller offered a platform bench, which could serve as a low table, could be utilized for extra seating, or could be used as a high base for deep shallow cases. The company also offered case units that were set vertically and provided maximum storage space per square foot of floor space. These included combinations of drawer and cabinet space that made them suitable for use in any room. It presented a drop-front desk with an ample interior supplemented by three large drawers, and a buffet that contained cork-lined trays, a high cabinet space, and drawers.

Another design departure was a radio cabinet that was horizontal rather than vertical and was intended to rest on a platform bench as either a single piece or as one of a group of cases. The radio panel had a drop-front door that served as a record shelf when the player was in use.

A home desk was another radical departure in design. It consisted of a container for a typewriter on one end, a top covered with leather, plastic, or a coated fabric, a working height extension slide file basket on the other end, and a storage unit above the desk surface and supported by slender columns. The entire desk rested upon a cradle of tubular steel. There were free-form lightweight tables with tubular aluminum frames supporting linoleum-covered wood tops, and a striking gateleg table in which a special wood hinge was worked out to eliminate the customary dropped edge that appears when the leaves of such tables are down. The table had two gatelegs on the sides to give greater stability. It also matched the company's case pieces and could be lined up with them.

A variety of sculptured forms in furniture was designed by Noguchi, one of this country's most distinguished sculptors. Among them was a coffee table with a wood base consisting of two members identical in size and shape. One of these members was reversed and joined to the other by a pivot rod to create a flowing form base, which also formed a tripod. The carved base was revealed for all by a heavy free-form plate glass top.

Many innovations were introduced by the architect Charles Eames, who in 1940 had teamed with Eero Saarinen to capture first prize in a competition for furniture design sponsored by the Museum of Modern Art in New York City. Eames mounted seats and backs on blocks of rubber to give them resiliency, utilized heavily plated metal parts and resin-impregnated wood surfaces so that his pieces were suitable for use both indoors and out.

As opposed to the experimentalists we have been discussing, there were the traditionalists who, while clinging to the major styles of the past, nevertheless made concessions in some areas of construction and materials to a changing mode of living. For example, some began using metals and glass and selecting woods in which contrasting grains could be dramatized, but they were reluctant to abandon the ornamentation that was for the most part anathema to the "modern" designers. And if we can judge by reading the furniture catalogs and those of the major chain stores of this era, their reluctance to yield fully to the new influences was shared by most people. The average homemaker was willing to accept a little unit furniture, "modern" chairs for the terrace, or a functional coffee table, but she still clung to the traditional for the preponderance of her furniture.

Nevertheless, as the forties progressed, functional furniture made further inroads. More and more occasional tables with plate glass supported by chrome-plated steel appeared in average homes. So did contoured upholstered chairs and settees encircled by frames of chromium steel. The gentle or pretty decorative effects of rooms began to give way to decorative schemes of sheer black and white, sometimes relieved by touches of color here and there, particularly in decorative adjuncts.

Whereas in the past furniture had been associated with such names as Chippendale, Hepplewhite, Sheraton, Adam, Phyfe, and a few others, some new names were becoming familiar to the public in the thirties, among them those of Donald Deskey, Eugene Schoen, Paul T. Frankl, Winold Reiss, Kem Weber, Walter Nessen, Wolfgang Hoffman, and Gilbert Rohde.

Firms such as Dunbar Furniture Manufacturing Company of Berne, Indiana were widely advertising "modern with a timeless accent." (Dunbar brought forth sofas with pillowed arms adjustable to any angle.) In 1933, Sears, Roebuck presented an "Art Moderne" bedroom suite that it termed "as distinctive as the architecture of the Chicago World's Fair." It was made of richly figured Oriental wood veneer resembling walnut with the center panels V-matched. On each side of the headboard, the bed featured lights housed in opal glass paneled compartments. Below them were twin cupboards, each with a swinging door and a shelf. An adjustable panel in the headboard was hinged at the top and could be raised or lowered for use as a backrest. Sockets for the electric light cord were built into the headboard legs. The dresser featured a tall hanging mirror and glass-topped compartments for jewelry and toilet articles. The latter were equipped with flexible aluminum doors that were opened by sliding them back into a concealed position at the rear of the dresser.

The right-hand side of the vanity in this suite was removable for use as a commode or night stand, and the left side had a plate glass top and a compartment with a sliding aluminum door similar to those in the dresser. This suite was featured in the Sears Building at the Century of Progress Exposition and was quite low in price. The highest-price piece, the dresser, sold for only $47.50, the vanity for $39.85, and the bed for $33.80. Other components of this suite included a chest, night stand, bench, chair, and vanity lamp.

By 1940 Montgomery Ward was offering a variety of furniture that represented a comfortable compromise between traditional and "modern." This included tables with blond finishes that were pristine in their simplicity and lack of adornment, upholstered chairs and sofas with maple frames of simple lines, hassocks with coated drill covers with contrasting color welts, including green with tan and maroon with red, and, of course, sunroom furniture with simulated leather covers and tubular steel frames.

Also popular in the 1940s was furniture decorated with wood inlays and with tops and end rolling to the front by means of rounded edges. Wooden knobs were used for pulls on drawers that were in effect large wooden cups recessed into drawer fronts. Limed oak was the darling of many homes.

Unless one has a very large home indeed, she is not likely to want to collect many pieces of furniture from these two decades, but when it comes to the decorative adjuncts of the home, that's another matter. There was a fantastic variety of lamps and other lighting devices, decorative wall plaques, mirrors, doorstops, clocks, centerpieces, and ornaments in general, and upon these the Art Deco influence was manifest and often striking. These objects reflected what was then the "modern" tempo and what is now considered the mood or the pace of the 1930s and even the early 1940s. Since Art Deco has been "rediscovered" (as are all art periods and fads eventually), the collector should be able to recognize and identify articles fashioned in this style.

Many adjectives have been used to describe Art Deco: frothy, saucy, carefree, vivacious, impertinent. Certainly the Art Deco mood was one of gaiety, often with a touch of impudence, belying what was in many quarters a severely depressed state of pocketbook and mind. We shall try to identify the spirit of this art and its background more fully in the chapter "Art and Photography."

As we indicated earlier, many objects created in the thirties represented a sort of amalgamation of Art Deco and modernism with a strange combination of curves and geometric shapes, the former a characteristic of Art Deco and the latter associated more intimately with the modernistic styles. In the hands of commercial manufacturers in this country, the combination was not always a successful one: Today, in fact, it often generates shudders. Yet in its day it served at least one purpose: It was a foil to the melancholia begot of the Depression. Moreover, there were numerous rooms in the thirties and even in the forties that set off Art Deco elements against modernistic ones, just as there were rooms in which the starkness of much functional furniture was offset by the introduction of pieces adapted from such traditional styles as those of Chippendale, Queen Anne, and others.

There was a touch of showmanship, of the theatrical, about it all, and the theatrical influence extended more importantly to a diversity of decorative adjuncts. This theatrical striving, the attempt to create something "new," resulted all too often in the creation of what may best be described as sheer novelties — interesting but scarcely destined to survive the test of time. Yet this mingling of styles, theretofore abhorrent to many who professed connoisseurship, has today become commonplace, so much so that it is recommended by antiques dealers (who, of course, have axes to grind) and even by interior decorators (who have at least hatchets to grind).

The spirit of commercial Art Deco was manifest in the thirties in many lighting devices and, in particular, in thousands of small table lamps, some of which even lent an air of frivolity to rooms that were otherwise almost painfully austere. This mood was reflected in numerous lamp standards, a large number of which were fashioned as undraped or partially draped lissome females in balletlike postures, or as dancing couples. The latter was a motif that had emerged in the late twenties and was enormously popular in the subsequent decade. Quite small lamps of these types were designed for use atop radio cabinets.

The majority of the less expensive dancing figures were made of either cast metal or glass, and they were widely vended around the country in gift shops and chain establishments. Sears, Roebuck offered one that featured a bronze-finished cast metal nude female dancer against a triangular pane of frosted glass at a price of just $1.85 in 1933. The 1933 Joseph Hagn Co. (now Americana Interstate Corp. of Mundelein, Ill., a subsidiary of Grolier, Inc.) catalog pictures one of composition and glass with a kneeling nude female attired in Egyptian headdress. When the light switch was activated, flames appeared to crackle behind the glass pane. Another in cast metal delineated a geisha girl holding a spread fan over her head; the bulb was concealed in a globe with a crackle-effect surface. Another was in the form of a metal dancing figure with outstretched arms against a frosted white opalescent glass background. This one stood 12 inches high, including a heavy metal base, and was offered at a price of $3.45.

Combination electric clock-lamps featured cast female nude figures in swaying postures, either on their bases or atop the clock.

A host of other novelty-type lamps made their advent in the thirties. Some heralded the advent of the age of air transportation, being figural-form airliners and zeppelins. There was an intriguing zeppelin clock-lamp with a swinging pendulum clock appended from the base of a frosted glass zeppelin. The clock was fitted with a Howard electric movement, and the combination cost $12.50.

There were interesting and inexpensive nautical lamps in sailing vessel form with chrome-plated sails and bulbs in the base that illuminated them. A Triside lamp that could be either utilized on a table or suspended from the ceiling had three silhouette-decorated parchment panels in a triangular metal frame and was available in 1934 for an astonishingly low 45 cents — less than the cost of a cord alone today.

Scene-in-Action lamps were popular in the thirties. They had round glass panels painted with various scenes in metal frames and on a metal base; an illusion of movement was created when the switch was turned on to illuminate the scenes. These were inexpensive, selling at from $1.98 to about $2.50 — a fraction of what they will cost now as collectibles. Some created the illusion of raging forest fires, water pouring over Niagara Falls, and sailing vessels breaking through moving waters.

Electric-lighted reproductions of old carriages, wagons, and ships were used by some interior decorators in the thirties to brighten up rooms. These ranged from replicas of the *Mayflower* to those of covered wagons and Queen Isabella's coach. Fire-Fleck Action lamps of metal and composition with translucent glass screens created the illusion of flames when the switch was activated. These featured such figures as Indian maidens and chiefs, and black-smiths and scenes such as fireplaces and even volcanoes. When the light was turned on in the volcano lamp, fire appeared to spout from the crater of the volcano and burning lava seemed to pour down its sides. Whether these were "fun" pieces or merely tawdry depended upon one's viewpoint.

An Aquarium Revolite presented the illusion of tropical fish swimming gracefully among submarine undergrowth.

Floor lamps, by and large, were stuffy and stodgy, crafted in much the same style as were those of the preceding several decades. They provided illumination but not much else.

Novelty clocks, however, were the order of the day. There were sleek Art Deco clocks in silver and black, but those created for the sake of novelty alone were, in many instances, fascinating if not of great value, either aesthetically or from a monetary standpoint.

There was an Elephant Mystery clock (though why it was a mystery remains itself a mystery) with a metal elephant holding aloft in his trunk an eight-day-movement clock with a swinging pendulum suspended on a jeweled bar. The Sportsman's clock, a Sessions movement in a hand-rubbed walnut case, boasted two sleek hunting dogs chasing a rabbit over the top. The Golden Girl was sheer Art Deco with a sensuous nude holding aloft an oval wooden-case clock with an electric Sessions movement. The figure was finished in 22-karat gold; this clock sold for $15.50.

A carved wooden panther of imposing proportions was depicted climbing atop a wooden-case Sessions clock. There were numerous varieties of novel kitchen clocks in the shapes of chefs, teapots, and other objects and figures. Cases were made of either metal or ceramics, including porcelain. The Liberty Bell clock of 1942 reflected the patriotic motif of wartime with a clock movement housed in a cast metal replica of the Liberty Bell, a cast figure of a doughboy on one end, and the inscription "God Bless America." Similarly, the U.S. Emblem clock was set into a cast metal shield of red, white, and blue with an eagle perched on the top and was lettered "God Bless America" and "Life, Liberty and Justice."

There was a Dice clock with a porcelain case; one of cast metal with a gnome on one end; another with a large cast metal police dog seated on its haunches, and a Lux clock with a case in the shape of a sunflower. The Kitty Cat Pendulette with a synthetic wood case depicted the face and paws of a white cat at its top. The Lucky Dog was also of synthetic carved wood in the shape of a doghouse with a Scotty's head at the top of the dial. Fitted with a Lux movement, the clock was animated, the dog's head moving from side to side as the minutes ticked away. And there were clocks in the shape of sumptuous residences, lighthouses, parasols, birdhouses, ships' wheels, and so on.

Onyx clocks were quite popular during both decades, some of them made of green Brazilian onyx. As prices went in those days, many of these were relatively expensive, selling at $25 to $50.

Decorated mirrored glass panels and mirror screens were used in the thirties in particular to create the illusion of space in cramped quarters. Victor White, a New York city painter, created some delightful decorations on metaled mirrors and executed a mirror-lined and canopied room in one New York residence. Screens and panels were designed as an integral part of the decorative scheme of rooms. Combinations of metals other than silver for the backs of the glass were utilized with effectiveness. These included, among others, copper, gold, and gunmetal. There were even beds with decorated mirror headboards in silver-leaf frames, and mirror door frames. The mirrors were decorated with everything from Oriental views to jungle scenes. Mirror screens were made by attaching silhouette patterns of the scenes to the reverse of clear glass plates cut to proper size, and the designs were then painted from the back. Some excellent painting of this type was done in oils. The completed paintings were covered with asphaltum and subjected to mirror baths for the deposit of metals — a process similar to that utilized in applying lusters to ceramics.

Much cheaper were Mirrorettes, which were handpainted silhouette scenes on plate mirrors. These were encased in simple frames and hung on walls, sometimes in pairs.

Dramatic effects also were obtained with lighted wall plaques, some of which were made of composition materials treated with a lustrous paint that gave them the appearance of blue-lighted pictures in shadow boxes. Other types of wall plaques were also used for decor, including large plastic ones depicting scenes that ranged from those of journeys in covered wagons to interiors of Colonial American homes.

For the sentimentalists of the thirties there was an abundance of poster-style illustrations with sentimental verses in gold frames. These eulogized the merits of mothers, wives, friends, sweethearts, and children or limned poetic essays on the preciousness of friendship, married love, prayer, smiles, and the ability to look on the sunny side of life.

For some reason doorstops flourished during the two decades although they are seldom used today except in a few homes in the hinterlands where, fortunately, the residents have not yet heard that they are no longer in style. They were fashioned of metals, wood, composition materials, ceramics, and glass; and they were produced in far more shapes than the uninitiate might imagine, such as the 1933 wood frame doghouse complete with metal dog. Almost every breed of dog, in fact, was fashioned into a metal doorstop.

There were cast metal doorstops in the shape of horsedrawn mail coaches, baskets of flowers, horses, cottages, cats, and quail. Most of them were inexpensive, only two or three dollars each. With a little effort and a fairly small outlay of cash, one could assemble a truly remarkable collection of these.

The berry bowl of shaded or decorated glass, to which the epergne had given way as a decorative centerpiece for dining tables, gave way, in turn, in the thirties to those made of what the manufacturers described as Pearlskin and Porsalana. These were actually composition substances that resembled glass and porcelain. These took the form of trees, flowers, and plants, some with leaves of glass and mounted on glass or composition bases. There were lemon trees, banana trees, water lilies, rock gardens, numerous bouquets, and flower bells. They did indeed brighten the table since they were profuse with color. A Chinese Centerpiece boasted red and turquoise glass flowers with jade green leaves. A Porsalana bouquet on a stone base had flowers in shades of rose, pink, and blue with green leaves.

And there were decorative ornaments for every conceivable purpose — some of which are difficult to conceive. They were placed atop tables, mantels, radio cabinets, milady's vanity, shelves, and in nooks and crannies around the home that one might think needed a touch of color, or the bizarre. These, too, were made of various substances, including metals, glass, ceramics, and composition.

In 1940 you could have purchased a Paradise Crane ornament of cast metal covered with silver and standing 12½ inches high for about $8. Pairs of cast metal pheasants with chromium finishes were available at around $7. There were horse ornaments galore, including those carrying riders — polo players and jockeys. An 8-inch-high silverplated horse mounted by a polo player sold for around $15.

There were many Art Deco ornaments, including dancing figures, girls in bathing suits, women in street clothes, and bare-breasted serving girls. They were made primarily of porcelain or earthenware. There were wooden stagecoach ornaments with metal wheels, replicas of sumptuous coaches from the days of Louis XIV, ox-drawn covered wagons, and a multitude of ship models with wooden hulls and decks and canvas sails. And, for good measure, there were also molded composition Hawaiian hula dancers and ukulele players.

We'll discuss some of the finer sculptured pieces and costlier ornaments in the chapter on Art.

Other objects given the Art Deco treatment in the thirties and forties included magazine baskets, hat stands, and garment hangers.

During the two decades, the major silver manufacturers introduced a number of new table service patterns, some of them reflecting the Scandinavian influence with its clean, simple lines. These tablewares in the "modern" manner differed sharply from the ornately decorated ones turned out under the earlier influence of Art Nouveau, such as, Gorham's striking Martelé.

We shall discuss some of the new patterns in a moment, but readers may be interested in knowing that the comic pages and the animated movie cartoons made a specific impact upon some producers of children's silver, and particularly upon such objects as spoons, mugs, and napkin clips.

In the late 1930s Wm. Rogers & Son, a division of International Silver Co., was making Walt Disney creations in juvenile silverplate. These included a mug on which Mickey Mouse was depicted playing a saxophone. For display purposes, the mug (or cup) was housed on a cart pulled by Mickey's dog, Pluto. Pluto also was attached to a cart with a Mickey Mouse knife, fork and spoon. A Baby Mickey Mouse Educator Set included a spoon and fork with Mickey's likeness on each. Mickey's likeness also appeared on a spoon and fork set held by a display figure of Donald Duck, and a figure of Mickey was featured holding a Mickey Mouse Educator baby spoon. A baby napkin ring, again featuring Mickey, was made by Rogers and came around the neck of a display figure of Pluto seated on a four-wheeled cart. The retail price in 1936 for an assortment of each of the items or sets mentioned above was $34.32.

Wm. Rogers & Son also crafted juvenile knives, forks, and spoons that were accompanied by holders in the likeness of nursery rhyme and children's story characters, including Humpty Dumpty, Peter Rabbit, Hansel and Gretel, Cheerio Chick, and the Little Corporal.

Along with Mickey Mouse, Popeye also captured the fancy of the designers for Wm. Rogers & Son, who, in 1938, were offering sets named after the noted promoter of spinach. These included spoons, forks, and knives of silverplate with a figure of Popeye in colors serving as the holder. The company also took a line from the radio comedian Joe Penner for its Kiddie Cups, which were packaged in cartons inscribed "Wanna buy a Kiddie Cup?" and with drawings of ducks. The cups themselves were decorated with nursery rhymes and characters from the old rhymes.

International Silver Company produced a variety of sterling baby spoons and napkin clips with handles in the form of jolly rabbits, ducks, parrots, mice, and monkeys.

In the 1930s Tudor Plate produced cups featuring nursery rhyme characters as well as a set of Uncle Wiggily cups, with decorations in the likeness of characters created by Howard R. Garis, who had copyrighted the names and the characters in his numerous volumes of *Uncle Wiggily* books that had delighted children for years.

Also in the early 1930s Community Plate made children's Winnie-the-Pooh knife and fork sets, cups, plates, porringers, and bowls named after the character created by A. A. Milne with the designs patented by Stephen Slesinger, Inc., of New York City. The knife and fork sets were packaged in special boxes, each of which contained a booklet with one of *Winnie-the-Pooh* stories.

International Silver Company created Mickey Mouse knife and fork sets in sterling silver with figures of Mickey cut out at the top of the handles.

Virtually all of the silver manufacturers introduced new lines or patterns in their tableware services during the two decades. The Towle Silversmiths of Newburyport, Mass. introduced Craftsman and Old Brocade patterns in 1932, and the attractive Candlelight pattern in 1935.

Alvin's new patterns included Romantique, Chapel Bells, Overture, and Mastercraft. The International Silver Co. presented its Continental and Modern design patterns with success. A new one by Gorham was Rose Marie, unveiled in 1934, following its The Hunt Club of 1930. Among the best sellers presented in silverplate by 1847 Rogers Bros. were First Love (1937) and Eternally Yours (1941). International Silver's best sterling sellers included the 1810 pattern (1930), Prelude and Royal Danish (1939), and Joan of Arc (1940).

In 1935, Community Plate introduced its Berkeley Square flatware pattern. Reed & Barton, and Dominick & Haff presented the Contempora design as a modern interpretation.

Some of the new patterns featured clean, simple lines, evidencing the Danish influence; but the traditional patterns that had been a favorite of many for years continued in popularity too. Nevertheless, one finds certain manufacturers in the thirties advertising silver "in the Danish manner." Decoration of most of these pieces was held to a minimum.

Silverplated novelties were popular during the period and included such things as tea bells, figural salt and pepper shakers, and console or centerpiece sets. One unusual centerpiece set consisted of a 14-inch-high glass tree, a silverplated swan, and a silverplated duck, all atop a hexagonal-shaped crystal mirror.

There was a new brand of metal in the thirties that is occasionally encountered today in antiques shops. It was produced as table service with a golden color and has puzzled some collectors. This was Dirilyte, and it was made by the Dirilyte Co. of America in Kokomo, Ind. This golden-colored metal alloy gave color to linens and china. Dirilyte was solid metal, not plated. A 34-piece service for eight sold in 1930 for $73.95 in a flatware chest.

Top: This chrome-steel coffee table (1940) featured an enameled wood top. **Center:** Chromium was lavishly used on furniture in the thirties. This table had an extension top, chairs were upholstered with Loydtex Leatherette. **Below:** These "modern" style tables of 1943, made of a combination of birch and figured birch veneer, were available in "strawtone," mahogany, or walnut finishes.

Top: Spring wind clocks, 1933. Below: Novelty clocks from early forties, including Elephant Mystery Clock (third row left), Teapot and Sessions Chef; Kitty Kat and Sunflower Pendulettes; Golden Girl; and Panther.

Top: Lighted wall plaques of the early forties. Made of composition materials, they were treated with a lustrous paint to give them the appearance of blue-lighted pictures. Below: Novelty statuary lamps of the thirties. These were of cast metal. (*Courtesy Americana Interstate Corp.*)

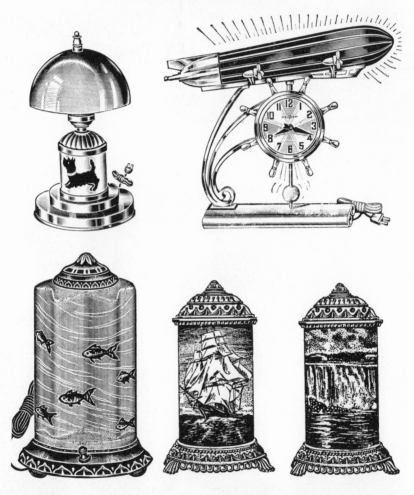

Top: Art Deco-type desk lamp with metal dog in bronze finish; 12 inches high; late thirties (*Courtesy Americana Interstate Corp.*) Center Left: "Scotty" student desk lamp was offered in 1940 for less than $2. Center Right: Zeppelin clock-lamp had swinging pendulum, zeppelin was of frosted glass with metal parts. It was fitted with a Howard electric movement. Below: "Action" lamps of the thirties. When lights were switched on, the fish appeared to be swimming, the ship sailing and Niagara Falls cascading.

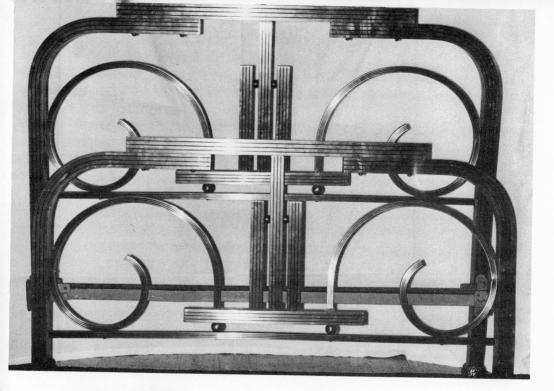

Top: Art Deco brass headboard and footboard with black accents. (*Collection of Maurice D. Blum and John J. Greer. Photo by Marlin E. Fenical.*) **Below:** Table, chairs, and extraordinary wooden screen designed by Charles Eames for Herman Miller, Inc., in the late forties. (*From the Herman Miller Collection. Courtesy Herman Miller, Inc., Zeeland, Mich.*)

Top: Bedroom suite in Art Moderne style offered by Sears, Roebuck in 1933 was displayed at the Chicago Century of Progress exposition. Below Left: "Modern" desk of unconventional design but great utility, including container for portable typewriter on 'eft; a working top; working height extension slide file basket at right, and storage unit on top. Designed by George Nelson for Herman Miller in 1940s. Below Right: Chess table in plywood and cast aluminum with plastic inserts in top designed by Isamu Noguchi for the Herman Miller Furniture Company, 1940s. Top revolves to open two pockets in the casting below it and also can serve as coffee table. (*Desk and table from the Herman Miller Collection. Courtesy Herman Miller, Inc., Zeeland, Mich.*)

Top Left: Photo taken of the Art Deco Exposition of the Arts Club of Washington, showing the skyscraper dressing table by Paul T. Frankel. (*Collection of Hal and Gretchen Glicksman.*) Right: Portable glass lamp with light inside base on marble-top Art Deco table. Chair is one of a set covered in neo-Art Deco fabric by Jack Lenor Larsen. Pieces in background are vacuum-cast neo-Art Deco display pieces by courtesy of Garfinkel's. Other pieces are from collection of Maurice D. Blum and John J. Greer. (*Photos by Marlin E. Fenical.*)

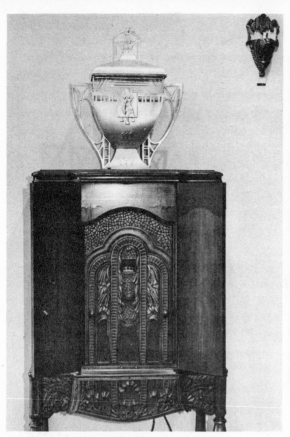
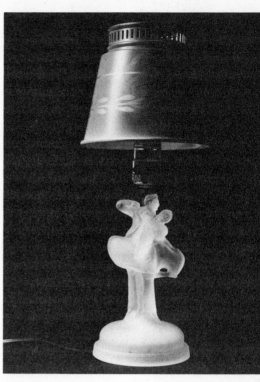

Top Left: Proto-Art Deco container on heavily carved Stromberg-Carlson radio. Metal wall sconce at upper right is of the "Roxy" school. (*Collection of Maurice D. Blum and John J. Greer. Photo by Marlin E. Fenical.*) Top Right: Art Deco lamp with dancing couple in camphor glass. (*Author's collection. Photo by J. D. (Don) Howard, Atlanta.*) Below Left: Reflecting the times was this La Paglia design by International Sterling Co. (*Courtesy International Silver Historical Library.*) Below Right: Flatware created for the Maharaja of Indore by Jean Puiforcat, 1930. (*Collection of Fred Hughes. Courtesy Minneapolis Institute of Arts.*)

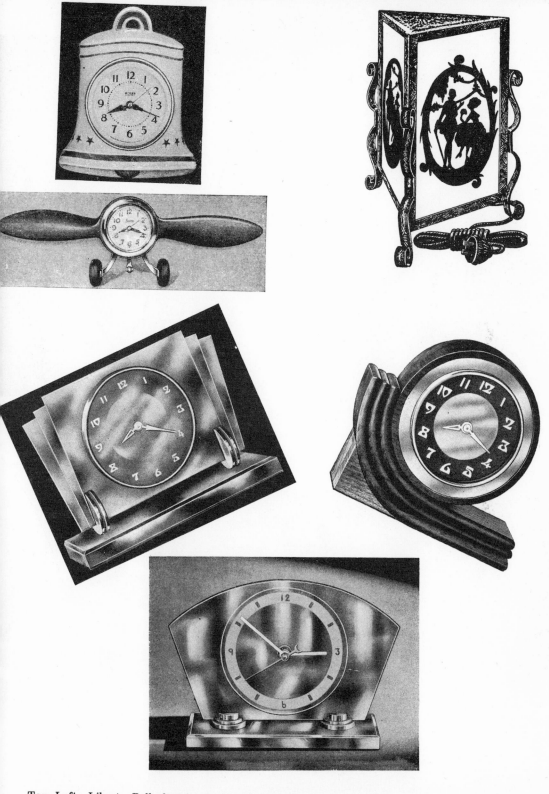

Top Left: Liberty Bell electric clock with white porcelain case and silver handle and clapper, and Airplane clock with carved wooden blades and chrome-plated landing gear; both of the late thirties. Top Right: Triside lamp of 1934 for table or ceiling use. Frame was steel, panels with silhouette figures of parchmentlike material. Below: Bennett Brothers, Inc., offered these ultramodern Walthams (top) and Hammond (below) electric clocks in 1940.

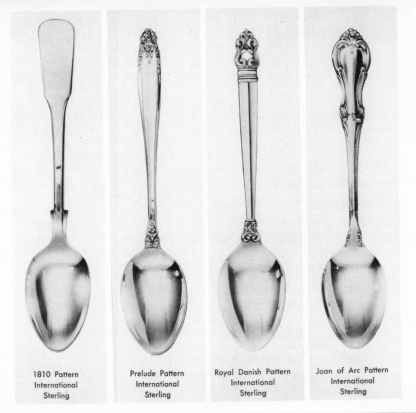

1810 Pattern
International
Sterling

Prelude Pattern
International
Sterling

Royal Danish Pattern
International
Sterling

Joan of Arc Pattern
International
Sterling

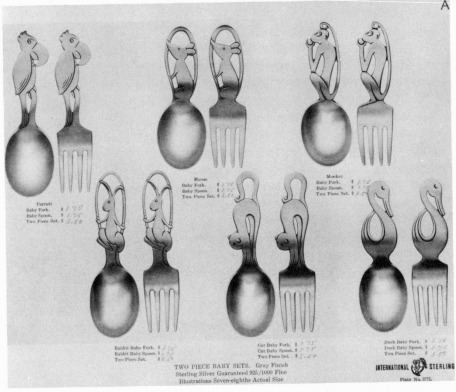

Parrott
Baby Fork. $ 1.75
Baby Spoon. $ 1.75
Two Piece Set. $ 3.50

Mouse
Baby Fork. $ 1.75
Baby Spoon. $ 1.75
Two Piece Set. $ 3.50

Monkey
Baby Fork. $ 1.75
Baby Spoon. $ 1.75
Two Piece Set. $ 3.50

Rabbit Baby Fork. $ 1.75
Rabbit Baby Spoon. $ 1.75
Two Piece Set. $ 3.50

Cat Baby Fork. $ 1.75
Cat Baby Spoon. $ 1.75
Two Piece Set. $ 3.50

Duck Baby Fork. $ 1.75
Duck Baby Spoon. $ 1.75
Two Piece Set. $ 3.50

TWO PIECE BABY SETS. Gray Finish
Sterling Silver Guaranteed 925/1000 Fine
Illustrations Seven-eighths Actual Size

INTERNATIONAL ⬧ STERLING
Plate No. 371L.

Top: International Sterling Company patterns of the thirties and forties. From Left: 1810 pattern, 1930; Royal Danish and Prelude patterns, 1939; and Joan of Arc, 1940. **Below:** Baby sets from International Sterling. (*Courtesy International Sterling Co. Historical Library.*)

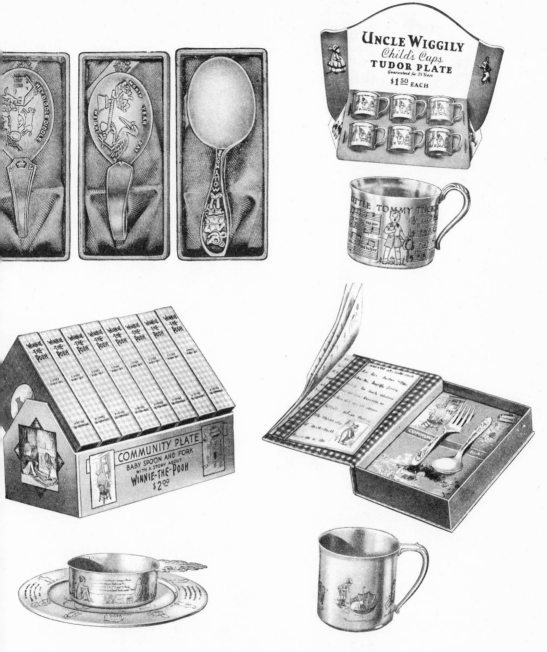

Community Plate's Winnie-the-Pooh baby sets in silver plate; Tudor Plate's Uncle Wiggily cups (above) and Nursery Rhyme Cup (1933). (*Uncle Wiggily name and characters © by Howard R. Garis. Reproduced by courtesy of Oneida Silversmiths.*)

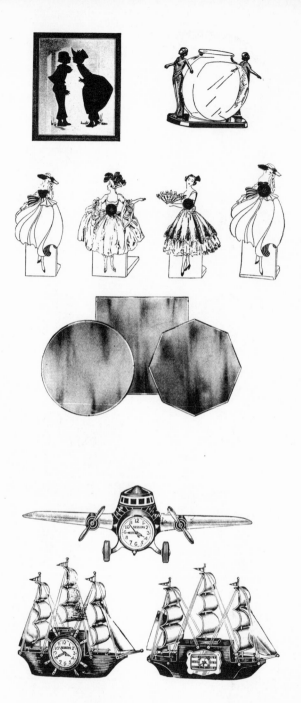

Top Left: Mirroettes with silhouette-type decoration from the thirties. This is "Love's Young Dream." Top Right: Glass aquarium, with cast metal figures, 1933. Second Row: Doorstops of wood and other materials could be decorated by do-it-yourselfers in the early thirties. These were offered by Thayer & Chandler, Chicago. Third Row: Circular, square, and octagonal Venetian mirrors of the late thirties. Below: Airliner clock with Sessions movement, and two Clipper Ship clocks with Sessions movements (1940). Airliner cabin was lighted and props were of metal. Ship models were metal and wood. (*Courtesy American Interstate Corp.*)

Top: Bennett Brothers, Inc., offered silver-finish horse ornaments at $12 each. Below: Decorative composition ornaments for the home in the early forties. Figurines are 18½ inches high.

THE TRIVIAL MOMENTS

TRIVIA has been spawned since the dawn of civilization. Trivia fascinated the Victorians, magnetized our grandparents at the turn of the century, captivated our parents during the Jazz Age, and exerted a pervasive influence upon children and adults alike throughout the thirties and forties. How many of us today, in fact, are entirely immune to its frivolous charms? It was a wise man who once wrote "He that shuns trifles must shun the world."

The reader already has encountered in this book more than a modicum of trivia and will encounter more in the chapters that follow.

Why, then, devote a separate chapter to trivia? The answer is because so much trivia produced during the period with which we are concerned does not fall neatly into pigeonholes in any of the other categories we have established. This, then, will be a chapter concerned with miscellaneous trivia that not only has some impact upon the times in which it was produced but is, by virtue of its peculiar interest or charm or perhaps by the sheer magic of nostalgia, of concern to some of today's breed of collectors.

For example, an event in May 1934 in a rural area of Canada created international headlines that continued, in one size of type or another, for a score of years. This was the birth of quintuplets to Mrs. Oliva Dionne. The youngster of today who has not heard of the Dionne quintuplets undoubtedly flunked his history courses. Almost as widely known as the quints themselves was Dr. A. R. Dafoe, the physician who brought them into the world and saw them through a series of crises through a combination of skill, ingenuity, and devotion.

It was, of course, inevitable that the purveyors of trivia should capitalize upon the popularity of the Dionne quintuplets — Annette, Cecile, Emilie, Marie, and Yvonne. And capitalize they did. Today a host of Dionne quint objects are collectors' items. Foremost among these are dolls, but these will be discussed separately and briefly in the chapter dealing with toys.

There were Dionne Quintuplet plates and cereal bowls, souvenir spoons, calendars, albums, scrapbooks, magazine articles, photographs, toys, hardbound books, and more. Those who wonder why Oliva Dionne should have attempted to make money on his own children need to acquaint themselves with the financial duress the parents underwent just to keep the infants alive, not to mention feeding, clothing, and otherwise caring for them as they grew up.

Today a full set of the five quintuplet souvenir spoons is worth $35 or more. A metal cereal bowl with the faces of the quints pictured in the basin and their names lettered around the side will fetch $15. A picture album account of the first two years of the babies is now valued at $10; a 4½-inch-diameter child's plate named after them, $12; and a book entitled Dionne Quintuplets Going on Two, $6 or $7. Even 1936 calendars picturing the quints are worth a couple of dollars or more, and a scrapbook of clippings about these children sold not long ago for $7.50.

Then there were the Campbell Kids, only they were not real live kids. They were dreamed by up an artist named Grace Weiderseim at the turn of this century. Although the origin of the Campbell Kids predates our survey, their commercial use flourished during the thirties and forties.

The first use of the Campbell Kids is said to have been on street car cards. Subsequently they made their appearance as dolls, as promoters of Liberty Bonds during World War I, and their likenesses appeared in a variety of other ways, but particularly as magazine advertisements for the Campbell Soup Co., of Camden, N. J., which utilized them heavily during the 1930s and 1940s.

Apparently the Campbell Kids had a last name only: First names are never mentioned. And the Kids are always pictured fullface forward. However, it has been reported that the youngsters were not called Campbell Kids in the first place and that their creator, who

later became known as Grace Gebbie Drayton, did give them first
names, Bobby and Dolly, and actually assigned to them the sur-
names of Blake and Drake. (See below.) At any rate, when they went
to work for the Campbell Soup Company, they became the Campbell
Kids and undoubtedly will be known by that name forever after.
Their frequent use in the company's advertising has won goodwill
for Campbell Soup from one end of the continent to the other.

According to the company, a number of artists worked on the
Campbell Kids after Grace Weiderseim, and these included Roy
Williams, Corrine Pauli, Dorothy Jones, the Studio of Paul Fennell
in Hollywood, the Studio of Johnstone & Cushing in New York City,
the Studio of Mel Richman in Philadelphia, and the studio of Bob
Cawley in Pennsauken, N. J.

The company's use of the Kids was frequently accompanied by a
jingle. The company itself says that one of the most famous of these
was written by Charles M. Snyder, and goes:

> We blend the best with careful pains
> In skillful combination,
> And every single can contains
> Our business reputation.

In a 1935 advertisement, three rather than the customary two
Campbell Kids were depicted — two boys and a girl — and the accompanying jingle read:

> "Come let's to bed," says Sleepy Head.
> "Tarry awhile," says Slow;
> He got a whiff of Campbell's Soup
> And didn't want to go!

Often, too, during the thirties, a single Kid was illustrated in the
ads, clad variously as a bandleader, football player, aviator, train
conductor, shopper, homemaker, chef, electrician, bowler, ship's
captain, card player, and so on.

Currently, Campbell Soup Co. uses the Kids in magazine and
newspaper advertising, television commercials, and as grocery store
promotional material.

Incidentally, Grace Gebbie Drayton created several comic strips
for newspapers, including one entitled *The Campbell Kids.* She also
created the widely known Dolly Dingle and characters known as

Bobby Blake and Dolly Drake, so that the Campbell Kids and Bobby and Dolly may indeed be entirely separate characters. The artist went on to also illustrate numerous books. The Dolly Dingle cutouts appeared in the *Pictorial Review* and are sought by collectors.

The dolls have been issued since early in this century, and all of them are collectible. But there were also Campbell Kids earthenware feeding dishes made by the Buffalo Pottery and adorned with brightly-colored decals of the Kids; bisque figurines made in Germany; souvenir spoons; and other objects. The Buffalo Pottery dishes are currently worth around $25 and may soon attain a greater value since Buffalo Pottery's star is on the rise in collector circles. The souvenir spoon will bring $5 or more, and the figurines $8.50 to $10.

Another delightful series of advertisements that appeared during the 1930s featured Brooksie, the white cow, and her companions of Brookfield Dairy Farm. The advertisements promoted Swift's Brookfield Butter, were in full color, and delineated Brooksie and her pals engaged in a diversity of activities in the Brookfield pastures.

Like the Campbell Kids, the Brookfield cows and calves were depicted in a great variety of costumes and poses. Brooksie was pictured doing everything from teaching school to leading a dance at a picnic. I've never encountered a collectible object made in the likeness of the Brookfield cows and calves, and if none was made, someone missed a bet. The color illustrations alone should be as collectible as are the advertisements for popular soft drinks and automobiles.

On the other hand, dolls — or at least doll cutout patterns — were made in the likeness of Elsie Borden, the Borden cow. A stuffed Elsie Borden cow doll, made as a Kreuger toy in 1942, was recently advertised at $22.

Also in the category of trivia are numerous novelty clocks turned out between 1930 and 1949, including a number of animated ones that now have fairly substantial value. We discussed some of these in the preceding chapter. Here are just a few more.

Immediately upon the heels of the legalization of beer in March 1933, the Happy Day animated clock made its appearance. Equipped with a 30-hour movement, this clock had a dial on which two male characters, each with a beer mug in his hand, were pictured standing across a beer barrel from one another. The men lifted their glasses as the clock ran. The works were housed in a square nickeled frame, and the clock sold for just $1.98.

A companion clock had an animated dial on which a boy shined a young woman's shoes when the clock was in operation. Still another featured a peanut roaster held by a vendor in action as two youngsters watched. All three of these clocks had alarms.

The early 1930s also saw the appearance of the Rickshaw electric clock made of cast metal with a coolie pulling a rickshaw in which a seated woman holding a parasol formed one end and a tall pagoda formed the other. This sold for $4.25 and was also available with an eight-day movement and an animated dial at the same price.

Another beer legalization memento was a cast metal electric clock lettered "Just Like Old Times" and with cast figures of a bar, a bartender, and a drinker with a beer mug in hand.

Under the stimulus of optimism generated as Roosevelt took office, the Prosperity electric clock was manufactured. This bore a cast metal replica of a knight in armor riding a steed over the top of the clock and holding aloft a banner lettered "Prosperity." The price was $2.35. Some of these clocks now bring $40 or $50 or more.

Replicas of early modes of transportation were extremely popular in the thirties, and the field of clocks was no exception. An electric model was made in the form of a four-wheeled coach, sans horses. Its price was $3.10.

There were Pendulette wall clocks adorned with characters from nursery rhymes, such as Jack and Jill and Mary and her lamb. These brought $1.28 and are probably valued at 10 to 20 times that amount today.

The Banjo clock was popular decades ago, but the Viola clock appeared in the early thirties, its shape exactly that of the instrument of that name.

New Haven made a Gondolier clock with a 30-hour movement. It had a blue and silver dial picturing the sun, stars, and moon and a gondola at its base.

An animated dial beer-drinker clock made by Lux is currently valued at $37.50, which will give you a good idea of the value of others of the same type.

There were novelty lapel watches galore during the late thirties and early forties in particular. The Tricky Grasshopper by Schwob was crafted with the figure of a giant grasshopper set with rhinestones as a fob-pin. Its price was $28.50.

Schwob also created lapel watches in the form of ice cubes of yellow 10-karat gold plate, and others with pin-fobs in the shape of Dalmatians, flowers, fleur-de-lis, flagstaffs, and bowknots.

Olympic made a line of novelty lapel watches in the early 1940s, including one with a bird of paradise pin-fob set with rhinestones. Clinton made one with a fob in the shape of two bananas. Ingersoll created a purse watch; one side of its case served double duty as a compact. In the war year of 1942 New Haven produced a lapel watch, called The Pentagon, with a red, white, and blue case.

There are also numerous collectible novelty knives in addition to the advertising knives discussed elsewhere in this book. A 1930 jack-knife had a case in the shape of a dog lying down. These wholesaled for 76 cents a dozen!

Coin knives were made in the shape and size of a silver dollar. The cases housed a stainless steel blade and a nail file. Together with a Waldemar chain, these sold in 1942 at $7.50, although similar coin knives without chain were available for less. The Pull-Ball knife had a blade that sprang open when a small ball at one end of the case was pulled.

There were "photo" knives in the thirties and forties (just as there are today) with photographs, usually of females in provocative poses, on their cases. These were called — what else? — "art poses." Some females were partially clad, some entirely nude.

There was a Waldemar knife with a compass embedded in the case, and there was a G-Man jackknife with a delineation of a G-Man, pistol in hand, on one side of the case and lettered with various symbols identified with the government agents. There were even comic strip character jackknives, depicting Popeye, Mickey Mouse, Dick Tracy, and others. In 1940 these were priced at two for $3.75 and were offered in stores on small cards, each containing two knives.

There were knives with cases of gold, with handles of bone, celluloid, stag and other horn, silver, silverplate, mother-of-pearl, and plastic.

In the late thirties Finnish Puuko knives were being imported and sold in this country for $2.15 to $3.95. These knives were handmade and were encased in sheaths of artificial bone ornamented in color. Many were adorned with interesting finials or stock ends.

There were novelty barometers either in the shape of various figures or with metal figures mounted on their stands. In the early 1930s Sears, Roebuck offered a Donkey Joker Barometer that could be hung on the wall and used as a toothbrush holder. These were made in Japan. The "barometer" was the figure of a donkey. Here are the instructions lettered on the front of this novelty: "If tail is dry, fine; if tail is wet, rain; if tail moves, windy; if tail cannot be seen, fog; if tail is frozen, cold; if tail is out, earthquake."

Musical toilet paper holders made their advent in the thirties. Made of enameled wood, inexpensive music boxes that played two tunes when the paper was unrolled were attached to the backs. They cost only $2.35 in 1934.

In fact, music box novelties of all kinds constituted one of the largest categories of trivia in the thirties and forties — but these represented a type of trivia that now has an appeal for a large number of collectors.

There were, of course, musical powder boxes in abundance just as there are today, and there were musical cocktail shakers and steins that we will discuss in some detail in the chapter entitled "A Collector's Miscellany." But there were also available traditional objects such as musical alarm clocks, musical revolving cake plates intended for holding birthday cakes and equipped with a unit that played *Happy Birthday.* In addition, there were bonbon dishes of metal with porcelain enameled plaques imbedded in their tops and removable compartmented glass trays; nursery lamps of decorated white metal with musical units in their bases; white metal cake platters with 22-note Swiss musical bases; castor sets of metal; clothes brushes; and, naturally, reproductions of singing birds in gilded cages, the more elaborate of which sold for well over $100.

Ceramic novelties literally poured from the molds of the potteries of the period. Cookie jars appeared in various whimsical shapes. There was one in the shape of an apple and another in the form of a strawberry, both equipped with arms and "human" heads. There were Dutch Boy and Girl cookie jars of porcelain painted in bright colors with the top halves removable. And there were jars in the form of cats, dogs, lambs, other animals, and clowns.

Among the novelty savings banks of the two decades were the Bubble banks made of a large clear bubble of glass with an animated figure standing inside on a wooden base. The banks held from $24 to $400, depending upon the type of coins deposited, and the total amount on deposit could be ascertained instantly by means of a coin gauge on the side. Sears, Roebuck sold these in 1944 for 98 cents. But you'll find much more about the toy banks in the chapter on collecting toys.

The current fad for so-called trivia, particularly the American versions of it, is reflected in the popularity of an "Americana and Collectibles" mail auction originated by Ted Hake, 115 South 21st

Street, Philadelphia, Pa. 19103, which offers collectors everything from pinback buttons to comic character items. Hake, a free-lance writer, established his auction some time before the current fad began and developed it into a thriving business with a clientele all over the country. He distributes catalogs describing and illustrating his offerings at regular intervals, suggests the current price range for most of them, and subscribers may then send in their bids at whatever figures they wish. Bids are competitive and the catalog lots go to the highest bidders. Hake will send interested readers a sample catalog free.

Hake may not obtain for the "Americana" items he offers (including hundreds of the objects mentioned in this book) the dollar volume obtained at the sales of such elegant auctions as those of Parke-Bernet and others handling scarce and rare antiques, but his individual sales probably exceed in numbers those of the long-established auction houses. Where and how he obtains his large and varied stocks is a trade secret. His sources may not be inexhaustible, but they are presently yielding a steady flow of the collectible things sought by those with less than a fortune to invest.

This chapter describes a mere sampling of the trivia of the period. The reader will find other types scattered throughout this book, much of it concentrated in the chapter entitled "A Collector's Miscellany."

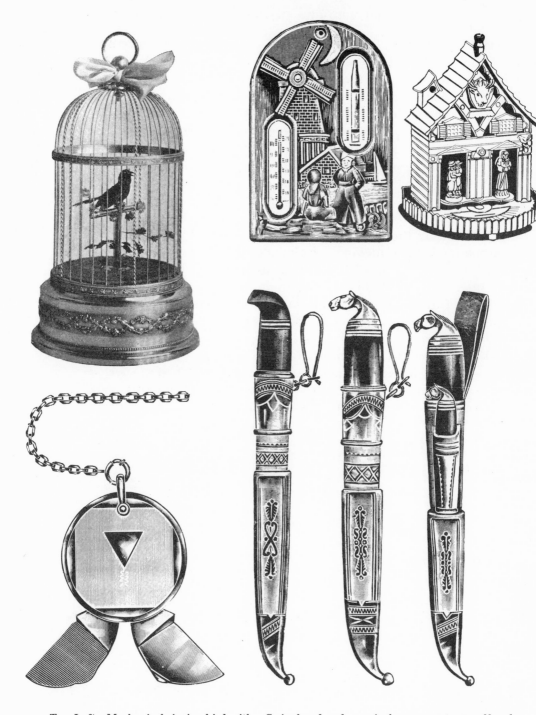

Top Left: Mechanical singing bird with a Swiss handmade musical movement was offered in 1940 by Bennett Brothers, Inc. **Top Right:** Weather forecasters of the early forties. The Weather Wizard at right is plastic and of a type in production for many years. This sold for a dollar in 1944. The musical clothes brush and toilet paper holder dates from the thirties. **Below Left:** Coin knife with Waldemar chain. **Below Right:** Three Finnish Puuko knives as offered by the Joseph Hagn Co.

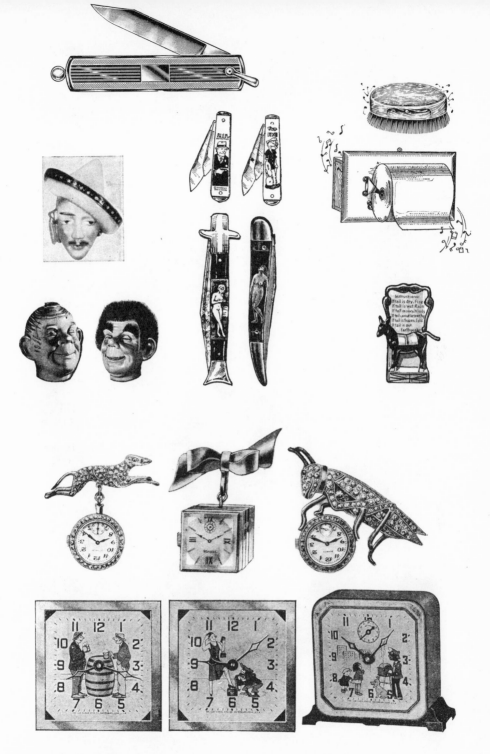

Novelties of the thirties and forties included these inexpensive clocks, watches, barometers, jackknives. The Ceramic Paddy was created by Paddy Novelty Co., Goliad, Texas. In 1941 it sold for $1.

During the thirties the Campbell Kids worked hard selling soup. (*Courtesy Campbell Soup Co.*)

Not two but three Campbell Kids appeared in this April 1935 ad. (*Courtesy Campbell Soup Co.*)

Musical novelties of the early forties, included porcelain powder box with a musical nursery lamp and a metal musical cake platter at right (top row). On second row are two powder boxes, one at left of wood and one at right of mirror glass, together with a piano-cigarette box. On bottom row are two porcelain and one plastic wood (center) powder boxes. Nursery lamp and cake platter were offered in the Joseph Hagn Co. catalogs and the others by Bennett Brothers, Inc.

10 COCA-COLA COLLECTIBLES

VISITORS to Atlanta, Georgia find a variety of attractions to compel their interest — the Cyclorama, that vast three-dimensional depiction of the Battle of Atlanta during the Civil War; Stone Mountain with its famed carvings of Generals Robert E. Lee and Stonewall Jackson, and Jefferson Davis; Underground Atlanta, a reconstruction of the underground city that existed before Sherman applied the torch — and many others. But for many a new 11-story building on North Avenue holds a particular fascination. It is the home of The Coca-Cola Co.

Housed in the company's archives, not open to the general public, are scores of mementos and records of mementos intimately associated with this popular drink through the years since 1886, when it was created by an Atlanta pharmacist, Dr. John S. Pemberton. These mementos, the great bulk of them produced for the company and distributed for many years through Coca-Cola bottlers, hold prime interest today for a rapidly-increasing group of collectors. They range from change trays and serving trays to bottles themselves and include such a diversity of objects as calendars, visor caps, blotters, rulers, bottle openers, ice picks, pencil sharpeners, thermometers, and a host of others.

These are among the objects that for decades have promoted Coca-Cola and have helped earn for this drink the goodwill of millions, not only in this country but over a large part of the world. This is not the place for a history of the company; the history has been related several times, always interestingly though not always with precise accuracy. Through the years The Coca-Cola Co. has spent substantial sums on advertising and promotion, and this investment has paid handsome dividends in sales and goodwill.

Substantial spending actually began with the purchase of the rights to Coca-Cola by Asa Griggs Candler in 1891 and the organization and incorporation of the company the following year, and it expanded with the beginnings of the Coca-Cola bottling industry in 1899 and for years thereafter.

Collectors today seek not only those objects that were created by the company for promotional purposes but also many that were created by the company for the use of those who sold the drink, such as dispensers, glasses, and other soda fountain and store adjuncts, including especially advertising signs and posters made of materials ranging from metal to cardboard.

While many of the objects now being sought, such as calendars and trays, have been produced continuously for years, and while certain very early objects are of major interest to collectors, a host of productions stemming from the 1930s and 1940s are now being collected. The record of these and others is preserved in the archives of The Coca-Cola Co. presently presided over by Wilbur G. Kurtz, Jr., whose knowledge about them is remarkable.

The collectible artifacts of Coca-Cola of the 1930s and 1940s may vary considerably in price from one geographical section to another and sometimes from shop to shop within the same locality, since the collecting of them is relatively recent, compared with the collecting of such things as Chippendale chairs and Ming porcelains. But prices are likely to become more stabilized soon, since all antiques eventually find their price niche as more dealers handle them.

It is highly doubtful that The Coca-Cola Co. suspected, when the production of these articles first began, that they would be avidly sought one day as collectors' items. That they are now being collected is a tribute to the popularity of the company and its drink and is also due in part to the whim of collectors who have little money to spend but who nevertheless want to ride their hobby even though on a smaller circuit than more affluent collectors. The prices in parentheses in the listings that follow represent typical prices asked recently for these collectibles by knowledgeable dealers.

Although serving trays have been produced since the latter part of the 19th century, some particularly attractive ones were made in the 1930s and 1940s, and collectors will find a record of these in *Metal Service Trays and Art Plates, A Catalogue since 1898,* issued in 1970 by Archives, Coca-Cola USA, a division of The Coca-Cola Co. Among those illustrated and described in this book is one with a lithographed drawing of a girl with a telephone receiver in her hand and lettered "Meet me at the soda fountain." Another depicts a bathing beauty (beauties of all types were favorites on trays promoting Coca-Cola). The 1931 tray depicted a farm boy with a dog. A likeness of movie star Frances Dee, attired in a bathing suit, graced the tray issued in 1933. In 1934 movie stars were featured again, this time Maureen O'Sullivan and Johnny Weismuller, both attired in bathing suits. Another popular motion picture star of the thirties, Madge Evans, decorated the 1935 tray. The 1936 tray, called Hostess, depicted a seated girl in an evening gown with a corsage. (Needless to say, virtually all figures depicted are showing drinking Coca-Cola.)

Another bathing beauty, running with her cape flowing in the wind, adorned the 1937 tray. An attractive brunette in a light summer dress and hat occupied the front of the 1938 tray, called Girl in the Afternoon. Again in 1939, the tray featured a bathing beauty seated on a springboard. In 1940, for a change of pace, the tray depicted a girl in a sailor cap and holding a fishing pole. She is shown seated on a dock, taking time out for the "pause that refreshes." A girl ice skater seated on a log in the snow decorates one 1941 tray, and another for the same year shows one girl seated in an automobile and another standing beside it.

The trays of the 1930s and 1940s will range generally in value on the collectors' market today for around $7.50 to $100, depending on condition and desirability. Those featuring Frances Dee and Madge Evans are at the top of the price range. Earlier and considerably scarcer trays will fetch higher prices, some considerably higher, and prices of more than $100 have been recorded for some.

A desirable collector's item from the 1930s is a china plate 7½ inches in diameter with an illustration of a bottle and a glass in the center and lettered "Drink Coca-Cola." This will bring $20. A variety of decks of playing cards were issued in both the 1930s and 1940s ($5). In 1942 special decks were issued for the men in service; one deck featured backs with attractive girls and another named Aircraft Spotters illustrated various types of planes to help enable servicemen and women to identify them ($5–$10).

Productions of 1930 included calendars, a series of lithographed nature study cards designed particularly for the use of schools, visor caps, a group of *A.B.C.* books *(Alphabet Books, Coca-Cola)*, blotters with four designs in each set, book matches, miniature bottles, steel wire bottle openers, the Starr bottle opener, rulers, pencils, ice picks, miniature Coca-Cola cases, and six-box folders. A particularly desirable advertising item of that year is a large clown cutout sign.

In 1931, new additions were pocketbooks and a series of handsome lithographed portraits of George Washington, General Robert E. Lee, Abraham Lincoln, and Benjamin Franklin.

In 1932, men's billfold wallets of leather were issued ($9–$10), as were a "giant" bottle (20 inches high), pencil sharpeners, tablets of paper, and a series of lithographed portraits of distinguished doctors. Advertising cutout signs issued during 1932 are now choice collector's items when they can be found. They were of the movie stars Jean Harlow, Joan Blondell, Lupe Velez, and Sue Carroll. Joan Blondell is still around and is still pursuing her acting career. The "blonde bombshell" Jean Harlow is still remembered by thousands although she died in 1937. Lupe Velez and Sue Carroll may not be as well known to members of the younger generation as they are to their parents or grandparents, but they were stars in the thirties. A Jean Harlow wall poster was produced in 1933.

A bottle-shaped pencil sharpener ($12) was produced in 1934 as were ice picks and metal thermometers ($15). Lithographed cardboard window displays presented Jackie Coogan and Wallace Beery, and a likeness of Joan Crawford (yes, indeed!) adorned a window hanger that year.

A pretzel bowl made its advent in 1936, and a Sesco opener in 1937. The following year Coca-Cola issued a school kit and another metal thermometer, this one measuring 6¾ x 16 inches. More pencils and the Golden Rule ruler ($1) appeared in 1939, followed in 1941 by a highly popular book, *Flower Arranging — a Fascinating Hobby,* written by Laura Lee Burroughs. The book was so popular that Volume 2 was issued in 1942.

The company saw to it that a variety of helpful things were made available in 1942 for the men who had gone into service following the attack on Pearl Harbor. These included mending kits, the playing cards mentioned earlier, and score pads, writing pads, notebooks, special pencils, and comic postcards. The pièce de résistance, however, was a game kit which contained a dart board, table tennis set, a set of Bingo cards, a Chinese checkers set, a regulation checkerboard, two decks of playing cards, a set of chessmen, and two sets of dice for backgammon.

The 1943 collectibles included a full-color series of twenty 13x15-inch cards, "Fighting Planes of the U.S." For dealers there were life-size cutout displays of the women in service — WAVE, WAAC, Marines, the nurse, and others. Another series of twenty 13x15-inch color cards, "America's Fighting Planes," came in 1944 as did some additional school materials.

Bear in mind that a number of the items listed had also appeared prior to the dates given for them, and their continued issuance indicated their popularity. Among the objects produced during the thirties and forties and even earlier were pocket knives, and prices of these various types have ranged recently from $3.50 to as much as $45; keychains (75¢–$1.50); thermometers ($10–$20), and a few watch fobs (prices now as high as $15), although watch fobs began to disappear from popularity along with pocket watches during World War I and the several years following World War I.

A five-gallon oak syrup barrel made during the 1930s and 1940s was offered recently at $55. The miniature bottles were originally made of glass. Those of plastic did not appear until the 1940s ($5 a crate).

In view of their fairly recent vintage, many collectibles of Coca-Cola are now commanding surprisingly high prices. A 1943 calendar showing women at various wartime jobs, for example, will bring $10. Cardboard signs of the 1930s and 1940s will bring from $5 to $25 or more, depending on size. A lighted metal sign showing a waterfall and lettered "Pay Cashier, Please" has recently been tagged $100. One will be lucky to find one of the 20-inch display bottles for less than $6 or $7, and the pencil sharpeners of fairly recent vintage will bring $5 or more. Bottle openers are worth around $3.50.

During the years numerous miniature metal trucks, delivery wagons and other toy vehicles have been produced, and the early iron ones have asking prices of $25 to more than $50. A crock fountain dispenser of the 1890s has been selling for $800, and a Tiffany leaded glass chandelier has been priced at more than $1,300, and is likely to go higher because of the short supply and heavy demand. Just as the name Tiffany holds magic for thousands of collectors, so does the name Coca-Cola.

The items mentioned in this chapter by no means constitute an exhaustive list of the collectibles of The Coca-Cola Co., but I hope they will help identify many of the promotional items used by The Coca-Cola Co. and Coca-Cola bottlers in the 1930s and 1940s.

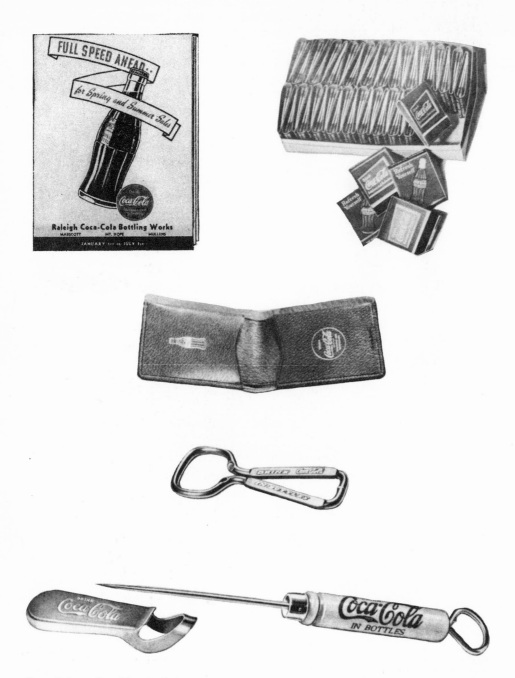

Coca-Cola collectibles include: pencil tablet of 1942 (top left); pigskin billfold (top center); book matches, which will bring about 25¢ a book today (top right); Steel wire opener, Sesco bottle opener and 10½ inch-long icepick (below). (*Courtesy Coca-Cola Co.*)

Blotters such as this one were distributed by the thousands. They are being collected today, though their value is still quite low (top left). **Top Right:** 1941 "Two Girls at War" tray is one of numerous pictorial metal trays sought by collectors. The thermometer is 16 inches tall and 6¾ inches wide and a desirable collectors item. **Below:** the giant 20-inch-high bottle and crown are sought by both bottle collectors and Coca-Cola specialists. (*Courtesy Coca-Cola Co.*)

11 MICKEY AND HIS FRIENDS

PROBABLY the world's best-known and most beloved 44-year-old "youngster" is a mouse named Mickey. Since he, like Jack Benny, is eternally young, it seems almost incredible that this delightful creature was fathered more than four decades ago by the late Walt Disney as the hero of an animated cartoon.

Disney, who had migrated from Kansas City to Hollywood in the late 1920s, first produced two silent Mickey Mouse short cartoons, then in 1928 released the first animated cartoon to use sound. It was entitled *Steamboat Willie,* featured Mickey, and was a fantastic success. Earlier, high school dropout Disney had produced as his first cartoon in Hollywood *Alice in Cartoonland.* It featured a combination of a live child actress and cartoon characters. This was followed by *Oswald the Lucky Rabbit,* a series subsequently taken over by Disney's distributor.

Success after success followed on the heels of Mickey. With *Snow White and the Seven Dwarfs,* the talented Disney created the first feature-length color cartoon. Its reported cost was $2.4 million, but the film grossed several times that. Disney created a series called *Silly Symphonies* and first used color in one entitled *Flowers and Trees.* It won him an Academy Award in 1932. A $2 million production, *Fantasia,* provided animation and visual interpretation for a two-and-a-half-hour concert by Leopold Stowkowski and the Philadelphia Orchestra and was an innovation in entertainment. Disney's *Ferdinand the Bull, Pinocchio, The Ugly Duckling,* and *Song of the South* made their impact upon audiences totaling millions.

Subsequently, Mickey Mouse and his garrulous friend Donald Duck appeared in the comic pages and the comic books, and a corporation was established to license manufacturers to produce a tremendous variety of objects in the likeness of or relating intimately to the Disney cartoon characters. Today there is a cult of Disney character collectors, and the earlier manufactured articles licensed by the Disney interests have ascended sharply in price.

These objects, ranging from watches to T-shirts and jewelry, are still being produced, and some idea of the market for them is reflected in the annual report of the Walt Disney Corp. which showed that for the six-month period ended November 1, 1970, the corporation's licensed manufacturers had sold $7.5 million worth of Mickey Mouse watches and clocks, $3 million worth of T-shirts and jeans, and $2 million worth of jewelry, cuff links, and suspenders!

Disneyland, of course, served to further enhance the popularity of Disney's characters, and a huge new $400 million enterprise, Disney World, built on a 2,500-acre site near Orlando, Fla., was opened late in 1971. The Disney interests own almost 25,000 additional acres in that area, located at the intersection of Interstate Highway 4 and U. S. Highway 192. This newest venture includes a Magic Kingdom, which is similar to Disneyland in California, and additional features known as Main Street, U.S.A., Adventureland, Frontierland, Fantasyland, Tomorrowland, Liberty Square, and also hotels, camping sites, and various recreational facilities.

Through the years, Walt Disney received numerous honors for his unique contributions to the field of entertainment, including honorary degrees and a special award from the Academy of Motion Picture Arts and Sciences for the creation of Mickey Mouse. And the International Numismatic Agency commissioned Ernest Trova to create a medallic sculpture of Mickey in connection with the character's fortieth anniversary.

Disney had his competitors in the field of animated cartoons, among them Paul Terry with his *Terrytoons,* the UPA Studios, Max Fleischer, and Warner Brothers, all of them successful but none quite so fantastically successful as Mickey Mouse and other of the Disney characters. It should be noted, however, that such Warner Brothers cartoon characters as Bugs Bunny, Yosemite, and Tweety and Sylvester have been licensed to nearly 100 manufacturers for the production of numerous products.

The range of Disney character collectible objects is vast. It includes dolls, windup toys, puppets, wearing apparel, silver wares, jewelry (including $15,000 bracelets made to order by the renowned New York jewelry house of Cartier), books, magazines, teapots, toothbrush holders, sheet music, cookie jars, comb and brush sets, and savings banks.

The original Mickey Mouse watch of 1932 by Ingersoll, which included metal bands with Mickey pictured on each band, is now valued at several hundred dollars. Subsequent Mickey Mouse watches made during the 1930s have been sold at prices ranging from $90 to as much as $300. The Mickey Mouse electric alarm clock of the early 1930s is quite scarce. It features a large cutout figure of Mickey that revolves around the dial each minute. The works are housed in a green metal case. Ardent collectors will pay as much as $500 for this clock. A later model is worth less.

The original Donald Duck wrist watch by Ingersoll and the original Big Bad Wolf watch also are now eagerly sought. Prices of both have fluctuated from dealer to dealer recently within a range of about $150 to $350. And later Donald Duck watches of the 1940s will fetch around $50 or so now.

There is also a Big Bad Wolf alarm clock, also made by Ingersoll and housed in a metal case with a dial depicting the Three Little Pigs and lettered "Who's Afraid of the Big Bad Wolf?" The 1934 version has brought as much as $400.

Collectors should remember that the Mickey Mouse and other character watches have been made over a period of years and some are still being produced so that values of the more recent ones should be a good bit less than those of the early models. Nevertheless, in the collector periodicals you'll frequently encounter advertisements of these character watches with no reference to date at asking prices of $75 or more, despite the fact that 1970 Mickey Mouse watches were available at a retail price of about $12.50, complete with the color likeness of Mickey and hands that point out the hour and minute.

The Mickey Mouse wristwatch with the cutout figure of Mickey on the dial, with a metal bracelet-band featuring a cutout of Mickey at each end, was retailed in 1933 for less than $2.50. In the same year Sears, Roebuck offered for 98 cents an Ingersoll Mickey Mouse pocket watch with a fob also featuring a picture of the mouse. In 1934, Montgomery Ward's catalog offered at $1.39 an Ingersoll Mickey Mouse pocket watch with a likeness of Mickey on front, back, and the fob, complete with box covered in lithographed paper, and at $2.98 a wristwatch with a leather strap adorned with two metal likenesses of the fabulous mouse.

Similar watches with some slight variations were made throughout the 1930s, all retailing for under $6.50. A De Luxe Mickey Ingersoll wristwatch with chrome case and metal link band had a list price of $5.55 in 1938, and a similar model with leather strap was priced the same.

A Mickey Mouse lapel watch by Ingersoll with a case finished in black and nickel and with a black lapel cord was offered in 1940 at $2.10. Some prices advanced a bit as the 1940s wore on.

In 1937, the Ingersoll Big Bad Wolf Watch (also called Three Little Pigs watch), in a pocket version with leather strap-fob lettered "May the big bad wolf never come to your door," was tendered at a wholesale price of $1.50 by one large wholesaler. Its list price was $3.30. In 1940 a large mail order firm was offering Ingersoll's Donald Duck pocket watches with Donald in colors on the dial and Mickey on the back at $1.58.

Also of interest to collectors are Mickey and Minnie Mouse sterling silver table utensils, largely spoons, knives, and forks, made in the 1930s. In 1937, International Silver Co. produced a sterling silver Mickey Mouse baby spoon and fork set, each piece 3½ inches long and depicting the Disney character on the handle. This set retailed, boxed, for $5.

(Incidentally, Molly Mouse — no kin to Mickey — sterling silver spoons and spoon and fork sets were being produced in the late 1930s, along with much other novelty children's sterling.)

Mickey Mouse and Donald Duck sterling photo rings were also made and now bring about $10 to $12 each.

Another early production licensed by Disney was a Mickey Mouse jewelry set that included a mesh bag, a necklace adorned with metal figures of Mickey, a bracelet, and a pin. This four-piece set was offered in its 1933–1934 catalog by Sears, Roebuck for 98 cents. In the same catalog, Sears offered a 22-inch-diameter Mickey Mouse shooting gallery with target, enameled steel gun, and six rubber-tipped vacuum darts at 89 cents; a Mickey crayon set for 23 cents; a set of four Mickey Mouse jigsaw puzzles for 45 cents; and a set of six assorted Mickey Mouse cotton handkerchiefs for 30 cents. These will bring several times their original prices today. The crayon set, for example, has recently been advertised at $8.50, and a single handkerchief has been offered at $10.

Numerous figurines and other items were made of ceramic materials, including bisque. A ceramic tea set was made in Japan early in the 1930s. The teapot alone from this set, decorated with an image of Mickey playing a guitar, is now valued at more than $10. Montgomery Ward offered the entire seven-piece set in 1934 for a dime! A choice item is a porcelain cookie jar made in the 1940s with a molded figure of Mickey on one side and of Minnie Mouse on the other. It was decorated in bright colors, stood 13½ inches high, and originally sold for $2. A Mickey and Minnie Mouse ceramic toothbrush holder with likenesses of both characters has a current price range of $35 to $45.

Mickey and Minnie salt and pepper shakers in ceramic are worth from $5 up. There was also a Donald Duck salt and pepper set.

Bisque figurines were turned out in profusion and in many sizes. These included figures of Mickey and Minnie Mouse, Pinocchio, Cleo the Cat, Ferdinand the Bull, Snow White and the Seven Dwarfs, and others. Figurines also were made of composition materials. A few recently asked prices for some of the figurines, a number of which originally retailed for under $1, may be of interest:

Mickey Mouse figurine 8 inches high with movable arms, $50; Mickey Mouse statuette with boxing gloves, $20; bisque figurine of one of the Seven Dwarfs, made in Japan and slightly over 3 inches tall, $7.50; 10-inch-tall composition figure of Ferdinand the Bull, $27.50; Mickey and Minnie Mouse chalk figures 4 inches tall, $12.50 a pair; 4-inch-tall figure of Minnie Mouse with umbrella, $12.50; 4-inch-tall chalk figure of Pluto, $5; bisque Pig playing violin, 3½ inches high, $6.50; bisque Pinocchio figure 4 inches tall, $6.50; bisque figure of Ferdinand the Bull, $6.50; bisque figurines of Snow White and the Seven Dwarfs, $50 a set; 7½-inch-high pre-1935 figure of Minnie Mouse in composition materials, $40; and bisque Mickey with baseball bat, $7.50.

Disney character dolls were manufactured in large quantities and a pair of Mickey and Minnie Mouse cloth dolls made by the Steiff Company in 1930 were tendered at an antiques show at $90 each. A 1930 set of five bisque baby dolls, including, among other characters, Mickey Mouse and Donald Duck, will sell for close to $100 in mint condition. A set of the Seven Dwarf dolls in rubber, each 5 inches high, is worth $50 or more on today's red-hot market. A doll Mickey Mouse with a bisque head and featuring Mickey playing a saxaphone is priced at $30. A Donald Duck rubber doll by Dell, on the other hand, was advertised not long ago at just $4.

A 1939 Pinocchio doll of composition, 36 inches high, is worth $75, but an Ideal wood-jointed Pinocchio 11 inches tall brings only $25.

Disney character hand puppets are less expensive. A cloth Mickey puppet is offered for $6 to $10 — the same price asked for similar hand puppets representing Minnie Mouse, Donald Duck, and Pluto.

Two-inch-tall lead figures of such characters as Pluto will bring about $3.50.

Although it is not widely known now, in exchange for labels from any three cans of Libby's Baby Foods, Libby, McNeill & Libby, of Chicago, offered in 1939 cutout cloth patterns for Disney rabbits, squirrels, and chipmunks based on models designed for *Snow White.* The cutouts were ready to be stuffed with cotton and sewn together. The patterns were colored with washable dyes and were sent in sterilized packages.

There were numerous Walt Disney character toys, including windups, a good many made in Japan, offered during the 1930s and 1940s. Others were made by American toy companies, including Marx. A 1938 Marx tin windup of Ferdinand the Bull is now worth around $15. A tin Mickey Mouse windup ferris wheel is valued at $25 or more. A Japanese-made tin windup golfing Mickey is valued at $10 to $12. A 1939 Pluto windup rollover toy has been advertised at $12.50 and another Pinocchio tin windup at $50.

Marx also produced a 1939 Pluto windup, now valued at $15 — the same price asked for a 1941 Marx Dumbo windup.

Among the numerous other toys produced were sand pails, now worth $4 to $5; a Pluto wooden pull toy valued at around $20; a Mickey Mouse airplane of hard rubber, which fetches an astonishing $20; a Mickey Mouse hard rubber fire engine worth about the same amount; a spinning top featuring Mickey and Minnie Mouse, Pluto, the Big Bad Wolf, and the Three Little Pigs in color, valued at more than $10; a 1939 Mickey Mouse Choo Choo train valued at $5 and a similar Donald Duck train, worth the same; (a windup train is worth $275!); a Donald Duck xylophone; a little known but fascinating Mickey Mouse plywood rocking horse (1937) with a rocker 3 feet long and that originally wholesaled for $99 a dozen; a Mickey Mouse Shoo Fly rocking toy of plywood, also made in 1937 and originally wholesaling for $108 a dozen; a Dopey (one of the Seven Dwarfs) 8½-inch-tall metal windup toy that walks and rolls its eyes (c. 1938), valued at $30; Donald Duck ceramic bank (about $5); a Dime Register Bank of the early 1940s that came in a series decorated with illustrations of Snow White, Mickey Mouse, Donald

Duck, and Dopey and that originally sold for less than $2 a dozen; a Mickey Mouse train made by Lionel around 1935 and consisting of an engine, a stoker car, and three circus cars; a Donald Duck wooden push cart ($5), and a series of Mickey Mouse Library Games, valued currently at $25, that included six volumes of card games in a box.

There are far too many other Disney character collectibles to include mention of them all here, but a sampling of these additional objects includes the following, with current values of some noted in parentheses:

Big Bad Wolf tin plate; sheet music published in 1936 (including "Mickey Mouse's Birthday Party"); Mickey Mouse bronze belt buckle ($18.50); Mickey Mouse comb and brush set with backs of chromium and black enamel (original selling price, $2.50); Mickey Mouse camera ($10); Mickey Mouse Christmas tree lights by Noma that originally cost $1.75 for a box of eight with shades decorated with a figure of Mickey ($40); Mickey Mouse metal lamps; Mickey Mouse Beetleware bowls ($7.50); Pluto plastic clock; soap figures of Pluto ($3.50); Mickey Mouse simulated leather bank in shape of a treasure chest, about 1935; Minnie Mouse Weather Wizard with calendar, 1940 ($10); Mickey Mouse mug picturing Mickey as a fireman ($14), and a Japanese bisque Three Little Pigs toothbrush holder ($20).

Also collectible are many Disney character comic books, magazines, hardbound books, and souvenir programs from the Disney pictures. As a random sampling of these, the *Mickey Mouse Magazine* published in 1934 is worth $12 to $15; the book *Walt Disney's Pinocchio* (1939), $2.50; *Mickey Mouse Stories* (David McKay Company, 1934), soft cover, $12.50; *Walt Disney's Story of Clarabelle Cow* (Whitman Publishing Company, 1938), hard cover, $8.50; *Walt Disney Presents Fantasia,* a souvenir program booklet, 1940, $12.50; *Donald Duck in the High Andes,* based on Disney's famous good neighbor cartoon; *Pedro, the Story of a Baby Airplane,* illustrated by Disney, and *Walt Disney's Thumper,* the story of a mischievous rabbit.

During 1934 and 1935 *Good Housekeeping* published Walt Disney's *Silly Symphony* cartoons as a full page in color. Perhaps no one is as yet collecting them, but they appear highly desirable acquisitions for the Disney collector. The same holds true for the Disney Mickey Mouse cartoons carried as full-color pages in *Good Housekeeping* throughout 1935.

There are scores of other Disney character objects either being collected or waiting to be collected. It should be recognized, however, that this is a boom speculation market at this time and that prices are likely to fluctuate quite widely from dealer to dealer for the same items. The possibility should also be taken into consideration that numerous Disney objects still being produced may be offered, perhaps inadvertently, by some dealers at higher prices than these things sell for in retail stores.

But the cult of Disney is well grounded and growing, and the earlier and scarcer objects may not become any cheaper in the future. It all depends upon the whim of collectors.

All of the Disney characters shown in the accompanying illustrations are copyrighted by Walt Disney Productions, and the author is grateful to the Walt Disney Archives for making a number of photographs available.

Mickey Mouse merchandise, from dolls to games, are all now collectibles. (© *Walt Disney Productions. Courtesy Walt Disney Archives.*)

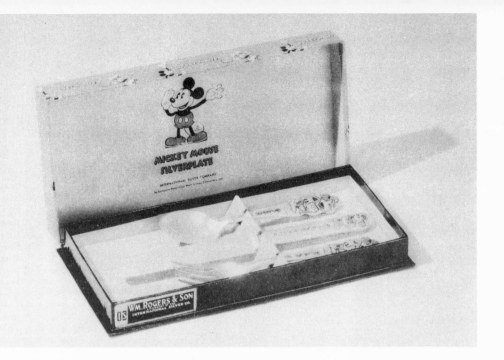

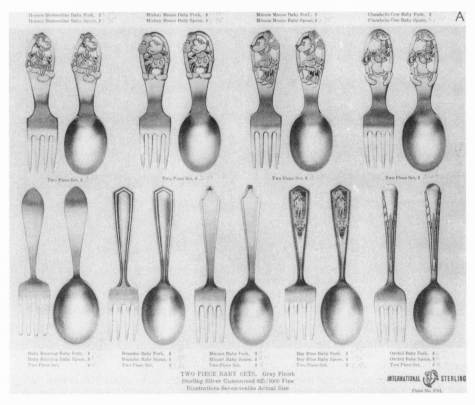

Top: Mickey Mouse baby set in Wm. Rogers & Son silver plate was advertised in 1934 at $5.90 a set. **Below:** Favorites for the very young were International Silver's baby sets. Those on top row from left were Horace Horsecollar, Mickey Mouse, Minnie Mouse, and Clarabelle Cow. Bottom from left: Baby Bunting, Brandon, Minuet, Boy Blue, and Orchid. (*Courtesy International Silver Historical Library. Disney figures © Walt Disney Productions.*)

Top: Mickey Mouse handcar made by Lionel. **Below:** The inimitable Mickey Mouse. (© *Walt Disney Productions. Courtesy Walt Disney Archives.*)

Top: Donald Duck, Mickey Mouse's pal. **Below:** Mickey and Minnie Mouse light shade featured cartoon panel. (© *Walt Disney Productions. Donald Duck courtesy Walt Disney Archives; light shade courtesy of Ted Hake, Philadelphia.*)

Top: Ingersoll's Mickey Mouse clock is a prime Walt Disney cartoon character collectible. **Below:** This famous plush figure evokes the movie cartoon era. (© *Walt Disney Productions. Courtesy Ted Hake, Philadelphia.*)

Top: From Left: Mickey Mouse lapel watch; Donald Duck pocket watch; and Mickey Mouse wristwatch with leather strap, all advertised in 1940. Second Row: Snow White Dime Register Bank sold in 1942 for less than $2 a dozen! Below: Montgomery Ward offered the Mickey Mouse wristwatch (on left) with two metal Mickeys on its leather strap for $2.98 in 1934; the 1938 version on the right went for $4.00. (© *Walt Disney Productions.*)

Top: Mickey Mouse objects offered by Sears, Roebuck in its 1933-1934 catalog. Center: Pinocchio doll sold in 1942 for $1.50. It was 11 inches tall, constructed of wood segments, and could sit, stand, and bow. Below Left: Scarce Mickey Mouse Shoo Fly rocking toy (wood), 1937. Below Right: International Silver Company's sterling Mickey Mouse baby spoon and fork sold in 1937 for $5 a set. (*Figures © Walt Disney Productions.*)

Top left is a plush Ferdinand stuffed with cotton; top right are two stuffed Dwarf dolls. Below at right are four Whistling Dwarf dolls with stuffed bodies, and at right is the Dopey ventriloquist doll, 20 inches high. All were advertised in 1940. (*Figures © Walt Disney Productions.*) Below is a set of Mickey Mouse dishes. (© *Walt Disney Productions. Courtesy Walt Disney Archives.*)

12 TOYS AND GAMES

ALTHOUGH we have already discussed a variety of toys and games in several specialized chapters, such a fascinating array of them (not related specifically to such things as radio shows or Walt Disney's cartoon characters) gushed forth from manufacturers' assembly lines during the thirties and forties that they deserve a chapter of their own.

Although mechanical banks have been collected for many years and the prices of some of the scarcer ones have risen into the hundreds of dollars, only in recent years has considerable attention been focused on "still" banks — that is, those that are not activated in some manner when a coin is deposited. These have been made in wondrous varieties over a period of many years, and the 1930s and 1940s saw the addition of some intriguing ones, as well as some mechanical and semimechanical banks.

In 1968 Hubert B. Whiting prepared an interesting color-plate book, *Old Iron Still Banks,* in which he described and illustrated about 450 of the earlier banks of this type, pointing out also that the tin banks are earlier and scarcer than the iron ones. Those discussed in the paragraphs that follow will largely postdate those in Mr. Whiting's book, but they are being collected right now, and indications are that their values will increase, perhaps considerably, within the next few years.

These later banks were made of a variety of substances, including tin, iron, brass, ceramics, and plastics. Hundreds of types were available in the 1930s and the decade following at retail prices under $1. Even a number of "action" banks were being marketed at under a dollar.

For example, in 1932, Montgomery Ward offered a Monkey Bank at 21 cents, and this obviously delighted many a child. Made of metal, the small bank, really a mechanical one, was adorned with two figures — a monkey and a parrot — on one side. One placed money on the monkey's tail and then pulled a lever, whereupon the parrot squawked and the monkey threw the coin into the parrot's mouth from which it dropped inside the bank.

For 33 cents Ward offered a Combination Bank of red steel, measuring 4⅞ inches high, 3¼ inches wide, and 1⅞ inches deep. The bank was opened by dialing the proper combination of four letters on the dial on the front. Ward also offered a lithographed steel Register Bank that accepted nickels, dimes and quarters, rang and registered the amount deposited, and opened when a total of $10 had been deposited. The price was only 49 cents. Particularly appealing was Ward's 1932 Three-Coin Register Bank, which operated similarly but was larger and had a separate cash drawer operated by a bottom lever. It cost only 95 cents.

In 1934 the Joseph Hagn Co. was offering for 78 cents its Popular Bank, made of cast metal and with cast figures of a very young courting boy and girl seated on a bench. There was a slot in the back of the bench for coins, and the metal was finished in a combination of ivory and gold. The bank was 6 inches high and 4½ inches long, and the company suggested that a pair of them would double admirably as bookends — an example of astute merchandising!

The American Savings Banks of metal came in several versions and were popular in the early 1930s. There were individual one-coin banks in this series that registered pennies or dimes, and there was also a three-coin bank that registered pennies, nickels, and dimes. The penny bank sold for 40 cents, the dime one for 58 cents, and the three-coin bank for $1.48. Bennett Brothers of New York and Chicago offered a handsome all-steel bank that registered and added nickels, dimes, and quarters and also accepted pennies, half-dollars, and bills in a special opening. The retail price was $3.80, and the bank could hold as much as $50, although it opened each time a total of $10 was deposited.

Numerous varieties of these registering banks were produced during the thirties and forties.

Not only the so-called "Piggy Bank" but numerous other banks in the shapes of animals had their heyday in the thirties and forties. Hagn offered a Fido bank for $1.10 in the form of a metal dog with a collar lettered with his name, and another at the same price in the shape of a white kitten with a ribbon about its neck. The frames could be unscrewed to empty the contents.

For very young children, there were unbreakable banks of plastic with perpetual calendars on their fronts. There were also metal banks in book shapes with "covers" bearing embossed designs of animals. Another book bank was bound in grained leather.

There was also the Scrappy Bank, named after the cartoon character. Available in the late thirties at 76 cents, this came complete with key in a cellophane bag. Its Bakelite case was decorated with scenes from the lives of Scrappy, his sweetheart, Margy, his brother Dopey, and his dog Yippy, and it was accompanied by a membership button for the Scrappy Thrift Club.

There were Popeye, Pinocchio, Lone Ranger, and other banks named after stars of the movies and the comic strips. Banks whose names indicate their shapes included the Drum (metal), the Baseball (Bakelite), and the Tank (wood). After the outbreak of World War II there were banks made in the likeness of and named after such famous fighting men as Eisenhower and MacArthur. There were Telephone banks of plastic and other materials; one in the mid-forties was in the form of a miniature dial phone with a coin slot in the top of the base. There was also a wall phone-type bank whose bell rang when coins were deposited.

In the early forties, Sears, Roebuck offered a Home Budget Bank for 98 cents. The interior contained six removable saving compartments with space for inserting titles such as "rent," "clothing," "vacation," and the like. Each compartment had a hinged cover and a slot through which coins were inserted. The overall container was of metal and resembled a squat document box.

Some of the banks above are worth from $20 to $40 on today's booming market.

Of dolls there was almost no end. We have already mentioned many of those made in the likeness of and named after motion picture, radio, and comic strip stars, and also those named after the famed Dionne Quintuplets. But there were others equally interesting.

Many types of dolls that had originally been created much earlier continued to be produced throughout the 1930s and 1940s: The Rose

O'Neill Kewpie dolls are one example and the Campbell Kids another. George Borgfeldt and Company, New York City, produced Kewpie toys and dishes in the 1930s under a patent obtained in December 1934. George Henry Hutaff, Jr., of Wilmington, N. C., obtained in January 1938, a patent for Bunny Hop dolls. Susie Q dolls were patented in 1938 by Ideal Novelty & Toy Co., Long Island City, New York, and a new patent for Kate Greenaway dolls was obtained in 1942 by Kate Greenaway Designs, Inc., New York City.

Taking its cue from the space age, the Viking Toy Company, Larchmont, N. Y., patented an Atomic Man doll in January 1947, and George Pal, of Hollywood, issued the popular Puppetoon dolls and marionettes in 1941.

Thousands of dolls of numerous types were issued during the two decades by such well-known companies as — in addition to the above — Kimport Dolls, Independence, Mo.; S. H. Kress and Co., New York City; Alexander Doll Co., subsequently known as Madame Alexander, New York City; Terri Lee Co., Lincoln, Neb.; McLoughlin Bros., Inc., Springfield, Mass.; American Character Doll Co., New York City; Nancy Ann Dressed Dolls, San Francisco.

There were far too many types to discuss here, but among the popular ones of the period were Cuddles with the Magic Eyes that moved from side to side; Princess Beatrix, which was quite popular and was made in numerous sizes; Tickletoes, a kapok-stuffed doll with rubber arms and legs; an automatic self-rocking doll that came in a cradle with automatic action; composition baseball and football dolls; Ideal's Magic Skin dolls of washable plastics; the Betsy Wetsy Nursing dolls that drank, wet, and slept; and a wide variety of costumed and talking dolls.

In passing, it might be noted that a set of Dionne Quintuplet dolls with molded hair and original dresses, bonnets, bottles, and rattles, plus playpen, has been advertised of late at $175; and a set of them carved in soap has been priced at $22.50. An Ella Cinders doll, 18 inches tall, named after the comic strip character of the thirties and made of composition materials, has been tagged $85. The General MacArthur composition doll will fetch as much as $50 and the rubber Sparkle Henty, 14 inches high, will sell for around $20.

Paper dolls of the thirties and forties will also bring several dollars each as will pages of magazines of the period with paper doll cutouts.

Because of the growing scarcity of the very early tin toys and the subsequent iron toys, tin windups produced during the 1930s and

1940s will now bring good prices from collectors — and there is a truly vast variety from which to choose. We can discuss only a few of the more intriguing ones, and the illustrations will give an idea of their diversity.

There were numerous windup animals, including monkeys that wagged their tails and tipped their hats; animals that turned around and opened and closed their mouths; and dogs that walked, wagged their tails and nodded their heads. There was a mechanical duck of celluloid that, when activated, shook a frog whose tail it had in its mouth (you're right: frogs don't really have tails of that sort!). Mechanical Sam, the Orchestra Leader, made of plush-covered metal, went through all the gyrations of a symphony conductor when wound and sold for only about half a dollar in 1940. Priced even lower was a mechanical boy and dog of metal and celluloid; when wound, the dog tugged at the seat of the boy's pants. And there were mechanical bicycle riders, machine gunners, dancing couples, tanks, drum majors, dogs with bones, dogs with shoes, boxers, clowns on horses, "furious" bulls, and pecking chicks selling in the late thirties and early forties at prices of a quarter to about $1.50.

The mechanical Tricky Taxi that could run around a table without falling off the edge made its advent during this period and sold for only about 50 cents. In the thirties Marx manufactured large quantities of mechanical vehicles ranging from express wagons to farm tractors, automobiles, and buses. Mechanical aerial acrobats were available at the outset of the thirties at a dollar or under. So was Funny Face, an 11-inch-tall lithographed man who not only walked and swayed from side to side when wound but whose facial expression also changed.

There were semimechanical musical Merry-Go-Rounds that were not wound but were sent whirling by a lever; small ones sold for $1.50 and larger versions for $3.50. A Sparking Airplane, with a spiral spring motor that propelled the craft and whose guns shot a stream of sparks, was available at 85 cents in 1942. It had a wing-spread of 18 inches and was 14 inches long. The Bimbo Dancer was a clockwork-movement-equipped, hula-skirt-clad figure 16 inches tall that went through the movements of the hula dance and the shimmy. It sold for $1.98 in 1934. Lionel was turning out a miscellany of clockwork toys during the 1930s, including an 18-inch-long Speedboat that will now bring $75 — nearly four decades after it was produced.

Lehman musical furniture was a hit of the forties. The individual pieces were equipped with music boxes that played when the furniture was set in motion. The items included children's rockers and rocking cradles.

Of interest, too, to today's collectors is a host of scientific and educational toys, including the famous Gilbert scientific sets and Erector sets; wood-burning outfits such as Pyrokraft and Burnitap; outfits for casting small toys (Gilbert produced some marvelous Kaster Kits in the late thirties and early forties); printing presses of various types, and the Lincoln Logs building sets.

Electrical toys of the late thirties and early forties fascinated many a youngster of those days, probably most of whom now wish they had kept what they had, because the values of these toys as collectors' items has climbed high. They included miniature electric ranges on which children could actually cook; miniature flatirons for ironing dolls' clothes; steam engines, ferris wheels, stride swings, and windmill pumps that operated in much the same manner as their full-size counterparts.

With the advent of the 1930s general interest in automobiles mounted annually as models changed and gadgets multiplied. Youngsters not able to drive a full-fledged car were delighted by toy vehicles that were miniature replicas of the vehicles their parents drove. Each Christmas during the thirties Santa delivered thousands of these.

There were toy replicas of Chryslers, Buicks, Packards, Pontiacs, Chevrolets, Fords, and numerous others. Many were equipped with electric headlights, instrument boards, ball-bearing gears, and rubber tires on disc wheels. Some even had spare tires. They were propelled, of course, by pedals.

There were also fire chief cars and fire trucks complete with ladders; drum trucks; velocipedes with sidecars; and handcars. Scooters were a favorite with the youngsters in those days also, but it is the toy vehicles that now are sought by collectors.

There is a growing fad today for collecting miniaturia. Miniatures in the form of doll houses, furniture, and furnishings will bring substantial prices if the pieces are well made. Such miniatures are still being made, of course, but they abounded in the thirties. Judging by the offerings in their catalogues of this decade, both Sears, Roebuck and Montgomery Ward enjoyed something of a landoffice business in this field, particularly during the Christmas season.

In 1933, Sears offered a 26-piece doll house set that included a four-room house, breakfast porch, and garage of fiberboard with 23 pieces of metal furniture. The house was 28½ inches long and 15¾ inches high, and the price was what today seems an incredibly low $1.79.

Sears also offered six-piece miniature wooden bedroom, parlor, kitchen, dining room, and bathroom furniture sets at 45 cents per set. A four-piece furniture set consisting of a 5-inch-diameter round table, two 6-inch-high chairs, and a plant stand, all made of sea-grass, sold for just $1.29. A 14-inch-long wardrobe trunk of wood with three drawers, two removable wooden hangers, a lock, and leather handles cost only $1.39.

Sears also offered miniature china tea sets of 18 pieces for 59 cents and 27-piece metal tea sets for 49 cents. Nineteen-piece aluminum tableware sets were available in 1933 at 59 cents a set.

The now widely-collected Tootsietoys were around in abundance in the early thirties. Montgomery Ward offered in 1931 a seven-piece parlor set of Tootsietoy metal furniture for only 95 cents, including a radio with doors that opened and a grand piano. A seven-piece dining room set could be purchased for the same price. Pewter Toot-sietoys in the shape of miniature automobiles, buses, tractors, fire trucks, tank trucks, trains and the like were offered in 1930 by the American Wholesale Corporation Division of Butler Brothers for 75 to 80 cents for a dozen pieces. The Tootsietoys had been popular for several years previously and constituted ideal inexpensive gifts for any occasion. Tootsietoy doll houses of container board were avail-able for about $2.

Children's musical instruments included the long-famous Scho-enhut pianos in various sizes. Their popularity was attested by the fact that they had been selling steadily for years and are still selling today. Schoenhut had been established in Philadelphia in the 1870s by Albert Schoenhut, who had come to this country from his native Germany and whose jointed figures and pianos became known the country over.

In its 1931–32 catalog, Montgomery Ward offered Schoenhut pia-nos at prices of from only 79 cents to $9.98. The latter price was for a 22-key, mahogany-finish model with a lifting lid. The instrument was 23¾ inches long and stood 21¼ inches high. The piano was accurately tuned and could be played by small children. Ward also offered a matching bench with a hinged lid for $1.39. Schoenhut produced both "grand" and upright models of its pianos.

The Schoenhut circus sets with wooded jointed figures and acces-sories also were being sold in 1930. A seven-piece set consisting of a clown, elephant, donkey, ladder, barrel, and stool was offered by the American Wholesale Corp. Division of Butler Brothers in 1930 for $16.50 per dozen sets, and a fine 12-piece set was priced at $3 a set. The same company offered Schoenhut's builder sets, construction toys of wood, at $4 to $8 a dozen sets. A Schoenhut Ski Jumper that hurtled over a goal post flanked by two United States flags was tendered at $8 a dozen.

Toy phonographs that actually played enabled youngsters of the thirties to enjoy the same sort of entertainment that their parents did on larger versions. Montgomery Ward was offering in 1932 The Little Dancer, an imported toy phonograph, with ten 10-inch double-faced records for $2.98. American Wholesale Corporation offered for $6.50 an American-made upright model 17½ inches high that also played the 10-inch records, and a Glenola table model with horn plus six 6-inch records for $3.95.

Adults are now collecting electric and other trains of earlier days, but in the thirties and forties they were the joys of children, especially boys.

Toy trains of one kind or another — clockwork, friction, pull, electric — have been produced for decades. The pull trains were novelties back in the days of the War between the States. Before the century was over, windups appeared, and engines powered by electricity puffed on the scene in the early 20th century. But the magnificently sleek and precision-made electric trains produced between the two World Wars have excited collectors' imaginations and are currently inducing them to loosen their purse strings.

Trains of the thirties and forties boasted parts of brass and plated nickel, accessories galore, and some cars fully equipped with miniature replicas of the same facilities as were offered in their full-size counterparts. They operated on "O," "HO" and standard gauge tracks, and the major brands were American Flyer, Ives, and Lionel. The Ives Corporation dates back to shortly after the Civil War, and the Lionel Corporation and the American Flyer Manufacturing Company were organized very early in this century. In the minority were several German brands. The manufacturers not only produced trains under their own brand names but occasionally under the names of major retail outlets for which they made them. The Ives Corp. was sold shortly after the Depression set in and Lionel acquired ownership later. In 1938 the A. C. Gilbert Company bought American Flyer, and in the late 1960s this line of trains was acquired from Gilbert by Lionel.

At the outset of the 1930s Montgomery Ward was advertising Dorfan electric trains, a German brand, as well as American Flyers, steam locomotives, and windup trains. Its 1931 catalog featured, for only 98 cents, a 28-inch-long windup with coal tender and three passenger cars hooked to the cast-iron locomotive, complete with six pieces of track. A steam locomotive that belched smoke and operated for half an hour on a single filling of fuel cost $9.95. It was made by Weeden Manufacturing Company, a pioneer in the production of steam toys and widely known for its numerous steam engines. A windup American Flyer with locomotive, tender, and two cars measuring 24 inches overall, together with eight pieces of track, a railroad station, tunnel, semaphore, and crossing and warning signs cost only $2.79. Wards offered that same year an American Flyer 43-inch electric train with tender, three cars and track for $8.98. A 57-inch-long wide-gauge Dorfan cost $18.50. It boasted a locomotive engine with electric headlights and cowcatchers at both ends, three steel coaches, electric-lighted, and 12 pieces of track. Transformers were available at $2.98 to $4.75.

The "O" gauge was the most widely-produced electric train during the two decades. The "O" refers to a track that measured 1¼ inches between the running rails. (The "HO" measured just half that distance.) The "O" gauge electric train was first made in the United States in 1910 by Ives. It was in the thirties that true scale-proportioned electric trains made their big impact, and, although their production was halted during World War II, they reappeared after the war. Collectors seek primarily those produced before production was suspended by the war. A newcomer to their production in 1930 was Louis Marx & Company, famous among today's collectors for a tremendous variety of other toys, including action ones.

In 1933 Sears, Roebuck advertised a three-car-engine-and-tender mechanical train with a battery-operated headlight and measuring 28 inches overall for $1.10. Its Lionel "O" gauge electric outfit, consisting of electric-lighted reversible locomotive, tender, and three cars with an overall measurement of 40 inches, plus 10 pieces of track and a transformer, cost only $8.98.

In 1941, Sears was offering an "HO" gauge Tru-Model (Gilbert–American Flyer) train kit, electrically operated, for $13.95. The kit included everything needed to complete a locomotive, tender, tank car, gondola, box car, and caboose that conformed to National Railroad Model Association standards.

Meanwhile, the completely-assembled scale models had definitely come of age, and every conceivable accessory was available. These included danger and crossing signals, depots, freight stations, bridges crossover tracks, crossing gates, tool sheds, signal towers, electric cranes, and so on. Lionel devised a gateman who automatically walked out of the door of his shack as the train approached, then returned, the door closing behind him, as the last car passed. Gilbert provided an Erector set for building an automatic and remote control whistle unit that operated automatically at any predetermined location at any time. In the late 1930s Lionel offered a coal elevator that loaded model freight cars by remote control. Gilbert–American Flyer produced a passenger and freight station with an electric audioannouncer and true-to-life sound effects of railroading.

In addition, there were automatic car unloaders, loading water tanks, block signals that permitted one train to follow another on a single track without danger of collision, cars that caught and discharged mail while the train was in operation, and automatic dump cars.

The country was not faced in the 1930s with the gruesome specter of inflation that has confronted it during the past few years, and prices of astonishingly efficient electric train outfits were, by comparison with today's prices, remarkably low. Lionel's whistling streamliner *City of Denver,* a replica of the Union Pacific train of that name, including a remote control power car, two illuminated coaches, an illuminated observation car, a remote control for whistling and reversing, and 12 sections of track, listed at $16.50 and was offered in 1939 by Wholesale Radio Service Co. for $11.75. The same company offered Lionel's remote control freight with six-wheel-drive steam-type locomotive heads and including the locomotive, dump car, floodlight car, coal elevator, a tender, oil tank car, caboose, unloading bin, Lockon, track, pair of switches, and transformer for $19.59.

In 1940 Bennett Brothers offered its customers the American Flyer New York Central Work Train with a die-cast locomotive and tender, a dump car, wrecking car, illuminated caboose, and 16 sections of track for $16.65. The outfit measured 63 inches long overall and was operated by a 100- or 150-watt transformer. The manufacturer's suggested retail price was $25. It also offered American Flyer's double-header freight train with two locomotives and two tenders and three cars plus 14 sections of track for just $9.30. Other models were available up to $56.68 list price for a big American Flyer Union Pacific model with a 16-wheel locomotive.

It may be interesting to note that a replica of the Sante Fe three-unit diesel locomotive with electric motors in front and bodies of bronze castings was made for exhibition at the 1939 New York World's Fair. It measured a total of 48 inches in length and was, of course, unique.

We have presented here only a small sampling of the ingenious toys of the thirties and forties. There were literally thousands of others, many collectible now at prices well above their original cost. They included a diversity of cap pistols and rifles; papier mâché Roly Polies that sold in 1930 for a dime to about 35 cents each; a diversified line of Arcade iron toys that ranged from automobiles to steam rollers; the outstanding Marx iron toys that included virtually everything from turnover tanks to climbing tractors; a miscellany of Wolverine automatic toys; Lyons Metalcraft construction kits that enabled their young recipients to build aircraft from monoplanes to zeppelins and blimps; Revotinas, those little decorated tin "music boxes" that a small child could play by turning a crank top; crank-operated church and cathedral organs that contained a spring mechanism and reeds; the Mystery Boat that ran for 46 minutes on a spoonful of Sterno heat; pull toys that did everything from wiggle to catapult; animals with voice boxes that were activated when they were pressed; Noma action toys — these and many others, a number of which you will find illustrated here.

Games of the two decades included not only many that had been popular for years, but numerous new ones. Some names will be familiar to readers who have reached their middle years. They included a variety of pinball games that became exceedingly popular in the thirties and whose popularity continued into the forties; Clown-N-Up and Poosh-M-Up, both bagatelle board games; Hoop-O-Loop, a mechanical hunting game; Archarena, a board game; Stop and Shop for the young grocery shopper; Down and Out, played with a wire chute and steel balls; Tip the Bell Boy, a semimechanical game; and games with names such as New York to Paris, Air Mail, Over the Garden Wall, Frantz Baseball, Poor Jenny, Lindy, Wings, Touring, Above the Clouds, Commando, Gusher, Contack, Touring, and Whoopee.

In the "Impact of War" chapter I'll mention a number of toys and games that stemmed from World War II. In the meantime, the reader may be interested in a few recently-asked prices for toys and games of those earlier decades. The following represent merely a sampling, and prices will often vary sharply from dealer to dealer:

Unique Art's Sky Ranger Zeppelin and Aeroplane, $30; green Lionel standard gauge #380 locomotive, $80; Lionel #384 steam engine with tender, $125; Wolverine pull-toy trolley, lithographed, $15; Chein's windup boy on skis, $15; Marx windup passenger train with engine, tender and three cars (c. 1935), $10; celluloid mechanical Hula dancer 6½ inches tall, $18; Chrysler Airflow miniature toy car (1930s), $10; cast metal police patrol car with rubber wheels, miniature (1930s), $14; Chein Roller Coaster (1930s), $19.50; Tootsietoy Buck Rogers Destroyer, $19.50; mechanical climbing tractor (1939), $15; friction Scottie dog (1939), $15; General MacArthur composition doll, $50; Lionel clockwork speedboat (1939), 18 inches long, $75; Popeye papier-mâché bank, $6 to $10; Marx tin windup large tank with popup gunner, $20; Girl on Scooter windup (early 1940s), $29.-50; Parker Brothers Quiz Kids game (1940), $5; and Howdy Doody dominoes, $3.

Top: The American Wholesale Corp. Division of Butler Brothers offered these Tootsietoy pewter toys in 1930 at 75 to 80 cents a dozen! **Below:** Marx metal action toys, offered in the 1931-32 and 1933-1934 Montgomery Ward catalogs. Original prices ranged from 25 cents to $1.59.

The railroad was still very much a part of the American scene, and no Christmas tree was deemed complete without one of these beauties beneath it.

Top: Metal and celluloid windup boxers; wooden Tootsietoy doll house, windup musical merry-go-round, and windup sparking airplane, from the early forties. The dollhouse dates from the early thirties. (*Courtesy Americana Interstate Corp.*) **Below:** Some of the numerous electric train accessories available as the thirties chugged to a halt, as offered by Fort Dearborn Mercantile Co.

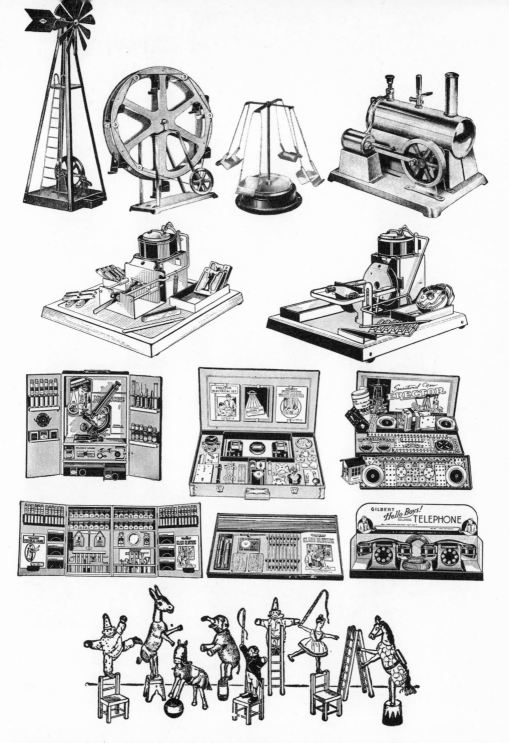

Top: Electric toys from 1950 included windmill pump, ferris wheel, giant stride swing, and reversible steam engine. **Center:** Educational and scientific Gilbert toys (1940). Top left is a metal casting outfit; at right is a larger set that cast hollow figures. **Second Row, From Left:** Advanced Microscope set, Advanced Electrical set, and an Erector set. **Bottom, From Left:** Inventor's Chemistry Lab, Glass Blowing set, and Telephone set. These boxed toys are difficult to find complete today. Similar toys and sets were produced over a period of years in many instances and the date a toy was advertised doesn't necessarily indicate the date it was first manufactured. **Below:** Famous Schoenhut Circus sets, produced over many years, shown here in their 1930 versions. Individual pieces now sell for more than complete sets sold for originally (less than $1.40 for 7-piece set to $3 for 12-piece set.).

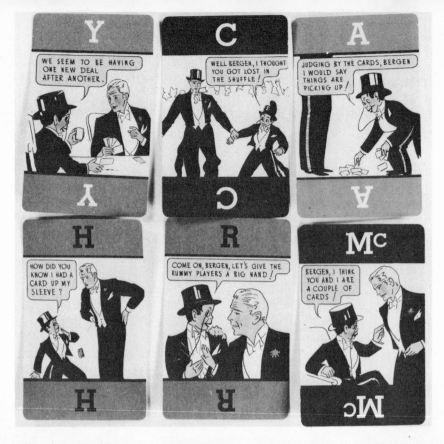

Top: Cards from an Edgar Bergen and Charlie McCarthy card game. (*Courtesy Ted Hake, Philadelphia.*) **Below:** The 13-inch Donald Duck doll played the tune "Don Donald" and the musical cradle played "Rock-a-Bye, Baby." Bennett Brothers offered these objects in its 1940 catalog. (*Donald Duck figure © Walt Disney Productions.*)

Top: Toy automobiles were advertised in 1933 by Joseph Hagn Co. Nash Model 12 is at top left and the renowned Stutz Model 138 at top right. Below from left are Essex Model 1714 and Franklin Model 10. Prices ranged from $9.70 for the Essex to $21.40 for the Franklin. Center: Glenola children's phonograph (1930) played actual small records. Below Left: the RCA Sound Control Studio was designed by National Broadcasting Co. sound engineers and offered by Bennett Brothers at $8.90 in the late thirties. This fabulous toy generated sounds resembling rain, train effects, gun shots, galloping horses, and police whistles. It was 26 inches long and 22 inches high. Below Right: Fire truck with brass railings and bell and ladder-raising attachment was sold by Firestone in 1930. It was 28 x 8¼ x 11 inches.

Top Left: Heavy cast iron motorcycles with riders of the thirties. **Top Right:** Popular toy banks. **Center and Below:** The Ideal "Cuddles" doll (1940) ranged in size from 16 to 25 inches and in price from $3.75 to $7.50. The 1934 four-piece reed toy furniture set sold for only $1.58 a set. The dolls' dishes and utensils date from the early forties.

Top Left: Games of the early forties included Gotham's Ice Hockey and Skip Ball, El Jumperino, and "home-style" roulette. **Top Right:** Ward offered this Ouija Board in 1931 for 98 cents. **Second Row:** Bennett Brothers wholesaled Contack at $1.15 and Monopoly for $1.50 in 1940. **Center and Below:** Ventriloquist dummies and character dolls. The Old Tom Heck dummy was offered by Joseph Hagn Co. in 1942 for $3.70. The Kayo, Dick Tracy, and Herby character dolls had movable jaws controlled by string, retailed at 70¢ each in 1940.

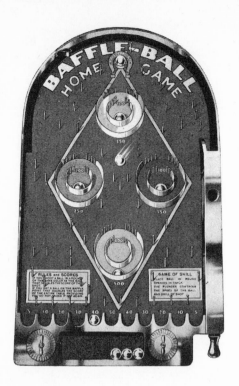

At top is the Baffle Ball game, one of the pinball games that took the thirties by storm. Below is a deck of novelty cards, and an Art Deco bridge set, which sold for $4.25 in 1933.

13 BUSINESS AND THE COLLECTOR

IN the Spring of 1971 the Board of Commissioners of Guilford County, N. C. announced that the county planned to reach back to Depression days and to sell to collectors souvenirs to remind the populace that the country had weathered financial slumps far more severe than the one that was continuing into the seventies. The souvenirs were "Depression scrip" that had been issued by that county to pay its employees and to meet other obligations during the 1933 bank holiday.

The scrip, stored in packing cases in the courthouse vaults for almost four decades, was then brought out and placed on sale to help finance Guilford County's 200th anniversary observance. The notes were in denominations of 25 cents, 50 cents, $1, $5, and $10, and about 800 uncirculated sets were offered for sale, priced at $1 to $4, depending on condition. All pieces had been perforated with the word "Paid."

"This scrip is a reminder that we have been through harder times than these and gone on to new heights," said Dale Montgomery, chairman of the board and also chairman of the Guilford County Bicentennial Commission.

Numerous businesses issued similar scrip during the Depression of the thirties to pay their employees and to meet other obligations, and this constitutes one of thousands of examples of business-related mementos of the thirties and forties that have now become collectible.

Dozens of these business collectibles have been discussed in preceding chapters with emphasis on radio premiums and objects relating to the business of entertainment in general. We will discuss numerous other miscellaneous ones in this chapter. Many, but by no means all of them, were offered as advertising and promotional adjuncts. They range from commodity and merchandise containers to advertising signs, from pocket knives to lithographed letterheads, and from serving and change trays to games and puzzles.

These business collectibles are not johnny-come-latelies: they have been around for several generations and date back to tradesmen's cards issued as early as the 18th century. These trade or advertising cards, incidentally, have been issued constantly through the years, the more desirable ones from this century having been lithographed in colors. They are worth from about a quarter to several dollars each, depending upon age, scarcity, and subject matter. Such cards from the thirties are collectible but their values, generally, are lower than those of earlier ones.

At the moment, there is a growing interest in tobacco and cigarette containers, primarily those of lithographed tin, some in novel shapes. Prices start at about a dollar and range up to several dollars each. Although the earlier tins will bring the higher prices, the mounting scarcity of these is focusing attention on many produced during the thirties and even into the forties. The Lucky Strike Flat Fifties tin in green with a red center, for example, will bring around $2.50 as will the Chesterfield Flat Fifties.

Some earlier tobacco containers were in the shape of lunch boxes or pails and were, in fact, used for just that purpose after the contents had been emptied. Typical is a U.S. Marine lunch box now worth $15. For those interested in collecting the tobacco tins, there are listed some recent publications on the subject in this book's Selected Bibliography.

Actually, all sorts of tin containers in novel shapes or with lithographed covers are now being sought. Interest in them has been stimulated by the restoration villages that feature re-creations of country stores. Tin containers are not recent inventions: The tin container for the preservation of food dates back to the early 19th century when King George III granted to one Peter Durand a patent for his principle of using vessels of various substances, including tin. Durand first utilized a cylindrical canister made of tin plate (iron coated with tin) after he had read a treatise written by Nicolas Appert, who in 1810 had been awarded a prize of 12,000 francs by Napoleon Bonaparte for his invention of a bottle to preserve food.

Although all the earliest cans were round, imaginative merchandisers were not long in devising novelty shapes and designs, producing tin containers in the shape of everything from sets of books to roulette wheels. The lithographic technique in the decoration of tin containers is said to have been first employed by the Somers Brothers in Brooklyn, N. Y., in the 1860s.

Hundreds of products were housed in these tin containers, and among the collectible ones is the log cabin-shaped can that contained syrup in the 1930s. The large size is now valued at $18.

But tin containers are by no means the only collectible ones. Those of wood, glass, ceramics, cardboard, and plastics are now sought, and a few collectors are even pursuing the paper cigarette packages of the early thirties; the designs of a number of them have now become obsolete or have been changed by the tobacco manufacturers.

Figural shapes in containers particularly intrigue collectors as has been witnessed by the boom in amassing recent-day Jim Beam whiskey, Avon products, and dozens of other figural containers. The Jim Beams and the Avons have been discussed at length in various articles and books, and we will merely note that indications currently are that prices of a number of the more recent figural bottles are declining, though those of the scarcer and earlier ones continue to show strength.

Lithographed containers, too, are being collected — if they boast some unusual feature such as shape or if the lithographing is devoted to scenes, objects, or people, or includes buildings since demolished, names of establishments no longer in business or names of streets no longer in existence. Although they may appear utterly inconsequential to many, both lithographed matchboxes and lithographed sugar sacks — the small sacks that contain individual servings — are of interest to a number of collectors. Even matchbook covers are collected. With the growing use of cigarette lighters in the thirties, the penny box of matches became scarcer. Today it has almost been replaced by so-called book matches. A collection of the boxes can be interesting if not particularly valuable. (Whatever collectors may say about intact contents, it is dangerous to mail boxes filled with matches.)

The wane of the matchbox, however, gave rise to a new collectible object — the advertising cigarette lighter — in the early 1940s. Inexpensive lighters with company names on them were given customers by several types of business, including swank restaurants, banks, and others. In its 1940 catalog, the Joseph Hagn Co. included this note addressed to advertisers: " 'Plain' Zippos, as a good-will gift, can be had with your trademark or any special insignia in metal with inlaid colors reproduced on the lighter. A longtime remembrance advertising — at a low cost! Write for quantity prices."

The beverage industry has consistently been one of the major users of promotional and advertising gimmicks, foremost among which have been serving and change trays and drinking glasses. We discussed Coca-Cola lettered trays in an earlier chapter, but dozens of other beverage manufacturers, particularly brewers, utilized metal trays to help put their message across. To bring top prices, trays should be in mint or new condition, regardless of age. Those in poor condition are rarely worth acquiring. But many will bring $10 to $20.

Among other soft drinks or "soda pop" concocters whose names were used on trays were Pepsi-Cola, Hires Root Beer, Nu Grape, Moxie, Dr. Pepper, Orange Julep, Double Cola, and several smaller and lesser-known companies. Most of these started utilizing trays earlier than the 1930s, but many of them, too, continued their use in the thirties and forties.

Beer and ale trays abounded both before and after the repeal of Prohibition, and there were few brewers whose names did not appear at one time or another on such trays. Just as trays were used to promote Coca-Cola, those bearing the names of other soft drink and of beer and whiskey producers were lithographed in bright colors, sometimes featured scenes but more often the likeness of a pretty girl, some rather scantily clad. Some trays were lithographed with a replica of the breweries; some featured dogs or sports scenes that had a strong appeal to men. Although the majority of change and serving trays were round, others were rectangular. The average serving tray measured about 12 to 18 inches in diameter; the change trays were much smaller, averaging about 4 inches, and there were some oversized trays. Miniature replicas of these trays with advertising also were used as ashtrays on tables in taverns, saloons, cafes, and elsewhere.

As with many advertising cards, many trays were produced with "stock" designs and were available to any advertisers who wanted to imprint their names on them. The specially designed trays, turned out generally in more limited quantities, are considered the more desirable by collectors. Some trays with striking designs were produced for Anheuser-Busch to promote Budweiser.

The use of trays as advertising adjuncts was not limited to beverage manufacturers of course. Some were used by dairies, machinery manufacturers, coffee firms, soap producers, and mail order concerns.

The change trays in general will bring $5 to as much as around $15. Random prices for serving trays include the following:

Southern Dairies serving tray, 1930s, $10; Ortlieb's beer serving, 1930s, $6; Chester beer serving, 1930s, $7.50; Miller High Life change tray, $7.50; Blatz beer serving, $8.50; Schlitz serving, $4; Budweiser serving with scene in color, $28; Carling's Black Label serving, $4.

Those figures will serve to indicate the very wide diversity of prices being asked for these more recent serving trays, but as the supply of the much older trays continues to diminish, many collectors think the prices of those from the thirties and forties will tend to stabilize, perhaps at $8.50 or above. It should be pointed out that although some trays are dated, many are not, and the absence of a date can provide a pitfall for collectors.

In addition to trays, the beverage industry utilized glasses, mugs, and pitchers for promotion. In general, well-decorated ceramic pieces will bring better prices than will such objects as glass mugs and drinking and shot glasses. Naturally, such collectibles from the 1930–1950 period will bring prices well below those prevailing for their counterparts from the early years of this century when saloons possessed an abundance of shot and beer glasses in various sizes, shapes, and designs, but values are moving up. A 1933 Huntsman's Ale pitcher with a hunting scene is offered at $13.50, and a Schlitz beer glass with a pictorial decoration and slogan is tendered at $2.25. A ceramic stein of the 1940s advertising beer is tagged at $5. Soft drink glasses of the thirties will fetch from a dollar up, and there are not many left at the dollar figure.

The beverage industry also utilized advertising mirrors, watch fobs, pocket knives, clocks, prints, thermometers, plates, bottle openers and corkscrews, letter openers, and other items for distribution either to retail outlets or ultimate consumers for the purpose of gaining goodwill.

Soda fountain dispensers are collectible, but apparently there are none dating in the thirties or forties that will come close to fetching the $800 or so at which an 1895 Coca-Cola syrup dispenser is currently valued.

Miniature advertising mirrors were utilized over a period of many years by numerous types of business. They were primarily round or oval (lozenge-shaped), contained a mirror on the front and lithographed advertising, which frequently included scenes, individuals, buildings, and the like on the reverse, and were intended to be carried in the purse. Most of the backs of these small mirrors were of celluloid. A few were made with small handles. Some mirrors were distributed by retail establishments, others as premiums by manufacturers. Mirrors of this type that date from the 1930–1950 period will be found at prices of 50 cents to about $2, but the majority were produced earlier and will range from around $2 to $15.

Of the objects for personal adornment used to promote goods and services, watch fobs and stickpins are in the majority; but by the thirties, wristwatches were replacing the pocket watch, so fobs from this era are scarce. The machinery and construction industries were the largest users of these but they also promoted soft drinks, stoves, automobiles, shoe polishes, and even shoes and flour. A good many fobs were of figural form, representing a miniature replica of the object they promoted. Fobs dating from the thirties and forties are now worth a dollar or two each; scarce earlier ones are valued at $7.50 to around $15.

Stickpins with advertising promoted everything from stoves to bicycle brakes. Other "jewelry" items included rings, charms, and decorative dress pins. In 1941 Armour & Co., Chicago, offered a floral spray dress pin with a Lucinore stone (a simulated moonstone), in exchange for a recipe folder from one of its cans of *Treet,* plus 25 cents for postage.

Pocket knives have been pressed into service by advertisers for decades and will be discussed in some detail in the chapter entitled "A Collector's Miscellany." In mentioning them here, however, it may be of interest that some are of substantial value, including one promoting Miller's High Life beer in the form of a decorated sheathed dagger made in Germany, which has been offered recently for $22, and one with a bone handle advertising Swift's canned dog foods, now valued at $9.

Buttons, too, have been used through the years for advertising. They were primarily of celluloid with pin backs. Among those of the thirties and forties is one lettered "Vote for Philip Morris" with a depiction of this cigarette manufacturer's famous trademark Johnny, and one with an illustration of Elsie the Cow issued by the Borden Co. Others were issued during the period by the beverage manufacturers, automobile makers, and cereal producers.

Many businesses also issued commemorative medals in observance of special events of which they were prime movers, or in celebration of longevity of service. Generally, those of greatest value were made of bronze, and their current values are roughly $3 to $10. Some medals were made of silver — but their distribution was invariably quite limited.

There is a growing interest right now in advertising signs and merchandise catalogs. Although scarce and desirable trade catalogs issued prior to World War I will frequently bring $25, $50, or more; those of the thirties are now chiefly in a price range of $2 to $10. Catalogs issued by such firms as Sears, Roebuck and Montgomery Ward in 1930 or 1931 will bring about $10, whereas the value of the same types issued after 1939 will drop to $5 or lower. However, these catalogs tend to increase in value each year, and it seems entirely possible that by 1980 a 1930 Sears or Ward catalog — the big annual ones — may bring $15 to $20.

Collectors seek the profusely illustrated catalogs that describe today's collectible objects, and many of those were utilized in the preparation of the illustrations for this book. Price lists without illustrations are of very little value. Catalogs of 20 or fewer pages, unless rare, will bring only a dollar to around $3 if issued between 1935 and 1945.

Within the past 24 months dozens of the early merchandise catalogs have been reprinted and have found a steady market. This may tend to depress somewhat the values of the early ones; but to my knowledge, there has been almost no reprinting of the catalogs issued during the 1930s and 1940s.

I believe that the value of desirable advertising signs, particularly those of metal with illustrations in color and those in figural form, will increase rather steadily in value within the next few years.

Most metal signs were painted on tin, and they were used by almost every conceivable type of business during the thirties and forties. Those with scenic illustrations, including sports and historic scenes, are often quite desirable. Some scenes were taken from paintings by famous artists of the past; others were done by contemporary illustrators of note.

Some metal signs were produced in figural forms, such as ther-

mometers, which were utilized by a number of companies, and bottles, which were used to advertise bottled drinks and certain medi-
cines.

Cardboard posters and placards in color and particularly figural
display pieces utilized by various firms in their retail outlets also are
of some value. Some businesses distributed cardboard advertising
pieces in the shape of Santa Claus during the Christmas seasons,
and those from the thirties are now valued at $5 to $15, depending
on size and condition. Such signs and placards issued by establishments no longer in business will usually bring a premium price.

To suggest other novel and specific collectibles relating to promotion and advertising of the period, we'd like to cite a few interesting
examples:

In 1936, Gerber Products Co., Freement, Mich., offered a Gerber
doll made of sateen, stuffed and trimmed, in exchange for three
labels from cans of its strained baby foods, plus a dime for handling.

In the same year, Cream of Wheat (which sponsored the radio
program "Buck Rogers in the 25th Century") offered a cloth cutout
"Rastus" doll 18 inches high, printed and ready to be stuffed and
sewed, for a dime in coins or stamps. The printed doll was in the
likeness of the company's trademark chef. A year earlier, this same
company had organized its H.C.B. (Hot Cereal Breakfast) Club and
offered members free cutouts of General Custer, his soldiers, Indians, Molly Pitcher, Davy Crockett, and other characters of historical
interest.

In the mid-thirties, the R. F. French Co., Rochester, N. Y., utilized
a character known as Hot Dan to promote its mustard and offered
without charge a Beetleware mustard spoon with a figure of Hot
Dan on the handle. The foot of the spoon could be hung over a jar
of mustard.

A variety of businesses offered ceramic pieces. Wheaties, for example, offered a nursery-rhyme-decorated cereal bowl, which now
has a value of about $6 (and also a Hike-o-Meter, now valued at $15).
In 1940 the Van Camp Seafood Company of Terminal Island, Cal.,
now the Van Camp Sea Food Co. Division, Ralston Purina Co., advertised for 50 cents a California pottery tuna baker and salad server
in the shape of a fish. The Ralston Purina Co., St. Louis, also featured
a promotional baby cereal bowl in 1931. It was decorated with a
rabbit, was lettered "Find the Bottom," and was available in exchange for a package top and 25 cents. Kellogg's Rice Krispies was
offering a set of six nursery rhyme plaques in color in 1940. Whea-

ties also offered, in 1934, a chromium sugar and cream set in exchange for a sales slip or receipt showing the purchase of two packages of Wheaties, plus 25 cents for packing and mailing. In 1931 J. & P. Coats Clark's O.N.T. Threads (The Spool Cotton Co., Newark, N. J.) advertised for only a nickel a set of cardboard parts that enabled the recipient to make animals out of its spools. The cardboard animal heads and tails were glued to the spools to create replicas of elephants, foxes, hippopotami, lions, zebras, and other animals.

In the mid-thirties, Old Dutch Cleanser, Chicago, offered to send a hammered silverplate-on-copper oval cake plate 10 inches in diameter to persons mailing in the windmill panels from three Old Dutch labels, plus 50 cents. The plate was manufactured by Wm. A. Rogers. The company also offered, in exchange for three windmill panels and 50 cents, a variety of Wm. A. Rogers silverplate sets, among them teaspoons, butter spreaders, soup and iced drink spoons, salad and oyster forks, and sugar spoons. In 1936 the company featured an offer of a series of plastic wall holders for its cans of Old Dutch Cleanser in exchange for windmill panels and 10 cents for each holder.

Games and puzzles were popular promotional objects. Procter & Gamble created a character known as Professor Quackenbush and in 1933 offered a Professor Quackenbush puzzle; its current value is $3 to $4. Other companies offered everything from playing cards to board games.

A Cattaraugus Cutlery steak set made of steel with horn handles was available in 1936 to promote the use of Softasilk cake flour. Its cost was just 25 cents plus a box top from the product. Food firms offered cookbooks galore either free or in exchange for box tops. General Foods advertised its Swans Down cake flour by sending a Beetleware flour scoop and a cake recipe booklet to anyone mailing in 20 cents. Quite a number of companies also offered free samples of their products. These were usually housed in miniature containers, which have become very collectible. Among these in the thirties was Larus & Bro. Co., Richmond, which made Edgeworth tobacco, and The Charles E. Hires Co., makers of Hires root beer.

The above represents only a sampling of the manifold objects utilized for promotion and advertising in the thirties and forties. Other collectible items include figural silverplated spoons, pictorial labels from packages, tokens, postcards, bottle openers, can openers, miniature banks, pictorial billheads and letterheads (and also itemized bills with prices), fans, shoe horns, buttonhooks, pen and pencil sets, letter openers, paperweights, spool and similar cabinets, books and booklets, tape measures and yardsticks, pencil clips, brushes, match holders, ashtrays, pencil sharpeners, measuring spoons, showcases, calendars, pencil cases, inkwells, and a variety of kitchen utensils.

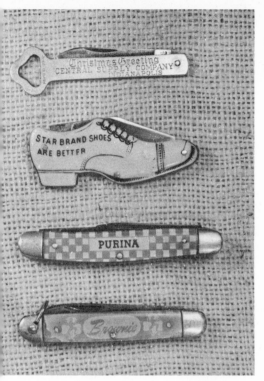

Top: Collectible advertising knives. (*Courtesy Ed Bardy, Traverse City, Mich.*) Below: Miniature political broom attached to New Deal slogan card; a Mr. Peanut costume decoration; Studebaker advertising button; photo mounts of men in service and of FDR, Churchill and Stalin; and 1939 New York World's Fair souvenirs. (*Courtesy Ted Hake, Philadelphia.*)

Top: These cigarette packages date from the thirties. **Center:** Cream of Wheat's cloth cutout Rastus doll of mid thirties; 1931 tobacco can. Edgeworth in this year also offered free sample packages. **Below Left:** Towle's Log Cabin Syrup tin containers of the thirties are now eminently collectible. The large size can is selling for $18! **Below Right:** French's Hot Dan mustard spoon (1931).

Top Left: Old Dutch Cleanser's Wm. A. Rogers silverplated cake plate and its wall can holder of the mid-thirties. Top Right: The 1931 Ralston Find the Bottom baby cereal bowl. Below: Trade catalogs of the thirties are collected both for their inherent interest and as valuable sources of information.

Collectible buttons galore. (*Courtesy Ted Hake, Philadelphia.*)

14 AUTOGRAPHS AND SUCH

AUTOGRAPH collecting has been a popular hobby for many decades, but the pursuit of the handwriting of noted personalities and handwritten documents of historic importance has been spurred almost furiously within the past few years. This results from several factors, probably foremost among which is the realization that choice autographic materials can prove excellent investments. Autograph letters are unique: There are no exact duplicates.

Outstanding autographic material has also risen sharply in value within the past several years, due not only to the increasing demand but at least in part to the astuteness of some dealers in the field of promotion and public relations. These dealers make certain that when unique or sensational material appears on the autograph market it is attended by the spotlight of publicity, and they see to it, when record prices are fetched by certain materials, that these prices are publicized.

One widely known major dealer who not only knows his field intimately but is adept in the practice of good public relations is Charles Hamilton of Charles Hamilton, Autographs, New York City. Some time ago Hamilton inaugurated with smashing success a regular series of public auction sales of autographs and allied material. His reputation has been so enhanced that his firm frequently manages to latch on to letters and documents of unusual significance or wide public interest more often than do shyer dealers who prefer to wait for business to come to them.

There are more dealers in autographs today than there were a decade ago. Among the better known and older ones are Walter R. Benjamin of New York City whose business was subsequently carried on by his talented daughter, Mary A. Benjamin, and Goodspeed's, of Boston, which deals both in autographs and rare books. Miss Benjamin wrote *Autographs: A Key to Collecting,* an admirable book for the beginner. Hamilton is the author of several books, among them *Scribblers and Scoundrels* and *Collecting Autographs and Manuscripts.*

There are numerous other highly qualified and dependable dealers, who issue catalogs at regular intervals. Among these are Kenneth W. Rendell, Inc., Somerville, Mass.; Paul C. Richards, Brookwater, Mass.; Carnegie Book Shop, Inc., New York City; Paul F. Hoag, Simsbury, Conn., and Conway Barker, La Marque, Texas. A number of other book shops also deal heavily in autographs, such as Argosy Book Stores, Inc., and the Scribner Book Store, both of New York City. Autograph collections also are occasionally featured by some of the country's major auction houses, and they are more frequently offered by Swann Galleries, Inc., of New York City, noted for its book auctions.

Technically an autograph is a letter or document in an individual's handwriting. It is also a signature alone. However, a signature is not essential for a handwritten letter to be considered an autograph letter. Letters and documents are sometimes signed with initials, and they are sometimes not signed at all.

If the almost universal substitution of the typewriter for the pen in writing letters, notes, and even postcards threw a monkey wrench into the autograph collecting hobby, it was only a temporary one. Dealers and experienced collectors are fully aware that busy men — a category that today embraces all professions from poet to President — rarely write letters by pen any more. The majority of their missives are typed by secretaries and, perhaps more often than not, signed by secretaries. Since the typewriter wrought a revolution in the practice of writing, this has been taken into account by dealers and collectors, and the experienced in both fields can tell a genuine signature from one that has been penned by a secretary — most of the time.

The typewriter actually has made legible handwriting almost nonessential, although illegible handwriting flourished for generations before the advent of this wonderful machine.

For a while the use of the typewriter sent the prices of desirable handwritten letters soaring while those written by machine and merely signed by hand were allocated quite low values. And while dedicated collectors still prefer the handwritten specimens, the prices of typewritten letters of importance or historical significance have risen rapidly within the past decade or so.

Of more dramatic effect upon autograph collecting has been the recent use of signatures written by automatic pens, used by United States Presidents for about 16 years. These signatures cannot be told from those written genuinely by hand, but they have now been accepted as legal.

This, however, is not the place to delve into the ramifications of autograph collecting. Suffice it to say that the majority of autographs dating in the 1930s and 1940s and being collected today were written on the typewriter and that at least some of them were signed with robot pens. When it comes to a choice of two letters by the same individual and whose content is equally significant, the one written by hand will fetch by far the greater price.

Those individuals whose autographs of the 1930s and 1940s are now being avidly collected represent, by and large, those whose accomplishments paralleled or were similar to those whose autographs are sought from earlier years.

They include statesmen, writers, inventors, military heroes, philanthropists, artists, explorers and other pioneers, genuises in the sciences, and villains.

There is a fad right now for collecting autographs of prominent Nazis from Adolf Hitler through Rudolf Hess, just as there is a fad for collecting Nazi military mementos.

Letters and documents written or signed by that arch conspirator and astounding egomaniac Hitler fetch high prices. Not very long ago a one-page document signed by Hitler in his headquarters and dated March 15, 1945, containing a military order, was offered at $500. It was signed just five weeks before his suicide. Another document issued from his headquarters in 1942 and designating a military appointee, countersigned by Hermann Goering, was offered at about the same price. A document dated 1938 in which Hitler appointed Hermann Goering, then the Luftwaffe commander, to the rank of Field Marshal, bore a price tag of $1,200.

Autographs of other top-ranking Nazis also fetch handsome prices. A document signed twice in pencil by Wilhelm Keitel, German Field Marshal, while he was a prisoner of the Allies in October,

1945, and addressed to the Allied prosecutor for war crimes was offered at $200. Keitel was subsequently hanged.

A four-page love letter written in 1941 by Heinrich Himmler, chief of the Gestapo, to his mistress was tendered at $475. It is fascinating to note that in this letter this terrorist, feared by millions, addressed his mistress as "my lovely, good little rabbit"!

A letter by Hitler's Deputy Führer Rudolf Hess, typed on his imprinted stationery in 1938 and thanking an acquaintance for an invitation, was priced at $125. A signed cabinet photograph of Hess had a price tag of $100.

Marshal Henri Petain, who commanded the French troops in World War I but was condemned for treason in World War II, does not fare nearly so well in the autograph market. An autograph letter signed by him in 1937 and addressed to a general was offered at only $30.

Autographs of figures associated with the Allied Forces in World War II also are in good demand. Sir Winston S. Churchill autographed a formal menu in honor of the officers and men of two British ships in London in 1940, and this menu, also autographed in pencil by Anthony Eden, was advertised at $165. A cabinet photograph signed by Churchill was valued at $250 by one prominent dealer.

General Dwight D. Eisenhower's autographs are eagerly sought. Recent prices include $95 for a signed portrait; $85 for a one-page typed letter signed from the Supreme Headquarters of the AEF in 1945 but merely expressing thanks; and $75 for a colored picture of the general used as a frontispiece for a book and signed by Eisenhower. Important letters relating to military activities will bring much more.

Letters of President Franklin D. Roosevelt are not rare, generally speaking, and thus, except for those of major historic or social consequence, do not always command prices as high as those of Presidents whose autographic material is much scarcer. Nevertheless, they are in demand, and a typed letter of one page dated in 1942 and expressing thanks to another well-known figure for his birthday wishes is valued at $85. Another typed letter dated 1933 from The White House and mentioning that he has directed General Johnson to "conduct an exhaustive study of price increases" in textiles was priced at $100. A 1938 letter to the then Secretary of Labor Frances Perkins was tagged at $175. And a fine signed portrait was valued at $150. This compares with only $40 asked for a signed portrait of his predecessor, Herbert Hoover.

Autographs of President Truman are popular, and a White House card inscribed by him in 1952, with the original envelope, is valued at $100. A handsome studio photograph of Truman inscribed to Louis Johnson and dated 1948 was tendered at $25 above that figure.

Letters of distinguished scientists, writers, composers, and aviators from the 1930–1950 period attract a host of collectors. A choice item was part of Albert Einstein's working manuscript for his unified field theory written in pencil. Some time ago this was advertised at $650. It consisted of a single page torn from a notebook and unsigned! His signature alone is valued at around $35.

Letters of Margaret Mitchell, the diminutive Atlanta author whose *Gone with the Wind* created such a sensation in 1936, are scarce. Not long after her book appeared, she was forced to adopt a practice of refusing to autograph copies, so great was the demand upon her. One of her typed signed letters, dated 1939 and discussing the Negro dialect used in her book, was valued by the owner at $250. Letters and even signed checks of another literary giant of the thirties, Thomas Wolfe, bring excellent prices, such as $250 for a 1938 letter signed in pencil. This was not long before his death. Wolfe-signed checks will fetch about $100.

Some letters by Ernest Hemingway will bring fantastic prices for a modern writer; one dated in 1949, discussing bullfighting, was placed on the market at $575.

Other authors writing in the 1930–1950 period whose autographic materials are rising rapidly in value include F. Scott Fitzgerald (autograph poem, $350) and William Faulkner.

That fantastically successful American composer George Gershwin, who created or helped create so many hits of musical shows, might be surprised at some of the prices his letters and notes now bring, as, for example, $275 for an autographed musical quotation from his *Second Rhapsody,* dated 1933.

The autographs of adventurers and pioneers, including those of our intrepid aviators are in constant demand. A cover signed by Wiley Post and Harold Gatty and carried on board on their around-the-world flight in the *Winnie Mae* in June 1931, was valued a couple of years ago at $200 and probably would bring more now. The asking price was $300 for a letter handwritten and signed by Charles A. Lindbergh, declining an invitation to a dinner given by the Roosevelt Memorial Association. Routine typed letters of his have been priced at $175 and more.

Although the signatures alone of famous persons were valued

generally at only a dollar or two a few years ago, many have now risen by several times that amount.

The writing instruments used by celebrities also have become collectible items today. These include the rather bulky fountain pens, which have been rapidly losing ground to the ball points, and some of the interesting and sometimes ornate mechanical pencils of the 1930s in particular.

This is despite the fact that fountain pens have been around for a long time and that millions have been made through the decades. Throughout the 1930s a variety of innovations were introduced by fountain pen manufacturers. The pen that drew up ink from a bottle into a sack inside the barrel gave way to the "sackless pen." Pens were made with visible ink sections to alert users when the ink supply was nearing depletion. Nonbreakable materials were introduced for use as barrels. Pen points were tipped with iridium, a metallic element resembling platinum and used in platinum alloys for gold points.

Pen and pencil combinations were made, combining both fountain pen and mechanical pencil in a single unit. Chaste black gave way to colors in pens — reds, greens, blue, and mottled black-and-white. Midget pens for use with a neck ribbon and with the owners' names lettered on them were popular in 1930. (Silk neck ribbons were available at 39 cents.)

Eversharp introduced what it called its "mystery feed" (things characterized as "mysterious" were far more novel in those days than they have been since the conquest of outer space). Parker went iridium one better and introduced tips of osmiridium. Waterman introduced a pen that it boasted wrote "one-third of a mile," and offered a 100-year guarantee on another. In 1934, Joseph Hagn Co., Chicago wholesalers, was offering a Chameleon pen — "the only pen in the world with two points." There was a point at each end of the barrel, and they were detachable so they could be used by two persons if desired; otherwise it would have been exceedingly difficult to use both points at the same time.

Numerous fascinating pen desk sets appeared with a great variety of combinations atop bases. These ranged from clocks to stalking tigers. Some with cast Art Deco figures are definitely collectible.

Mechanical pencils were marketed in amazing variety. An intriguing one was a pencil–lighter combination. The barrel contained a removable wheel-type lighter. These wholesaled for only $1.50 a dozen in 1934! There were mechanical pencils with 10-sided barrels and 4-inch leads — four times the length of those in the usual mechanical pencils of the period — at 88 cents a dozen whole-sale.

Telescoping purse pencils were popular in the thirties among the ladies. When one pushed the end into the barrel, this action also caused the tip to be drawn inside, thereby reducing the total length to only 2½ inches. This type in sterling silver retailed in 1934 at $3 to $6 each.

Pencil sharpeners have undergone little basic change in recent decades, but a few novelty types appeared on the market in the 1930s that would be interesting to find today. One was a gun sharpener in the shape of an automatic pistol. Pencils were inserted in the muzzle and then turned to sharpen the points. A hinged, nickel-plated top lifted to release the shavings and to disclose an eraser.

Another sharpener was designed in the form of a miniature globe of the world. The globe rotated on its axis and was accurately charted and enameled in colors. The sharpener was in the globe's base. The entire piece, including base, stood only 3½ inches high.

Another interesting writing adjunct was the stationery cabinet. Montgomery Ward offered a very inexpensive one in 1940 with three drawers. The cabinet was covered in artificial leather in pastel col-ors. It sold complete with 24 sheets of paper and 24 envelopes for less than a dollar.

Letter openers, once also called paper cutters, have been made in tremendous variety for many years, and a number of novelty types appeared in the 1930s and 1940s that would add interest to a collec-tion of these handy devices. A number were made of metal in the shape of swords with a tassel in the hilt. Others were manufactured of bone or ivory. An inexpensive combination set containing a bone letter opener and a bookmark was offered by Sears, Roebuck in 1934 at only 23 cents. Hagn offered a paper cutter in the shape of an army rifle in 1946. It was made of metal with a polished bronze finish, and the bayonet served as the cutter.

Library sets containing a pair of scissors and a paper cutter were popular during the period. The majority were housed in a leather container or sheath. Many such sets are still around today — and in use.

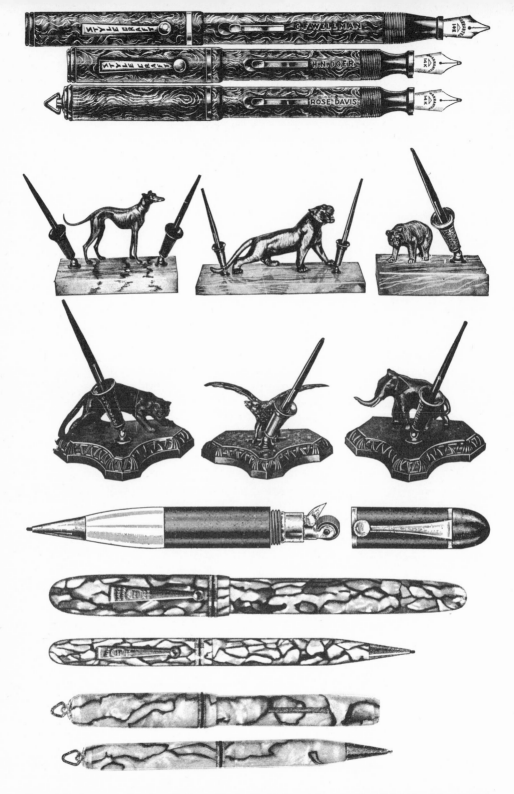

Top: Montgomery Ward sold these Style Craft fountain pens in 1931 for 79¢ to 89¢ each. Center: These writing sets mounted with Eversharp pens were offered by Joseph Hagn Co. in the early thirties. Whippet at top left is solid bronze. Tiger in center was finished in brass on onyx base and sold for $62.25. Sets on bottom went for $13 to $15.30. Below: Fountain pens and combination mechanical pencil and cigarette lighter of the thirties.

ROUND THE WORLD FLIGHT
of the "WINNIE MAE"

Pilot
Wiley Post *Wiley Post*

Navigator
Harold Gatty *Harold Gatty*

Top: Pencil sharpeners of 1934 in shape of gun and globe. At left below, a bottom view of the globe, showing sharpener. Center: Army Rifle Paper Cutter (1946). (*Courtesy Americana Interstate Corp.*) Below: Cover carried by Wiley Post and Harold Gatty on board their around-the-world flight in the Winnie Mae. It's postmarked June 21, 1931 and signed by both Post and Gatty. It is priced at $200. (*Courtesy Kenneth W. Rendell, Inc.*)

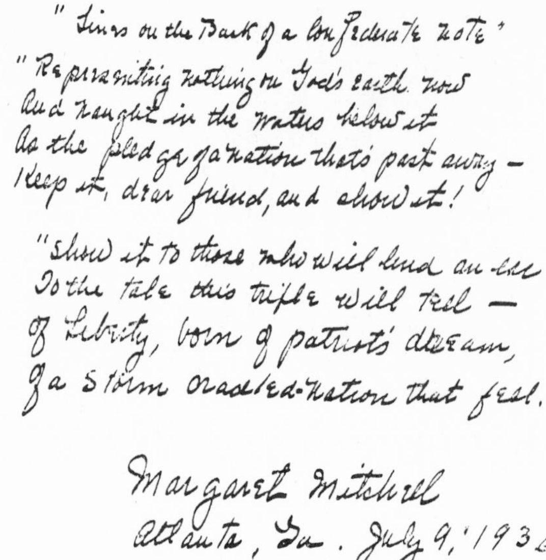

"Lines on the Back of a Confederate Note"

"Representing nothing on God's earth now
And naught in the waters below it
As the pledge of a nation that's past away —
Keep it, dear friend, and show it!

"Show it to those who will lend an ear
To the tale this trifle will tell —
Of Liberty, born of patriot's dream,
Of a storm-cradled-nation that fell."

Margaret Mitchell
Atlanta, Ga. July 9, 1936

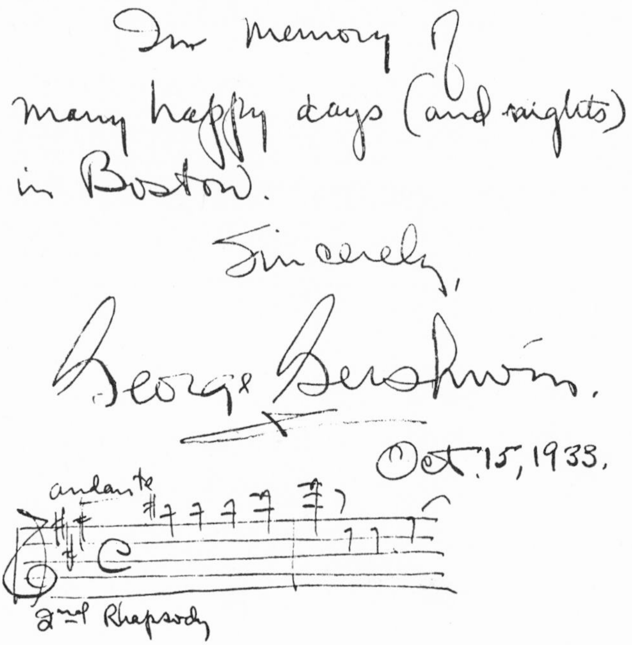

In memory of
many happy days (and nights)
in Boston.

Sincerely,

George Gershwin.

Oct. 15, 1933.

andante

2nd Rhapsody

Top: Autograph manuscript poem by Margaret Mitchell, author of *Gone with the Wind*, dated July 9, 1936. Priced at $75. Below: Autograph musical quotation from George Gershwin's *Second Rhapsody*, signed by the composer, priced at $275.00. (*Courtesy Paul C. Richards, Autographs.*)

Hegewaldheim, 28. VII. 41. 22^{30}

Mein Lieber!

A love letter of four pages, one of which is reproduced here, by Heinrich Himmler, chief of the Nazi SS, dated July 1941. Priced at $475 by Kenneth W. Rendell, Inc., by whose courtesy it is reproduced.

15 THE SMOKER'S WORLD

FOR a profession that has traditionally cautioned its members to adopt a chary attitude toward publicity in any manner that might be construed as undignified, the medical profession of late has raised a mighty howl and cry about what it has termed the perils of smoking. The profession has kicked cigarette smoking in the teeth and has done very little better by the cigar and the pipe. I don't know whether, as a result, there are fewer smokers today than there were last year, but I do know that mighty few of them smoke in doctors' waiting rooms. It also seems certain that many have kicked the habit and others are trying. I do not propose, however, to debate the perils or the merits of smoking, which is best left to the knowledgeable. I do propose to introduce you to some of the intriguing adjuncts of smoking that flourished in the 1930s and 1940s; and although there do not seem to be many collectors of these at present, there are likely to be more before long, especially when the fascination of smoking accessories is recognized.

Prior to World War I, smoking was largely a man's world, but it was not long thereafter that the ladies poked a hole through the curtains that shrouded this sphere, just as they did through the curtains of the barber shop and the saloon. By the 1930s many ladies were more adept at blowing smoke rings than was the average male, and the manufacturer of smoking adjuncts no longer designed his products solely for the man of the family but tried to appeal to the female as well. This was particularly true of those who produced such things as cigarette cases, lighters, dispensers, boxes, and ashtrays. These objects passed from the stage of mere utilitarianism to that of decorative imperiousness. They not only performed their function; they imparted charm or color or at least novelty to the home and to the purse.

The cigarette case evolved from the cigar case, and in the 1930s it became a sleek and glistening object brought forth from milady's purse to excite admiration, envy, or at least interest. Cases appeared in silver, plated silver, and baser metals enameled to impart an aura of elegance. Two-tone cases appeared, usually black and white, as did some made of rolled gold-plate with enameled panel designs. To fit the male's inside coat pocket, producers turned out new long shapes, some measuring more than 6 inches in length, to hold 20 cigarettes in a single row, while smaller versions were made for the ladies to hold 10 cigarettes on each side.

Chromium-finished cases with Art Deco designs were popular in the 1930s, some of these appearing in a color combination of tortoise and black. An oblong or a square case was a matter of personal preference since both shapes were available. There were envelope-style cases, too, with foldover tops that snapped shut; some were decorated with jewels. There were inexpensive but colorful cases set with rhinestones or imitation jade. Many featured raised signets upon which the owner could have his or her initials or name engraved.

By the end of the thirties a wide variety of combination compacts and cigarette cases were being turned out for the feminine smokers. These not only conserved space in the purse but made it easy for a lady to smoke and powder her nose at the same time. Some were made of cloisonné and others of gold plate. Most of them held 10 cigarettes, loose powder, cake rouge, and a mirror.

Cases with engine-turned designs and golden bronze finishes were popular in 1940. Although standard cases usually held either 10 or 20 cigarettes, some appeared with a capacity of 13, their producers obviously not being superstitious. For the male there were cases covered in steerhide that had a special appeal to masculinity. At about the same time, the pop-up case was being advertised. One simply slid back a narrow top and a cigarette popped up, activated by a spring, for easy extraction. For those concerned about baggy pockets, there were "featherweight" cases; one manufacturer described his as being made of "aeroplane metal" and promised that it "will not bulge or weight down pocket." There were also "wafer thin" models that held a dozen cigarettes and opened automatically when top and bottom of the case were pressed simultaneously. There were models in which a spring automatically lifted up one cigarette when the case was opened.

There were some cases whose exteriors boasted a simulated wood grain effect, such as Carpathian elm burl and walnut, but a few lightweight cases were actually made of wood. And for those who in the forties were hip, even though the word was unknown at the time, there was the Flippy case of lucite, whose cover was graced with the likeness of a scantily-clad female. When the case was opened, the lass did a strip tease. The cases were variously lettered "Call to Arms," "Sailor Beware," "Take Off," "Caught in the Draft," "Girl He Left Behind," and "Here Comes [sic] the Police." And for the sports there were racetrack models with horse and jockey ornaments.

After the initial popularity of the black-and-white cases wore thin, a riot of colors appeared, often in combination, on cigarette case covers. These included pink and green, tortoise, emerald, ruby, amber, sapphire, red, green, yellow, solid black, solid white, white and straw, gold, gold and black, tortoise and black, black and "smoked pearl," cream and blue, cream and brown, white and blue, solid blue, and others. The cases will now bring $2 or $3 to $40 or more, depending on their material.

More interesting, however, than the individual cigarette cases are the combination cases and lighters, which also were produced in tremendous abundance. Many of these came as boxed sets and were favorite gifts for special occasions. Some sets contained a case and separate lighter and also a pocket knife and Waldemar chain. There were even combination case-lighter-compacts. Most combination lighter-cases had the striking mechanism mounted on top of the case, which opened on one side. Some strikers were mounted on one side of the case top and were ignited by pressing against the other side, such as the Permaplate Slide-a-Light combination.

Many quite elegant (and relatively high-priced) sets and combinations bore the Evans name. They were streamlined and stylish. Pickwick offered a series of quite inexpensive combinations that retailed in 1940 for as little as $1.50. Ronson produced some very elegant models in both individual cases and combinations. Its Dureum Twenty model sold for $27 in 1940. Dureum is a metal alloy with a natural gold color.

Most interesting of all, however, from the collector's standpoint are the novelty lighters of the period — upon which designers truly lavished their imaginations. There were lighters in the form of airplanes, caddies (complete with golf bag), cannons, knights in armor, world globes, lamp posts, ships' helms (ignited by turning the wheel), cameras of Bakelite, lipsticks, flasks, elephants, trained seals balancing balls that contained wheel lighters, Bengal tigers whose hinged heads contained wheel lighters, lighthouses with the lighter in a domed top, bottles, dice with lighters under a removable cap, sports trophies of antimony, camels that concealed lighters on their humps, pistols whose lighter ignited when the trigger was pressed, bullets, decanters, and numerous other objects.

A hit of 1940 was a musical marine lighter in the shape of a ship's helm. It contained a Swiss musical movement in the base, which was activated when this table lighter was lifted. The movement was supplied with assorted tunes. When the wheel was given a partial turn, the cap of the lighter was released and the wick ignited. Dunhill in the same year featured a Fan Dancer Silent Flame Lighter with a nude fan dancer atop it (for the delectation of the male users, the dancer held her fan atop her head). The fan dancer ornament stood on a square base that contained two flashlight cells. There was a trick to operating the lighter. The "lighting stick" had to rest against a metal railing around the top while its protruding tip simultaneously contacted the metal ornament. This pippin sold for less than $2.

In 1940 also, Dunhill was offering a Silent Flame table lighter that offered no mystery, only dignity. To operate it, one merely removed a fluid-containing cylinder from its receptacle atop a round, high base and touched its tip to a chrome ring at the top. The flame resulting was large enough to light a cigar or a pipe and was extinguished by replacing the cylinder in its receptacle.

Then there was the somewhat mystifying Lektrolite Glopoint that ignited cigarettes without a flame. One unscrewed the top of the oblong round lighter, pressed the cigarette inside, and puffed. Lektrolite offered a midget model of this type in 1940 that sold for $1.20. It also produced a key chain Glolite in chrome with a rhodium-finished snake chain and fine link keyholder with monogram tag attached.

Zippo advertised a diversity of models in its windproof line, which was offered over a period of many years. In a somewhat similar category were the small Sure-Fire Storm-Proof lighters that ignited a wick by the turn of a wheel.

Ronson built a lighter into a pencil housed in a chrome, engine-turned case with pocket clip and monogram shield, and these were available at $6.50 in 1940. The lighter was built into the end opposite the pencil tip.

The Joseph Hagn Co. offered a number of lines of novelty lighters, including one in the shape of a watch with a lapel cord available. The wick ignited when the crown was pressed. These sold for 70 to 85 cents in 1942. In this same war year a lighter was produced in the form of a miniature 50-caliber antiaircraft shell of solid brass. This was a flint lighter of the wheel type. For the sports fans there were Blackstone Giant Sport lighters of antimony with embossed squares on the case depicting such sports articles as boxing gloves, a base-ball bat, tennis racket, and golf club.

Hundreds of thousands of lighters were manufactured during the two decades in the conventional shapes, primarily oblong or oval, with bright enameling and of a diversity of materials by such well-known companies as Ronson, Evans, Match King, and Zippo. In the early 1940 Evans was making modernistic lighters of Brazilian onyx with felt-covered bases in cube and bell shapes, and in 1938 Ronson marketed watch lighters that combined a lighter with a built-in stem-wind, stem-set watch. Another Ronson novelty of that period was a miniature of a modern bar, atop which rested a cocktail shaker and glasses. The lighter had two compartments, each of which held 15 cigarettes, which were automatically elevated for easy removal as the lids were raised. The center section was a touch-tip lighter. The contrivance was handsomely-enameled in a grained walnut effect with chromium-plated relief bands, and the retail price was $25. A junior size model also was available for $16.50.

A novelty in the early 1930s was an electric Smoker-ette that dispensed lighted cigarettes. It featured a lever that was drawn forward, held for a few seconds, and released to eject the cigarette ready for puffing. The dispenser held 60 cigarettes and was priced at $3, complete with plug-in cord.

The collector who wants to pursue something relatively new in collectibles associated with smoking can have a field day with the lighters, and since they are far smaller than a breadbox, space limitations will prove no problem. Apparently very few have been on the collectors' market so prices have not yet been established, and values become strictly a personal matter between buyer and seller.

Novelty dispensers and cigarette boxes, newcomers to the collecting scene, are also fun to collect. There were some remarkable dispensers in the 1930s. A 1933 cast metal elephant dispenser finished in red, green, or ivory ejected cigarettes when its tail was twisted. It had a capacity of 20 cigarettes, and it cost only $1.25.

In 1934, the Joseph Hagn Co. was offering a wooden dispenser in the shape of a house with lithographed windows and doors. The roof was lifted to eject a cigarette.

In the same year a quarter would have bought you a 20-capacity metal dispenser with an enameled dog on the front and polished brass handles. One cigarette at a time was ejected by tilting the dispenser slightly forward. The Joseph Hagn 1940 catalog featured a Triggerette, a "modernistically"-shaped dispenser available in a variety of colors. When you turned a revolving disc in its top center to the right or left until an opening in it was aligned with a cigarette in the container, the cigarette would pop up. The same catalog illustrated a Pull and Puff ejector that held 25 cigarettes and was made of imitation onyx. One lifted the cover on the oval container and pulled forth a slew of cigarettes simultaneously.

The Ro-Tray was an oval leatherette container that ejected one cigarette at a time when the top was turned. A novelty type featured a wooden box made of a combination of woods with male and female figures on top. A lever in the back of the container not only ejected a cigarette when pressed down but also turned the heads of the two figures toward one another with tongues protruding. The cost was less than a dollar. A combination ejector-ashtray of wood with floral decoration dropped a cigarette forward when the top was lifted.

There were scores of different types of cigarette boxes and other containers, including a diversity of delightful novelties in the 1930s and 1940s. Many featured animals. The American Wholesale Corp. Division of Butler Brothers of Baltimore offered one in its 1930 catalog in the form of an antimony elephant with a brass-lined barrel container on its back. It was priced at a dollar. The Quick Trick box with a replica of a duck on one end was popular in the 1930s. Cigarettes were stored in a box on the opposite side of the base. One tipped a small knob on top of the outfit and the duck dived down and picked up a cigarette in its bill. Sears offered this for only 85 cents.

So-called white metal cigarette boxes with molded figures atop their covers were produced in the 1930s in imitation of the earlier ornate jewelry boxes. Hagn offered one in 1934 featuring an unclad maiden partially shielded by a towel and holding what appeared to be a cocktail shaker. One side of the box featured a golfing scene panel in color. The boxes had cedar linings and sold for $5.75.

Art Deco cigarette boxes were featured in the 1940 catalog of the Richter & Phillips Co. of Cincinnati. These sported a lissome nude seated on a metal base and holding a crystal glass box above her head. The boxes measured 4 inches wide and 4½ inches high. There was a companion ashtray set with the same lass or her twin holding aloft four glass ashtrays. This would indicate that the influence of Art Deco lasted longer than some have indicated.

There were a variety of embossed antimony boxes that sold for well under a dollar in the 1930s, and there was a wooden trick cigarette box that held a 20-pack load. The cigarettes appeared and disappeared mysteriously — unless one knew the secret of the end panel. There were modernistic boxes of lucite, roll-top wooden boxes, and combination memo-calendar-boxes. An intriguing novelty of the early 1940s was a "cigarette tree" for the dining table or terrace. The tree was made of glass with glass curlicues that each held a cigarette on the branches. Half a pack of cigarettes could be placed on each tree, which stood 11 inches tall, including the planter base.

And of course there were numerous musical cigarette boxes, among them a walnut container that held 47 cigarettes and had a miniature music box in the base. The box began playing when the lid was raised. Another type that's still around was in the shape of a miniature grand piano that played two tunes when the top was lifted.

Ashtrays provided another fruitful field for the designers. They were produced in almost every conceivable shape and size, and novelties abounded. Decorative animal ornaments were favorites and ranged from hound dogs to elephants. One of the latter stood on its rear legs to hold a barrel receptacle for ashes. Another was in the shape of a dachshund, whose metal body formed a low-slung tray supported by the creature's feet.

An interesting combination ashtray and paperweight in highly polished brass consisted of a vessel held in the outstretched arms of an Egyptian sprawled lengthwise. The 1933 catalog of the Joseph Hagn Co. illustrated a four-compartment tray atop which stood a full-length female nude, nearly 10 inches high, made of Britannia metal finished in ivory. The inserts were housed in a Britannia metal base with an Oriental bronze finish, and with gold or silver finish optional. These brought $6.50 each.

A 1933 tray of metal with a removable green glass insert was presided over by the mischievous-looking figure of a crow. The Jack R Better ashtray had two metal jackasses that held cigarettes between their long ears. The Lucky Horseshoe tray was just that: a tray in the shape of a horseshoe with a heavy cast metal horse on the rim. One very similar was called Turf Favorite.

Novelty smokers' sets appeared in the thirties. Some included cigarette box, ashtray, matchbox, and separate base in plated silver. Sears offered in 1933 at the total price of a dime a three-sectioned set of cigarette holder, match holder, and ashtray, the pieces representing dice and made of ceramic. The Humpty Dumpty set consisted of a tray on a metal shaft with a footed base. The tray housed a revolving ash receiver of colored glass covered with metal, an open ash receiver with cigarette rests, and a metal cigarette container. The 1940 Richter & Phillips catalog presented an intriguing smoker's set on a silverplated base fitted with a crystal glass holder and four ashtrays and graced with a 7½-inch-high metallic-ebony horse. A companion piece featured the horse with a covered cigarette box of crystal. The horses were well modeled. The latter set wholesaled for $9, the former for $13.50. The Red Cap set was made in the form of a red cap porter carrying two suitcases, one for matches and the other for cigarettes. There also were wooden cabinet smokers with humidor compartments and Art Deco carvings.

Bennett Brothers in its 1944 catalog presented a perfectly fascinating tobacco humidor in the form of a drum with crossed drumsticks forming the handle. The humidor was of hand-turned walnut with a contrasting maple base and lid; it carried a suggested manufacturer's retail price of $7.50. (A cigarette holder was made in similar shape.) Other wooden humidors were made in the shape of bowling balls and butter prints.

Pipe rests and rack sets in novelty shapes are not peculiar to the thirties and forties but some conversation pieces were turned out during those decades. There were combination pipe racks and clock sets with the clock in the shape of a ship's wheel and anchors serving as the pipe rests; swan sets with pipe rests in the shape of bronze swans; and combination pipe racks with humidors and "knocker" trays with cork knocking knobs. There were racks in the shape of a pilot's wheel made in combination with a glass humidor. The Texan combination of 1944 featured a walnut humidor with horseshoe ends, which served as stalls for pipes.

There were racks carved in the shape of a boat, and there was a Red Cap pipe rack set similar to the smoker's set described above.

Of great appeal was the Galleon pipe rest. This had a miniature ship with billowing sails mounted on one end of a chromium-finished base and the pipe rest on the opposite end.

Pipes have been collected for many decades, and there were some products of the thirties and forties that will appeal to all except those collectors who seek nothing less than a century of age. Novelty shapes predominated in the early 1940s. There were pipes shaped as revolvers; those with bowls in the form of a skull, and there were folding pipes that required a minimum of pocket space for toting about. The Churchwarden pipe had a stem 11½ inches long. There were some fascinating Danco imported briar pipes, especially those with bowls in the shapes of fish and shoes. These were distributed in the 1940s by the Danco Corporation, of New York City. Danco's Peasant pipes were also charming. Another development of the early forties was the "air-conditioned" pipe with an aluminum shank and "air-conditioning" chambers.

Finally, those who lived through the Depression years of the thirties will remember the cigarette-making machines that enabled one to buy bulk tobacco and papers and roll his own. These were quite inexpensive gadgets, and in 1931–1932, Montgomery Ward was offering one called the Target, complete with two packages of Target tobacco for only 98 cents. There was a special one made specifically for use with Brown & Williamson tobacco that sold for $5. The machine-rolled cigarettes saved money but always managed somehow to dribble a few shreds of tobacco into the smoker's mouth.

Any of the objects described in this chapter could constitute a varied and conversation-provoking if not immensely valuable collection.

As mentioned earlier, tobacco tins are now being collected, and on a widening scale. Most of those now sought predate the period with which we are concerned, but some continued to be made into the 1940s. Among these were some of the lunch box tins, which were originally used for tobacco and whose purchasers often utilized them subsequently for lunch boxes, since this is the shape in which they were made. The Fashion tobacco tin–lunch box was made as early as 1855, according to Marvin and Helen Davis in their book *Tobacco Tins* (privately printed, 1970), but continued to be made until 1943. These containers came complete with wire handle, and scarce ones will now bring as much as $25.

Tobacco tins were made through the years in a great variety of shapes and sizes, both for store counter use and as pocket tins. Although we tend to think of the latter as chiefly oblong and fairly thin containers, others resembled milk cans, canisters, milk pails, and other objects. Among the most delightful of the tobacco tins were the Roly Polies made by Mayo's Tobacco Co.

Most readers will remember the names of many of the better-known brands of tobacco that came in tins, among them Half and Half, Prince Albert, Old Colony, Kentucky Club, Velvet, Edgeworth, Lucky Strike, Hi-Plane, Bulldog, Old Bond, and Stag. Some are still being produced.

Top: Trigger, Scottie, Watch, and two Art Deco lighters of the thirties and early forties.
Below: Cigarette cases from the same period.

Cigarette lighters of the thirties.

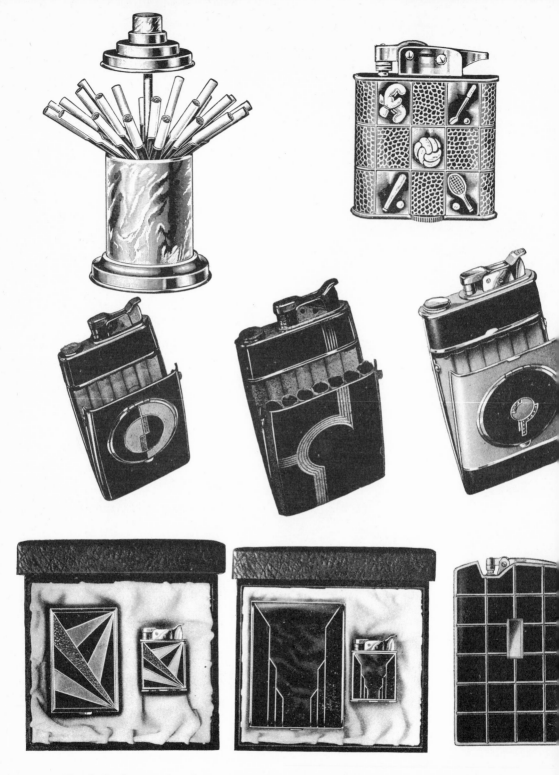

Top Left: Inexpensive cigarette container of the thirties ejected cigarettes when top was lifted. **Top Right:** Blackstone Giant Sport lighter (1942). (*Courtesy Americana Interstate Corp.*) **Below:** Note the Art Deco or "modernistic" design influence of these combination cigarette case-lighters and boxed sets. These Evans cases date from 1933. The Ronson Dureum Monarch combination (bottom right) is from 1940.

Ash trays, containers, and ejectors.

Smoker's accessories include Danco fish
and shoe pipes and Ronson Touch-Tip
Bar lighter (1938) and Ronson Penciliter.

1940 smokers' sets. Crystal cigarette box (top left), crystal ashtray set (below) with decorative nudes. At right are smokers' sets with well-modeled horses on silverplated bases.

16 POLITICS AND APPLE SAUCE

THE beloved Will Rogers said wryly many years ago, "All politics is apple sauce." But politics in the 1930s and 1940s was, to use the familiar parlance, dead serious.

Bitterness marked the Hoover–Roosevelt campaign and the subsequent, and unprecedented, campaigns by the man who, thanks to newspaper headline type, became known the world over as "FDR." No love was lost in the Truman–Dewey set-to, which, due to the overzealousness of one of the nation's major newspapers, created in itself one fascinating collector's item — a copy of that paper whose headlines proclaimed Dewey the winner.

The gadgets, paraphernalia, trivia, and miscellaneous trappings of political campaigns have been collectors' items for decades; those utilized in the presidential campaigns of the thirties and forties are no exception. There are hundreds of collectors of and scores of specialized dealers in political Americana, and right at this time interest in this field is on the upswing — and so are prices. In general, scarce older mementos of politics are valued considerably above those of recent times. Nevertheless, there are certain rarities of campaigns during the 1930s and 1940s that will bring excellent prices.

Many collectors will tell you that the heyday of political ballyhoo began during the presidential campaigns of Benjamin Harrison (who was himself far less colorful than were the campaign gadgets his supporters used), and William McKinley, who was engineered to victory in 1896 by the resourceful Mark Hanna, and won a second term in 1900 — a term cut short by a bullet from the gun of anarchist Leon Czolgosz.

There are dozens of mementos available from the McKinley–Hobart and McKinley–Roosevelt campaigns and from the subsequent campaigns of both successful and unsuccessful candidates, including Theodore Roosevelt, Alton B. Parker, William Howard Taft, Woodrow Wilson, Charles Evans Hughes, Warren G. Harding, James M. Cox, Calvin Coolidge, John W. Davis, and Al Smith.

The Roosevelt–Hoover battle in 1932 produced numerous collectible objects. There were Hoover–Curtis and Roosevelt–Garner buttons galore, jugates with illustrations of the pairs of candidates, badges, thimbles, ribbons, bumper plates, photographs, pocket knives, stickers, clocks, and assorted gadgets, each designed to drum up votes. In his campaigns to follow, Roosevelt shared the spotlight with, first, Henry A. Wallace and then Harry S. Truman. By and large, the Roosevelt mementos were more colorful than those of Hoover and of Roosevelt's subsequent opponents, Alfred M. Landon, Wendell L. Willkie, and Thomas E. Dewey.

Although Hoover forces utilized the symbolic elephant in varied forms and issued such things as pictorial knives, cane heads, and keys, the slogans were not particularly colorful, utilizing such phrases as "Be Safe, Keep Hoover," "Who? Who? Hoover" (on miniature owls) and "Press on with Hoover."

Gadgets of the first Roosevelt campaign were less flamboyant than those of his subsequent forays when his supporters used such slogans as "Don't Change the Pilot" (harking back to Abraham Lincoln's comment, "It is best not to swap horses while crossing a stream"), "He's Good Enough for My Buck," "Youth for Roosevelt," "Defend the New Deal," "It's Good to See the Home Fires Burning," and "I'll Bet My B.V.D. on F.D.R."

His supporters made lavish use of Roosevelt photographs, the United States flag, and the stars and stripes shield. "New Deal" mugs were popular, and manufacturers produced white metal clocks with Roosevelt at the helm of a ship, and various bits of trivia. Ugliness cropped out in some of the later Roosevelt campaigns as a result of the bitterness some powerful groups bore him, though perhaps little of this reflected the unrefined humor of the Warren G. Harding nose thumber — a small figure of Harding that thumbed its nose and had a tail that plopped out when the head and feet were pressed.

Roosevelt forces utilized one rather crude button with the picture of a jackass in the center and lettered at the top "Land (on) Your." This small button will now bring about $12. In the battle with Landon, Roosevelt supporters produced a button lettered "We Can't Eat Sunflowers, Disgusted Republican, Let's Lose with Landon," and in the fight against Willkie, a button was issued lettered "Watch Willkie Wilt." Another was lettered "Willkie for President of Commonwealth and Southern," and still another, "Win What? with Willkie."

Landon forces utilized numerous buttons on which a photograph of the candidate was enclosed in a replica of a sunflower, and also one that pictured Landon atop an airplane flying over the White House and lettered "Land on Washington."

Willkie supporters sported buttons with such slogans as "Caution, We Need Willkie, Not Dictatorship," "Eleanor, Start Packing, the Willkies Are Coming," "Roosevelt for Ex-President" and "1st Term Good, 2nd Term Good Enough, 3rd Term Good for Nothing." Willkie backers made lavish use of the phrase "No Third Term." A crude Willkie button pictured an outhouse in the center and was lettered "Project #Ump-000 Sponsored by Eleanor."

In two unsuccessful campaigns, Dewey backers used buttons with such saccharinelike phrases as "God Bless America" and "I'm on the Dewey Team." But they also pursued the theme "No Fourth Term," and in the race with Truman one button was lettered "Truman Was Screwy to Build a Porch for Dewey."

Truman backers went in heavily for the reproduction of likenesses of their candidate on buttons, badges, and placards. A campaign ribbon with a Truman photo button at top and a medal below will now bring about $8, and the well-known button lettered "I'm Just Wild about Harry" now sells for around $15.

Unusual Hoover campaign gadgets included an "official" cigar and a pair of plastic dice.

A Roosevelt electric clock showing the President holding a ship's wheel and lettered "Roosevelt at the Wheel for a New Deal" was extremely popular. The cast metal was finished in bronze, silver, or gold, and the timepiece was 13¼ inches high and 9¼ inches wide. This clock was made by Windsor and sold originally for $4.78.

Other miscellaneous collectible mementos of the political campaigns of the two decades include a diversity of posters, which usually featured a portrait of the candidate and a campaign slogan; slogan bridge score sheets used by Hoover; lettered auto reflectors;

stamps; a Willkie aluminum ashtray lettered "Win Votes Every Day for Wendell Willkie; contribution certificates given those who contributed to campaign funds; license plates; ceramic and glass mugs and cups (Landon used a glass cup with his portrait and lettered "Elect Landon, Save America," and the FDR mug had an embossed photograph of the candidate with the phrase "New Deal"); tumblers, including the one used by the Willkie forces and lettered a bit too optimistically "The Winner"; tin and tinfoil lapel tabs; photographs of candidates with either genuine or facsimile signatures, and many other objects. Although many of these are intriguing and values are on the rise, they do lack much of the robustness and variety of the gadgets used in earlier political campaigns. Herbert D. Loomis wrote two excellent brief articles on some of the mementos of earlier campaigns for *The Antiques Journal* in 1971, one entitled "Political Buttons" appearing in the March issue and the second, "Ballyhoo," in June. There was also an excellent article on these earlier objects entitled "Campaign Collectibles" in the November 1948 issue of the magazine *Antiques,* and the same magazine published in its November 1939 issue an article by Dr. Edward A. Rushford on torches and other lighting devices utilized in political campaigns in the days before electricity.

There are two good reference books for the collector of political buttons. One, *Political Campaign Buttons in Color,* by Otho D. Wearin (Leon, Iowa: Mid-America Book Company, 1970) has 24 color plates of buttons with prices. The newer one, *The Illustrated Political Button Book,* by Dick Bristow (Santa Cruz, Cal.: published by the author, 1971) illustrates hundreds of buttons from the time of McKinley through the Nixon–Humphrey battle and establishes a numbering system that he hopes will be adopted by other collectors to simplify communication among them. The book also contains a price guide to values. The author plans to revise the guide annually and to add supplements of additional items.

"Brummagen" is a word frequently encountered by the collector of political Americana. This refers to reproductions, fakes, and questionable items. The Bristow book contains a pictorial section devoted to reproductions and redesigns followed by descriptions of them. Generally, only the costlier items are reproduced, but a number of Hoover, Roosevelt, Dewey, Willkie, and Truman buttons are included in the brummagen.

In the normal course of events, as we have indicated, the older collectible items — other things being equal — will bring higher prices than more recent ones; but the increasing interest in political Americana has forced prices of many political objects, including buttons, of the thirties and forties, to relatively high levels. Hoover, Roosevelt, Truman, Landon, Garner, and Willkie buttons that were fetching only a few dollars at most several years ago are now bringing $15 to $25.

Admission badges to the major political party conventions should not be overlooked. Some were elaborate, and values are going up.

As a rule, mementos associated strictly with city and state elections are of quite limited interest except in the states involved.

Today one will encounter at virtually every antiques show one or more dealers specializing in political Americana, and a visit to these booths will give the reader a better idea of the variety of political objects that are collectible than can a brief chapter such as this.

Political buttons. **Top Left:** Truman and Truman—Barkley. **Top Right:** Dewey and Dewey-Bricker. **Center:** Willkie and anti-Roosevelt. **Below Left:** Roosevelt and Roosevelt-Wallace. **Below Right:** Landon and Landon-Knox. (*Courtesy Dick Bristow, Santa Cruz, Calif.*)

17 ART AND PHOTOGRAPHY

AMONG the manifold developments of the 1930s two especially are of interest to today's collectors. One was the emergence of projects (and also institutions) devoted not only to the encouragement of "modern" art but to making it available for the enjoyment of the masses. The other was the flowering of photography as both an art form and a hobby for a considerable segment of society.

The New Deal Administration, seeking to provide employment not only for bricklayers and shoe clerks but for members of the professions who, without premeditation, found themselves unable to earn a livelihood, inaugurated in 1935 a Federal Art Project under the Works Progress Administration. This new program was based, in part at least, on the premise that painters, designers, and sculptors, as well as salesmen, textile workers, and electricians needed to eat. (The long-held assumption on the part of many that artists and writers can exist solely on a liquid diet is both erroneous and slanderous.)

The Federal Art Project put large numbers of artists to work and at one time supported more than 5,000 of them. As a corollary the Treasury Department set up a bureau charged with the procurement of art for use in public buildings. Edward Bruce, himself an artist as well as a businessman, was placed in charge of this program, the results of which may still be viewed today — and with appreciation — in many of our public structures.

The art programs generated some remarkable results, foremost among them being the fertilization of a group of "modern" movements in art that before long had introduced a new vigor and a robustness to the art scene in America. Art took many directions simultaneously as centers for creative art were established in a large number of cities. The diversification proved healthy, stimulating an appreciation of art among many who theretofore had ignored the modern movements, probably because they did not understand them and therefore found it simply impossible to appreciate them.

The program as a whole was provided comfort and aid by the Museum of Modern Art, which had been established only in 1929 in New York City and whose total energies were devoted to promoting creative art of the present era. Other museums and institutions also played important roles in the extension and development of art in the United States, among them the Whitney Museum of American Art, opened in New York City in 1931; and in Merion, Pa., the Barnes Foundation, established by Dr. Albert C. Barnes, assembled in its gallery a remarkable collection of modern art masterpieces, including a fine array of Western art.

Heterogeneity was probably the keynote of the art of the thirties as artists veered off into new paths in the realms of posters, book and magazine illustration, painting, and especially murals, and sculpture. So-called "modern" art movements elsewhere over the world, but particularly those originating in France, had their influence here, and these included Surrealism — the art of the subconscious and fantastic which originated in the twenties and peaked in the thirties and of which Man Ray, Marcel Duchamp, Salvador Dali, and Joan Miro, were among the chief practitioners; and Cubism, originated by Picasso and Braque.

How diversified the new American art had become was evidenced at an exhibition called "New Horizons in American Art" on which the federal government and the Museum of Modern Art collaborated in 1936. Abstract paintings truly flourished in the late thirties and the early forties, and there were those who drooled over them and others who damned them in toto.

Certainly one of the outstanding painters of 1930 and for some time thereafter was Grant Wood, the Iowan, whose best-known work is *American Gothic*. But there were scores of others whose names today are known even in the hinterlands, among them Thomas Hart Benton, Rockwell Kent, Guy Pène du Bois, John Steuart Curry, William Gropper, Georgia O'Keeffe, Jackson Pollock, Walt Kuhn, Leon

Kroll, Reginald Marsh, and John Marin, to mention only a few among a host. And, of course, there was "Grandma" Moses (Anna Mary Robertson Moses), who had begun to paint at the age of 76 and who had her first "one-man" show in 1939. And there was also Norman Rockwell, who still refers to himself as an illustrator and who began drawing covers for the *Saturday Evening Post* — that wondrous magazine that refused to be embalmed — as far back as 1916. *Post* covers with Rockwell illustrations are sought by collectors today. A 25-year-old book, *Norman Rockwell, Illustrator,* became a best seller when it was reprinted in 1970 by American Heritage Publishing Co., Inc., at a retail price of $20, although it was made available to advance subscribers at $12.95.

Edward Hopper, who had produced some stark paintings that depicted the emptiness of the American scene in the twenties, turned out some fine works in the thirties focused upon grim but potent urban views. Charles Burchfield also ranked high among the artists who portrayed life in America in a post-realistic manner. Highly individualistic styles were developed by Grant Wood and Thomas Hart Benton, some of whose outstanding work embodied an admixture of grimness, humor, and satire. Satire also pervaded much of the work of William Gropper, intimately concerned with manners and morals, whose lithographs had their roots in the cartoon, and who therefore conveyed in his work a social commentary that was caustic in its severity.

An abundance of other fine talent either emerged or matured during the thirties and forties to make these decades among the most fruitful in the history of American art. Their names and work will be encountered in numerous books dealing with modern art, and their paintings are not now available for a pittance. We will not discuss them further here since this chapter is intended to deal primarily with the objects of the two decades that are within the reach of those whose treasure house is less than opulent.

One movement, or style, however, that flourished in the thirties and lingered on into the forties and that is now intimately associated with this period has come to be known as Art Deco, upon which some emphasis already has been placed in this book and which is being "discovered" and rediscovered in the seventies — discovered by the younger generation for whom its manneristic qualities hold a peculiarly modernistic appeal, and rediscovered by their elders, who remember it, some vaguely, and in some of whom at least it evokes a nostalgic mood that combines a feeling of both yearning and annoyance.

The name itself was given the style after it had stopped flourishing and is derived from *L'Exposition Internationale des Arts Décoratifs et Industriels* (The International Exposition of Decorative and Industrial Arts), held in Paris in 1925 at which the new style was first presented in an organized and international exhibition. The style has been called by other names, but it is Art Deco that is here to stay.

Art Deco was the first widespread popular style to follow Art Nouveau into so many varying channels from painting to industrial arts, and although many of its characteristics had evolved earlier, it did not reach maturity until the mid-twenties. Those who contend that the movement had spent itself by the arrival of the thirties have failed to examine sufficiently the production of the thirties. During this decade Art Deco, in either undiluted or diluted form, was evident in objects at almost every hand, though it is true that a multitude of them were commercially produced on assembly lines, were intended for consumption by the masses, and lacked the creative vigor of many earlier pieces.

Although to a minor extent Art Deco bore kinship to Art Nouveau and to other styles, it developed a variety of characteristics that were peculiarly its own. William Morris would have abhorred it, since that guiding spirit of the Arts and Crafts Movement in England loathed the machine and the new materials to which the machine gave birth. Art Deco utilized both and, to a large extent, became dependent upon both. Mass production was in high gear in the thirties, and it was natural that manufacturers, always eager to ride the crest of a popular movement, should have adopted (and adapted) Art Deco. The style is not an easy one to define although many have attempted it. In the diversity of media in which it was embraced, it utilized elements and materials that were as diverse as those that molded the changing moods of the years through which it evolved and flourished.

In his interesting book, *Art Deco* (Studio Vista, Ltd.–E.P. Dutton and Co., Inc.), Bevis Hillier allocates to Art Deco such influences as Cubism, Expressionism, Futurism, Vorticism, the art of the American Indian, the arts of Egypt, and the colors of the Russian Ballet. But Art Deco, as we have said, also developed its own peculiar characteristics to set it apart and entitle it to some appellation of its own. Whereas artists and artisans of the Art Nouveau movement had favored asymmetry, those of Art Deco returned largely to symmetry, although in later commercial versions they created, under the influence of functionalism and modernism, geometrical arrangements that tended to yield an impression of rigidity not found in the earlier fluid lines of Art Deco. The designers seem to have been striving for a compromise between the angle and the curve. Ultimately "modernism" simply supplanted Art Deco.

But thus far insufficient attention seems to have been paid to the influences that had perhaps the greatest impact upon both the Art Deco and modernism movements. These were the mood of the times themselves, the pace of living, the affectations, pastimes, and morality.

The pace of living quickened in the twenties and, after some hesitation at the outset of the period, finally burst into an almost frenzied speed in the thirties. This quickening, leading to the futuristic movement, is evidenced in the design of automobiles and aircraft, in car hood ornaments, in sculpture, poster art, furniture. This design is characterized by a word that has become a part of today's vocabulary — streamlining. And this is the realm in which Art Deco and modernism are locked in a shadowy embrace.

But Art Deco, particularly in the commercial productions of the thirties, embraced such qualities as impishness, frivolity, vulgarity, puckishness, and jocoseness. These qualities are evident particularly in the myriad trifles of the period ranging from costume jewelry to smoking accessories. And even though many such productions may be characterized today as frankly vulgar, this does not make them less fascinating to the collector of trifles, a breed whose ranks swell daily. One characteristic these American versions or adaptations of Art Deco did not have — snob appeal.

Along with a tendency to frivolity, much American Art Deco also was robust and vibrant, and occasionally shocking. Many objects combined masses of sharply contrasting colors, black and white, red and black, white and green. Others featured zigzag lines likened to the lightning flash and still others the stepped pyramidal shape compared by Hillier to that of Aztec temples. Generally, pastels were eschewed in favor of vivid colors, which, combined with touches reminiscent of Egyptian pageantry, have been said to reflect, at least in part, the influence of the stage and costume designs created by Leon Bakst and his cohorts for the Russian Ballet, founded and so magnificently nurtured by Sergei Diaghilev.

There are many individuals who contributed to the development of the new style. The contributions of some were primarily to the type of Art Deco witnessed at the Paris Exposition of 1925; those of others to the evolving modernistic style that became enmeshed with functionalism. They included Paul Poiret, the French fashion dictator; talented designers of glass such as Maurice Marinot and Simon Gate; such multitalented designers as Le Corbusier, Donald Deskey, Kem Weber, and George Nelson; such designers of silver as Charles Boyton and those employed by L'Orfèvrie Christofle; the Saarinens; the sculptors D.H. Chiparus and Jean Dunand; the painters Fabius Lorenze, John Vassos, and Rockwell Kent — these and scores of others, some of whom are likely to remain anonymous until historians of the period dig more assiduously into sources of the art.

Although the Art Deco movement was an international one, making inroads into most of the civilized countries of the world, its impact was particularly strong in France, that country in which so many art movements of the past have originated. Artists participating in and part of the movement in that country could be generally separated into two categories, according to Judith Applegate in her comments in the catalog of the Art Deco exhibition arranged by the Finch College Museum of Art, New York City, in January and February 1971. There were, she says, "the exotic romantics" and the "modern romantics, who were more aligned with a machine aesthetic and industrial production than with the whimsies of fashion or decorative effect." But, as she also observes, there were many who fell between the two extremes, combining in their work the elements characteristic of both.

The Finch College Museum of Art exhibition was one of several Art Deco exhibitions held in 1971 that focused attention anew upon the creations of the twenties and thirties. Its success was due in large measure to the efforts of Mrs. Elayne H. Varian, Curator and Director of the Contemporary Wing, and her associates who brought together a diversity of Art Deco objects ranging from furniture to glass, ceramics, and graphic arts.

A second exhibition was held from July 8 through September 5 at the Minneapolis Institute of Arts and was organized by Bevis Hillier and David Ryan, the museum's Curator of Exhibitions. It featured nearly 1,500 works of all types. Those displayed at the Finch College Museum of Art formed a part of this exhibition.

As could be expected, the exhibitions drew both praise and condemnation. Of the Minneapolis show, John Canaday wrote in *The New York Times:* "It left me feeling that to have reached adolescence and to have spent your youth with Art Deco all around you was to have been victimized by its perversity and vulgarity." And he added: "Art Deco (being pseudo in everything) was a pseudo-snob style that discarded snobbery's prerequisite of exclusiveness to cater to a 1920s audience that had come into so much money and was so numerous that only a style of consummate vulgarity could succeed with it commercially."

Unquestionably there are many other critics who agree with Mr. Canaday though they may not write as breezily, but there are also those who view the style not merely as a historical one, which it was, but also as one that mirrored its years; and whether that is good or bad depends upon one's taste and the mellowness of one's memory.

At any rate, the two exhibitions served to direct attention to the fact that whatever else it was, Art Deco was a diverse art that sometimes tended to splinter into subdivisions, all held to the parent body by an intangible but nevertheless real umbilical cord.

Not as large in scope but nevertheless important was still another 1970 exhibition, one held at The Arts Club in Washington, D. C., in June in which more than 250 Art Deco creations were on display. The Washington show was assembled and coordinated by Maurice D. Blum, a principal in the large Washington decorating firm of John J. Greer–Maurice D. Blum Associates, Inc.

Messrs. Blum and Greer themselves had assembled their own outstanding collection of Art Deco, which was featured in the exhibition along with objects from the striking collection of Mr. and Mrs. Theodore Davidov of Bethesda, Md., and others. This exhibition also attracted major interest. A number of the illustrations in this book depict objects in the Blum–Greer collection, which were supplied through the kindness of Mr. Blum.

In sculpture and molded ceramic figures, the lithe-limbed, wholesome, athletic type female is encountered almost as frequently as is the insouciant female head with flowing locks in Art Nouveau. In sculpture, movement is a keynote. There are dancers galore — nude, seminude and diaphanously draped — all imbued with an obvious *joie de vivre.* Their arms are aloft; one or both hands often clutch the hem of the flowing skirt. Illustrated in this book is an ivory and bronze torch dancer, wearing silvered bloomers and with breasts bare. Her head is thrown back and in each uplifted hand she holds a lighted torch. Standing 14 inches high on a truncated onyx marble plinth and inscribed "P.K.," the figure brought $875 at a Parke-Bernet auction in 1971. Shown in the same photograph is an ivory and bronze female archer signed F. Preiss. She wears a gilded tunic and a red kerchief: The impression of motion is obvious, since she is ready to release an arrow. This figure, on an onyx marble plinth and black marble base, is 9¼ inches tall and brought $375 at the same auction.

Typical, too, of the sense of movement conveyed by Art Deco statuary is the illustrated pair of skaters in ivory and bronze. Signed Jaquemin and standing 13 inches tall, they were sold by Parke–Bernet for $400.

Paul A. Straub & Co., Inc., of New York City offered in the mid-thirties a diversified group of European faience figures ranging between 8½ and 21 inches high in dancing postures that caught the vibrant spirit of Art Deco. Some of these also are illustrated here. Today they will bring many times their original small cost on the collectors' market.

Hundreds of Art Deco sculptures were produced in France and others elsewhere abroad that centered on dancing figures. The female dancers also were incorporated in figural lamps. Names found on these sculptures include D. Chiparus, Lorenzel, R. Paris, G. Rigot, Barthelemy, Gori, and Pierre le Faguays.

In addition to the dancers, the skaters, and the archers, there were sculptures in ivory or bronze, or a combination of ivory and bronze, of bathers, troubadors, skiers, nymphs, and young women in street dress, tennis garb, and pajamas. Figures of women wearing ankle-length skirts and holding large dogs in leash were quite popular in the early thirties as a theme for productions in ceramics, and many variations of these will be encountered in trade catalogs of the period.

Art Deco was the theme for the 27th annual National Antiques Show in New York City in February 1971. A number of sculptures of the types just described were displayed, including the ivory and bronze figure of the dancer, signed D. Chiparus, illustrated here.

In the United States the movie star Jean Harlow typified the female figure popular for use on small decorative articles. Inexpensive flapperlike figurines of ceramic showed young women in bathing suits, sailor suits, and even sarongs. Some figures were made of composition materials and of plaster, erroneously called chalk.

In addition, there were numerous figures of lithe, running dogs and of other animals that were utilized as table decorations or were used to adorn the top of the radio cabinet. Cast Art Deco figures also appeared as clock ornaments, were incorporated with jewelry, or were used as architectural ornamentation.

One of the most remarkable assemblages of Art Deco in this country is known as the Coda Collection. It was brought together by Mr. and Mrs. Theodore Davidov and Mr. and Mrs. Roy Copeland of England, who have a working arrangement in collecting (and also selling) Art Deco. A number of their decorative pieces, including some mentioned above, have been sold at auction through Parke-Bernet.

Mrs. Davidov grew up with Art Deco: Her mother had a collection of pieces. Several years ago, before the boom in the decorative pieces got under way, Mrs. Davidov, herself an artist, began quietly collecting fine objects in this mode. Today her home is furnished in Art Deco, and her collection includes even Art Deco dresses. Her collection of jewelry and figures and figurines of porcelain and other materials is outstanding. Mrs. Davidov has become one of the country's most knowledgeable authorities on the style and the artists of the period.

In the field of architecture, Art Deco made some impact but primarily in decorative elements as just noted. But a sort of streamlined modern architecture did develop, especially for the skyscrapers that seemed to climb to dizzier and dizzier heights in the metropolitan centers of the nation. These structures as designed and built in the thirties managed to evade the aura of uniformity that had characterized a large part of the commercial architecture both prior to World War I and following World War II. The stepped pyramid likened by Hillier to the Aztec temples found its niche. In New York City the 56-story Chanin Building built in 1929 was a forerunner, and the McGraw–Hill Building of 1930 was a typical example. Others followed during this decade. The Art Deco and the modernistic influences are found in Radio City Music Hall and the Chrysler Building in New York City, among others.

The traditional materials of the building industry began to be abandoned in favor of reinforced concrete, structural steel, aluminum, and other newer ones. Some of these new materials yielded both economy and strength, but they also were utilized in such a manner as to accord prestige: They imbued the beholder with the idea that their architects and those who dwelt therein not only were keeping up with the times but were actually outpacing them. The tall commercial buildings became both towers of strength and of modernity, and the eclectic late Victorian styles became obscured in the mists of a contrived antiquity.

In architecture, as in other arts and crafts, the role of the machine gained momentum, particularly in the design and construction of apartments and smaller dwellings. Among the major new processes was prefabrication of both small and large elements. This helped hold down costs. It also bestowed strength, although at a sacrifice of some degree of individuality. But social questions also had emerged as a consequence of the Depression: How to provide an aesthetically satisfactory dwelling place for the growing masses of low-income families. The multiunit apartment structure emerged as one answer, and then came the multiunit, multibuilding complex that has continued to gain in importance since World War II and has now escaped the confines of the cities and has sprawled over into the suburbs.

Because the sword of Damocles had not yet descended on the motion picture industry in the thirties, as it subsequently did, not only the movies but the movie houses flourished. Many were built as showplaces, designed to dazzle no less than did the flashing limbs and flamboyant costumes of the inordinately luscious girls who decorated the extravaganzas filmed for the delectation of the masses. The neon light led to the creation of marquees that beckoned the populace with an appeal as irresistible as were the songs of those sea-nymph Sirens to the crew of Ulysses long ago. Marble and onyx temptations in lavish lobbies provided a further lure as did resplendent lounges which afforded milady not only the opportunity to reapply her lipstick and mascara but to indulge with female companions in the ages-old art of gossip.

But as the fourth decade of this century neared its close, the sword of Damocles began its descent, and scores of those palatial edifices were cleft by its blade in the years that followed, to the sweet sorrow of many who had patronized them in the years of their youth.

The entrances to and the lobbies of other public buildings built in the thirties were lavish, too, adorned not only by marble and onyx architectural elements but by sculptures and murals that reflected the spirit of the times, sometimes in gargantuan proportion. The Art Deco and "modernistic" influences were evident in the decoration of doors, gates, and grilles. As Arnold Lehman points out in an article, "New York Skyscrapers," in *The Metropolitan Museum of Art Bulletin* for April 1971, even mailboxes were utilized to serve as significant examples of the decorative style of structures.

Many of the decorative innovations of the thirties are even now exerting their influence on architects in their designs for the approaches to and the lobbies of public buildings, including even hotels, such as Atlanta's fabulous Regency Hyatt House. In its design architect John Portman exercised an ingenuity that was flamboyant but hypnotically alluring.

In the thirties, too, the art of the poster was rejuvenated and became as individualistic as it had been during the days of Art Nouveau. This art was stimulated by the Federal Art Project, and the poster was pressed into the service of a wide variety of causes and projects. Striking posters of the period will one day, perhaps in the not distant future, provide a new focal point for the collecting of nostalgic art; and those who begin seeking examples now may discover one day that their acquisitions were not only rewarding for the pleasure they gave but also as investments. To a lesser extent, the Art Deco influence was extended to the dust jackets, covers, and title pages of books.

Although examples of photography as art can be found as far back as the past century, the thirties and forties saw the true flowering of both photography as art and photography for the masses. The candid camera became the rage. Newspapers and pictorial magazines abandoned their bulky Graflexes, Speed Graphics, and their 8x10-inch studio cameras for the much more portable Rolleiflex, Leica, Exacta, Zeiss Ikon and other miniatures utilizing 2¼x2¼-inch or .35 mm. film.

The earlier stilted, posed group shots largely typical of pictorial coverage of conventions and other group assemblages gave way to unposed closeups of individuals engaged in such normal activities as gnawing ravenously on chicken thighs, hoisting a cup that cheers, or poking a forefinger into the nose. Needless to say, many such shots were not altogether flattering to their subjects, but they did afford novelty for readers and viewers.

Picture magazines, foremost among them being *Life,* sprang up to fill a growing demand for pictorial journalism; and newspapers accustomed to the slower services of independent engravers installed their own engraving departments to close the time gap between the snapping of photos and the appearance of cuts in print.

Although the carrier pigeon was experimented with on a few occasions, some newspapers began utilizing the airplane for speedy delivery of film for processing from distant places when the importance of the event warranted it, and often when it did not. Such transport of photographs taken at Saturday football games for printing in Sunday newspapers was one example.

Camera clubs cropped up all over, enlisting the majority of their members from the swiftly swelling ranks of amateur photographers. They sponsored competitions and salons in every region of the United States. Numerous entries in the salons represented candid shots, others carefully contrived pictures, some of which indeed were entitled to the rank of art. Photography of the nude became a highly popular pastime, not only at camera club meetings but in the apartments of young bachelors who seemed to have become suddenly addicted to the camera.

Color processes, pioneers among them being Eastman Kodachrome and Dufaycolor, were developed for amateurs, and by the late 1930s color photography was the rage. The movie camera also became a joy to thousands of amateurs, who shot literally millions of miles of movies of their children, their vacations, and their home life and foisted these with gusto upon their relatives, their neighbors, and anyone else they could entice into their homes long enough to enable them to set their projectors in motion.

Scores of new cameras, still and movie alike, appeared on the market throughout the thirties and forties. Familiar names, in addition to those already mentioned, included Argus, Kodak Retina, Dollina, Agfa Clipper, Regal, a variety of miniature Kodaks, Gevirette, Foth Derby, Perfex, Reflecta, Baldina, Reflex Korelle, Jubilette, Voightlander Brilliant, Purma, Falcon, Ikonta, Contax, Univex, and many others.

Accessories for both still and movie cameras multiplied — and bathrooms, clothes closets, storage spaces, and guest rooms were converted into home darkrooms in whose recesses amateurs plied their talents and enriched the tills of the camera and the film producers.

But the professionals and the more talented of the amateurs managed to preserve on film much of the history of two exciting decades, and the giants among those dedicated to photography as art, such as Edward Steichen, created art in much the same sense as it was created by Leon Kroll and Georgia O'Keeffe and Max Ernst.

No major war in history was ever captured on so much film as was World War II, nor was one ever captured so dramatically. Much of the credit for this goes not only to the newspaper and magazine photographers but also to experts within the armed services. A fine record of this accomplishment is preserved within the covers of *The U.S.A. at War: U.S. Camera Annual, 1945,* edited by Tom Maloney and published in 1945 by *U. S. Camera* and Duell, Sloan & Pearce.

Early photographic apparatus of all types, including cameras and darkroom equipment, has been collected for several years, and there are some who are now beginning to collect prototypes and the earliest models of the miniature cameras. It may be surprising to the layman to realize what an overwhelming proportion of those produced in the early thirties are still operable and capable of producing first-class results. Some of the photographs with which this book is illustrated were taken with a 1934 Rolleicord that I first placed in service as a newspaper photographer–reporter in North Carolina.

I'm willing to venture the guess that outstanding and historic photographs of the thirties and forties will become increasingly collectible, because they serve as documentary evidence of things as they were and not as many would like to remember them as having been.

There is already a brisk trade in photographs of movie and other entertainment stars of the period. There are also some collectors of sports photographs. The next progression should be to photographs that record the everyday history of that era — the homes, the public buildings, the vehicles of transportation, the unusual or novel events, and the faces of the people.

Of course the paintings are desirable and are being collected in numbers; but not everyone can pay $6,000 for a Dali colored ink and watercolor work, which is what his "Deux Figures Surrealistes," painted in 1939, brought at a Parke-Bernet auction in 1971, or $8,500 for Diego Rivera's painting on Masonite, "Campesino," completed in 1936, which is what it fetched at a Parke–Bernet sale. But many drawings, etchings, posters, and book illustrations are available for far smaller sums. So are the minor ceramic sculptures mentioned earlier.

John Vassos, an outstanding Art Deco illustrator, did this gouache "Traffic Ballet," 1927, for *Dance Magazine*. Collection of Ted McBurnett. (*Courtesy Finch College Museum of Art.*)

Top: Art Deco nymphets. **From Left:** chrome figure on ashtray; gilded figure holding ashtray, and two Greenies, one of which is of Egyptian influence. (*Gilded figure from collection of Marlin Fenical, others from collection of Maurice D. Blum and John J. Greer. Photo by Marlin E. Fenical.*) **Below:** Mirrored head in front of mirror with blue glass. (*From collection of Mr. and Mrs. Theodore Davidov, of Bethesda, Md., as shown at the Art Deco Exhibition in Washington. Photo by Marlin E. Fenical.*)

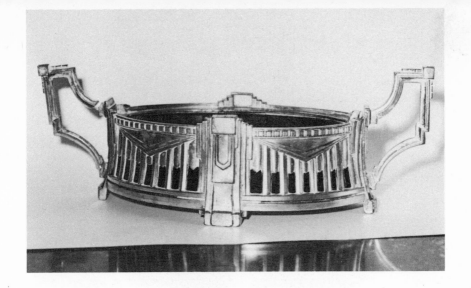

Top: French Art Deco blue glass and white metal container. **Below:** Bronze Art Deco figure with nickel finish on black lacquered wooden base; signed A. Bouvaine. (*From collection of Maurice D. Blum and John J. Greer. Photos by Marlin E. Fenical.*)

Watercolor on paper with stylized figures, by Alfred Tulk, 1931. (*Collection of Stanley Insler. Courtesy Minneapolis Institute of Arts.*)

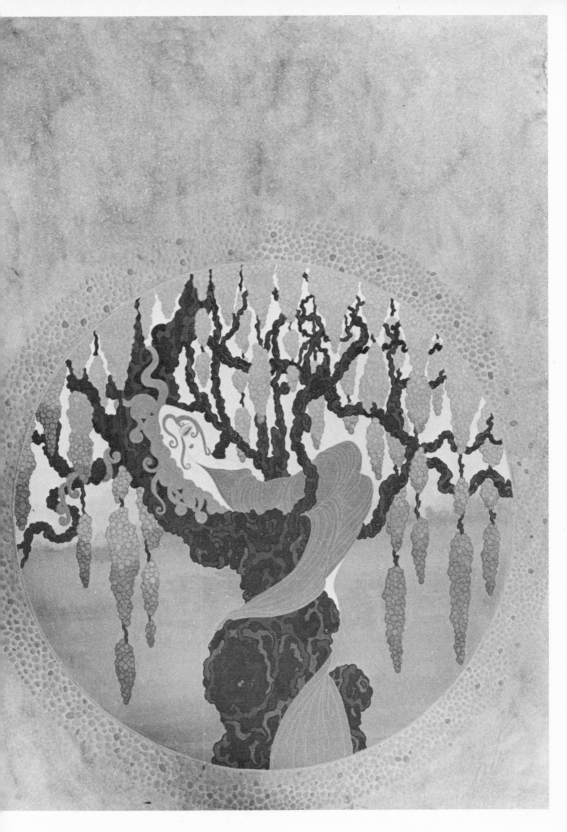

"L'Ete" by Erté (Romain de Tertoff), gouache, signed, *c.* 1928. (*Courtesy Minneapolis Institute of Arts; loaned anonymously.*)

French bronze and ivory sculpture of Art Deco dancer by D. Chiparus on an onyx base. (*Courtesy National Antiques Show, Madison Square Garden, New York City, and Pearl Winick.*)

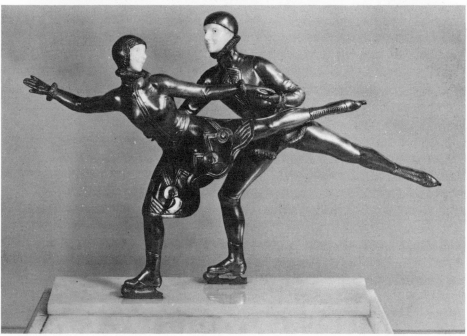

Top: Art Deco sculpture signed F. Zucchet. (*Collection of Maurice D. Blum and John J. Greer. Photo by Marlin E. Fenical.*) **Below:** This bronze and ivory figure group of two skaters is typical Art Deco. Signed Jacquemin and posted on a truncated marble base, the sculpture brought $400 at a Parke-Bernet auction in 1971. It was from the Coda Collection, Bethesda, Md. (*Courtesy of Parke-Bernet Galleries, Inc., New York City.*)

Top: Art Deco ivory and bronze sculptures from the Coda Collection, Bethesda, Md. The archer (left), signed F. Preiss, fetched $375 in a 1971 auction at Parke-Bernet Galleries. The torch dancer, inscribed P. K., commanded $875. (*Courtesy Parke-Bernet Galleries, Inc., New York City.*) **Below:** Art Deco porcelain figures were sold in the thirties by Paul A. Straub & Co.

Bronze medallions from the collection of Dr. Robert Pincus-Witten, New York City. Top: "Abundance," by Pierre Turin. Below: "Defense du Canal de Suez," Raymond Delmarre, 1930. (*Courtesy Minneapolis Institute of Arts.*)

Bennett Brothers, Inc., offered these cameras in early forties. **Top Row From Left:** Agfa Unifo Clipper, Univex Twinflex, and Dehel folding camera. **Second Row:** Falcon-Abbey, Falcon-Flex, and Falcon Automatic No. 6. **Bottom:** Univex Mercury and Corsair II.

Cameras of the thirties included the Purma Special, Super Baldina, Voightlander Reflex, Rolleicord, and Exakta, Jr.

Top: Eastman's inexpensive and popular 1934 Jiffy Kodak Six-20 with f6.3 lens sold for $17.50. Below: Univex movie cameras, projector and accessories of 1940, from Bennett Brothers catalog. The Univex Model Cine 8 with f4.5 Ilex Univar lens went for $20.

THE
IMPACT
OF WAR

BETWEEN the time the Japanese bombed Pearl Harbor on December 7, 1941, and the devastation of Hiroshima by an American atomic bomb on August 6, 1945, an era within an era had been created and destroyed.

The impact of war changed not only the American way of life but the life of the world. The upheaval that began when Japan launched its belligerence against Manchuria in 1931, intensified when the bellicose egomaniac Mussolini plundered Ethiopia in 1936, and headed down the long road to its climax when the vertiginous Hitler invaded Austria in 1938 shattered brutally the sweet illusion of peace in our time.

Though the passage of time may have dimmed the memory, life in the United States between the declaration of war on Japan on December 8, 1941, and the acceptance of Japan's surrender on August 14, 1945, experienced a metamorphosis, many of whose effects still linger. The transformation was similar to that endured and supported during World War I — but more intense and affecting an even greater percentage of the populace. It was the regimen to which the conflict subjected us that led to the creation of what today have become collectible objects, and I'll touch only upon the paraphernalia of war and the by-products of a controlled economy.

To the alphabeticized bureaucracy from which our meager blessings flowed in those war years we now owe many of these collectible mementos. A large number of them may be chalked up to the mental and physical peregrinations of the OPA, which stood for Office of Price Administration, and from its multitude of War Price and Rationing Boards established in cities and hamlets throughout the land.

The rationing of a host of important commodities ranging from gasoline to sugar was controlled by the issuance of ration books containing coupons, each good for a specific amount of a specific commodity. I have more than one reason to remember these. In the early days of the OPA I was War Price and Rationing Editor for a metropolitan newspaper and dwelt on a day-by-day intimacy with those who promulgated and those who executed rationing policies. And then on one memorable morning, I awoke with a need to use my own ration book only to discover that my young son, irritated beyond reasonable bounds by some restraint exercised upon him the day before, had eaten the damned thing.

Today the ration books are being offered as collectors' items. A recent ad offered one for $20. The price seems high by comparison with what certain other mementos of this period are bringing, but it must be remembered that most individuals in those war days — when shortages of many foods, gasoline, and alcoholic beverages existed — used their ration books down to the last coupon. Hence, they are scarce today. World War II windshield gasoline ration stickers are being offered now at $1 for three.

Although there seems to have been little trading in them yet, the probability is that one day the numerous orders, directives and other miscellaneous memoranda issued by the various emergency wartime bureaus will be collected also. These include the paper items stemming from agencies such as the OPA, the War Labor Board, Office of Defense Transportation, War Manpower Board, and others, including even the Selective Service System.

Posters of the war already are in demand. A variety of new themes was utilized for posters, and many talented artists turned their energies to their creation, foremost among them probably being E. McKnight Kauffer. But there were also posters by such outstanding artists as Ben Shahn, who had supported "causes" before (notably in his powerful painting "The Passion of Sacco and Vanzetti"), Henry Koerner, and Symeon Shimin.

Thousands of posters on the bulletin boards or walls of factories engaged in defense production warned workers of the dangers of careless talk. Blood, of course, was urgently needed in treating the wounded, and a diversity of posters solicited blood donors. And, of course, there were recruiting posters galore. There were illustrations of soldiers under fire, soldiers praying, aviators, generals, and admirals. Many posters were issued under the auspices of the War Production Board, Office of War Information, and Office of Civilian Defense.

There are still many readers who will remember the posters that solicited "Bundles for Britain" and for the relief of United China (alas, united no more!).

A large poster titled "Lidice" by Ben Shahn is presently valued at around $40. One of a battle scene with a prominent display of Japanese and Nazi flags and the slogan "Get the Jap and Get It Over With" is tendered at $25. Many others will fall into the $7.50–$15 price range.

There were novel posters, too. The house organ *Table Topics,* (published by Rosemary, Inc., of London and New York), reported in its July–August 1941 issue that whereas many London restaurateurs placed signs on their establishments reading "Open as Usual" after they had been damaged by Nazi bombs, one individualistic operator, after the front of his restaurant was blown off, posted one reading "More Open Than Usual."

Because they were published in such vast quantities, few newspapers of the war period are in demand, although copies of those headlining the German and Japanese surrenders and President Roosevelt's death will bring about $2 a copy. There are numerous items relating to Roosevelt that are collectible, in addition to the political campaign mementos discussed in an earlier chapter. A decorative tile was issued commemorating the historic Atlantic Charter conference of Roosevelt and Churchill in August 1941. The tile depicts the wartime leaders on shipboard and measures 6 inches square. It is now valued at $60 to $65.

Roosevelt was also the country's most famous stamp collector, and publicity relative to his philatelic activities stimulated this hobby vigorously. As a tribute to his activity in this field, more than 40 countries have issued Roosevelt commemorative stamps, Tom Mahoney reported in an article in the Spring 1970 issue of *Minkus Stamp Journal.* Many stamps were suggested, he added, by the Franklin D. Roosevelt Philatelic Society of Hyde Park, whose membership numbers about 200 Rooseveltiana collectors.

The Mahoney article reflects exhaustive research and will provide excellent background for those who collect stamps issued dur-

ing the Roosevelt Administrations from the very first one authorized
by him five days after his inauguration and commemorating the
150th anniversary of the Proclamation of Peace that ended the Rev-
olutionary War.

In the spring of 1970 the Roosevelt Philatelic Society mentioned
above sponsored under the name of "Duplex 11" its 12th annual
exhibition that featured 120 frames of prize-winning collections of
major interest to collectors of stamps issued during the Roosevelt
era and of those honoring the President himself. Although only
slightly more than 180 new stamps were issued during Roosevelt's
12 years in office, the collector can limit himself to these and the
subsequent issues commemorating Roosevelt and events of World
War II and still amass an impressive display.

Hundreds of enterprising merchandisers cashed in on the war by
creating scores of articles with a patriotic appeal or relating to the
emotions of longing and sadness engendered by the conflict. The
chances are that many of these will soon flow to the shelves of
antiques and curio shops from which they will wend their way into
collectors' hands.

One example is milady's compact. Many of these were issued with
a patriotic motif during the war years. Typical was one manufactured shortly after the war began. It featured a red, white, and blue
enameled reproduction of the United States flag and was lettered
"God Bless America." In a similar category were cigarette cases,
many of which carried military insignia. Crushproof inexpensive
cases were available in early 1942 with Army, Navy, Marine, and
Air Corps insignia in colors; they sold for around half a dollar.

There was an abundance of patriotic jewelry, much of it designed
for wives, sweethearts, and mothers of the boys in service. Costume
pins were turned out in profusion. One, gold-filled, was in the shape
of two crossed rifles with the linked letters "US" at the bottom. There
were small sterling silver pins with Army, Navy, Army Pilot, Navy
Pilot, and aviation insignia. Of course there were rings with their
insignia for the men in service. Some of 10-karat yellow gold were
selling in 1943 for under $25. Goldplated and sterling silver lockets
with military insignia on their fronts and space for two photographs
inside were available at about $3 to $3.50.

Inexpensive charms and pendants were turned off the assembly
lines at a rapid clip. There was a brooch in the shape of a torpedo
made of mother-of-pearl and goldplated metal, plus Navy insignia.
Similar brooches with Army and Air Corps insignia were fashioned

in the shape of bullets. These wholesaled for $6 a dozen. Capitalizing on Winston Churchill's famous "V for Victory" sign, sterling "V" pins were produced as costume accessories. There were lapel pins in the shape of Uncle Sam hats, "God Bless America" shields, and a variety of United States flags, some of sterling.

Novel items included a drum majorette lapel pin with a flag attached and an American eagle tie clasp holder. There was also a lapel pin with an American eagle at the top and red-white-and-blue trimmed drums below. Another pin featured a replica of the Liberty Bell in the talons of an eagle.

Bracelets also were turned out with military insignia, and similar insignia adorned numerous cigarette lighters, which were favorite gifts for those in service. Among the large producers of the latter were Evans and Match King. There was a table lighter in the shape of a pursuit plane. (Just before the declaration of war, there were even "neutrality" costume pins lettered "Keep U.S. Out of War" on a shield atop which the American eagle perched.)

To keep fresh the memory of loved ones in service, there were picture frames adorned with insignia of the various services, and to keep fresh this memory plus that of one's own face, there were patriotic mirrors, decorated, naturally, with a flag. For mothers with sons at war, these could be had with the lettering "My Son Is Serving His Country."

Plaster service plaques hung in many a home during the war years as did a variety of cloth banners, among these being one lettered "Remember Pearl Harbor." There were cloth flags of all sizes from tiny ones on stands that could be placed on tabletops to big ones hung outside the home and raised on flagpoles. After Pearl Harbor, A. C. Sherman, who had earlier done an oil painting called "Old Glory," created a new painting of the flag that was reproduced on heavy coated stock and sold framed.

The likeness of the popular hero General Douglas MacArthur turned up on all sorts of gadgets, including plaques, composition busts, and savings banks. There was also an Eisenhower bank. Both banks were of metal cast in the form of busts of these two military leaders.

A choice item for collectors interested in the mementos of the war would be a Liberty Bell Clock, with the dial and works housed inside a cast metal replica of the bell swinging from a support and placed on a walnut base upon which also stood a cast replica of an American GI. The clock was equipped with an electric movement, and inscribed upon the bell was — what else? — "God Bless America." There was also an electric clock housed between propeller blades and another with a case in the shape of a plane. Also popular in 1942 was an electric clock surmounted by a replica of a cannon and fitted with a Howard movement. It sold for around $8.

A rash of model planes appeared not long after the war started, most of them fashioned after famous American warplanes, including the Boeing Flying Fortress, Grumman Avenger, Republic Thunderbolt, Lockheed Lightning, and DeHavilland Mosquito Bomber. The models were made to scale and ranged in price from a quarter for one with a 27-inch wing span to $2.70 for those with 42-inch wing spans.

In addition, there were models of other implements of war, including the famous General Sherman tank and jeeps with gun trailers. Kits were available for youngsters who wanted to build scale models of the Air-King Lockheed XP–38 Interceptor, the Bell Air Cobra, Curtiss P–42 Pursuit plane, and others.

Numerous toys were influenced by the impact of war, among the least harmful and most creative being a Victory Garden set that consisted of packages of vegetable seed, tiny flower pots and saucers, and a shovel, rake, and hoe.

Among the amusing bits of trivia to emerge during the war was one called Hotzi Notzi, which was a bent-over plastic figure of Hitler with a pincushion on his seat. Some enterprising dealer recently discovered these and offered one at $12. Another was a plastic skunk with Hitler's face. Describing it as Der Phew-rer, the Joseph Hagn Co. offered samples for 45 cents.

There were, of course, wartime games, such as Commando, played with tops, but toys rather than games will attract the greater interest.

Paper items stemming direct from the conflict offer wide possibilities for collecting. These include official battle maps of the various campaigns, both Allied and Nazi. Those of real value are signed by well-known military figures. Some time ago one of the well-known autograph dealers offered five signed maps at $125.

Another dealer has offered a printed broadside of General Eisenhower's message to the men embarking on the Normandy invasion, signed by Eisenhower at the top, for $100. Surrender passes lettered "Allied Pacific Theater Surrender Pass," printed in both English and Japanese, have been tendered at $7.50. All types of propaganda leaflets, including those dropped from planes, are collectible. A

Nazi propaganda leaflet illustrating the Dunkirk position of the British and citing reasons for surrender is priced at $15. Five dollars has been asked for a pornographic Nazi propaganda leaflet flown via rocket to U. S. troops. A 1939–40 series of 10 anti-Nazi Dutch postcards by Tom Smith illustrated in cartoon form, with uncomplimentary poses of Hitler and other Nazi bigwigs, is valued at $16.

World War II photographs are growing in interest. A short time ago one measuring 5x6½ inches and showing the execution of a Nazi spy was advertised at $10. A collection of 37 original photographs of Hitler at rallies, greeting youngsters, and so on, taken prior to his invasion of Poland, was priced by a dealer at $150 for the lot. Another series of 32 issued by the Nazis for propaganda purposes is priced at $125.

Nazi documents of all kinds are currently in great demand in the United States. This coincides with a fad for Nazi weapons, flags, insignia, and other memorabilia. Interestingly, collectors in England went through this same collecting phase but most have now "graduated" to collecting older militaria, whereas American collectors are still high on the Nazi kick.

Autograph dealers within recent months have issued catalogs offering photographs, letters, and documents signed by top Nazi leaders at substantial prices. A signed photograph of Admiral Erich Raeder, sentenced to life imprisonment during the Nuremberg trials, is priced at $75. The same price was asked for one of Field Marshal Erwin Rommel signed in pencil. Signed photos of lesser Nazi military men are priced $35 to $50.

An ornate document issued from Hitler's headquarters in 1942, signed by both Hitler and Goering and announcing the appointment of Dr. Karl Eckerle as Chief Justice of the Nazi Luftwaffe was valued at $475! An autograph letter signed by Rommel in June 1943 and addressed to his wife was priced at $325. It consisted of two pages on his personal correspondence card and describing the situation in the East as "so tense that it might explode any day." A typed message on Hitler's imprinted correspondence card, dated Berlin, April 1943, and expressing appreciation for congratulations, signed by Hitler and with his stamp, had an asking price of $175.

The price for a printed portrait of the top Nazi war criminals at Nuremberg, signed on the reverse by 19 of them, was $1,500. A holograph letter by Hitler accompanying a gift of flowers bore the same price.

Nazi military objects will bring excellent prices, though they are likely to vary from dealer to dealer. An officer's Afrika Korps pith helmet with insignia in mint condition is priced at $19; a 2x3-foot Nazi flag at $12; a youth dagger with a swastika inlaid in the grip and etched "Blut und Ehre" ("blood and honor") at $13.75; a flag used on Panzers for aerial recognition at $12.50; a captain's uniform with an Eidelweiss badge plus a hat at $35; and a complete sheet of Nazi stamps, "Kraft durch Freude" ("Strength through pleasure") at $15.

Incidentally, Nazi officials and illustrations of Nazi meetings are pictured on a series of premium cards that were distributed with Schwarz Weiss cigarettes during the 1930s.

Nazi medals will bring prices varying from a few dollars to more than $100 each. A few will bring substantially more than $100. A Luftwaffe Goblet of Honor made of silver and extremely rare has sold for as high as $1,800, it is reported by Edward L. Beard in his book *Nazi Medals* (published by Pioneer Guns, Norwood, Ohio). The Nazi medal collector will find this book helpful since it not only describes the medals but contains a guide to their values.

In a category by themselves are thousands of small objects, primarily ceramic and metal — the majority falling into the category of trivia — that were produced in Japan during the American occupation of that country. The majority are stamped "Made in Occupied Japan," but some are stamped only "Made in Japan" or "Japan." These little objects were produced between the latter part of 1945 and the spring of 1952 when the treaty ending the occupation of Japan became effective.

Turned out by carloads were miniature ceramic figurines, animals, steins, Toby jugs, vases, banks, tea sets, pianos, containers and boxes of various types, dolls, and the like. A number of small windup toys also were made. A concise but excellent presentation of the background of these Made in Occupied Japan trifles appeared in the November 1971 issue of *The Antiques Journal.* The author, Professor Bill Poese, pointed out that many of the small objects were originally made in pairs and that, although huge quantities were turned out during the years of occupation, the total quantity is nevertheless limited so that the chance of rising prices in the future appears good.

Right now scores of these trifles may be found in antiques shops and at flea markets at prices of from around a dollar to three or four dollars. Some of the better and larger pieces will bring more, a nine-piece ceramic demitasse set having been priced at $25. The pieces are by no means in the category of either treasures or art, but, by virtue of the fortunes of war, they are unique, and they could prove good small investments if bought now while prices are low and held for a few years. A number of the windup toys already are selling at $10 to $25. They have one added advantage: Because of their low cost, they are not likely to be reproduced or faked for some time.

Aside from museums, there are few collectors of the major implements of war, such as tanks and bombs. But there is one exception: military planes. There exists a small but dedicated group of hobbyists who not only seek out the old World War II planes but restore and fly them. Just as is the case with classic automobiles, the hobby of buying, restoring, and maintaining military aircraft is an expensive one. A single purchase often involves the expenditure of more than $50,000.

In the summer of 1971 *The Wall Street Journal* cited data from the Federal Aviation Administration's aircraft registration department to indicate that some 2,000 of these military planes were then being flown by hobbyists.

Collecting models of the planes is much cheaper.

It should be added here, too, that in addition to keeping the boys in service well equipped with such reminders of home and the homefolk as picture lockets, wallets, cigarette cases, and the like, our entrepreneurs also wanted to keep them happy. One result was the issuance of numerous pinup girl pictures in glorious color. Some of these represented drawings by well-known illustrators, and those of the scantily-clad girls, it is said, sold "like hotcakes." They possessed, it was advertised, a "morale-building appeal." It has been suggested, however, and probably by wise persons, that what it made them want to do most of all was to get out of wherever they were and come back home fast.

Top Left: window sticker encouraged families to buy war bonds. Top Right: Among the collectibles of the period are postage stamps. (*Courtesy Miss Barbara R. Mueller.*) Below: World War II ration books are eagerly sought by collectors. (*Courtesy Charles L. Leonard, Cincinnati, Ohio. Photo by J. D. (Don) Howard, Atlanta.*)

Military motif dress accessories and lighters . . . and one neutrality pin.

Picture frames, service plaque, mirrors, V-Garden Set, 10 x 12″ cloth banner, U.S. Emblem clock, reflecting patriotic fervor. The button is from the collection of Ted Hake, Philadelphia.

Top Left: 1944 toys included U.S. fighter tank and a field artillery cannon that fired toy shells. Top Right: Uncle Sam pottery bank of 1940s with blue band on hat appealed to the patriotic mood. Below: Gold-filled blouse pin, electric Cannon clock, Forstner Komfit Bracelet with Army Aviation insignia, plaster plaque of General Douglas A. MacArthur, and "Der Phew-rer" composition skunk with Hitler's face.

Joseph Hagn Co. offered these costume pins in 1943 (top and bottom left). (*Courtesy Americana Interstate Corp.*) **Center:** Sterling silver service badge (1942) sold for $1.25 by Fort Dearborn Mercantile Co. **Below Right:** At the outset of the forties those who wanted neutrality sported pins such as this one.

The war had its crazy moments, as witnessed by this "girl next door" (*Courtesy Americana Interstate Corp.*) and a Hotzi Notzi pincushion. (*Courtesy Ted Hake, Philadelphia.*)

Top: The phrase for which collectors look, and a collection of Made in Occupied Japan ceramic pieces. (*Courtesy Bill Poese.*)

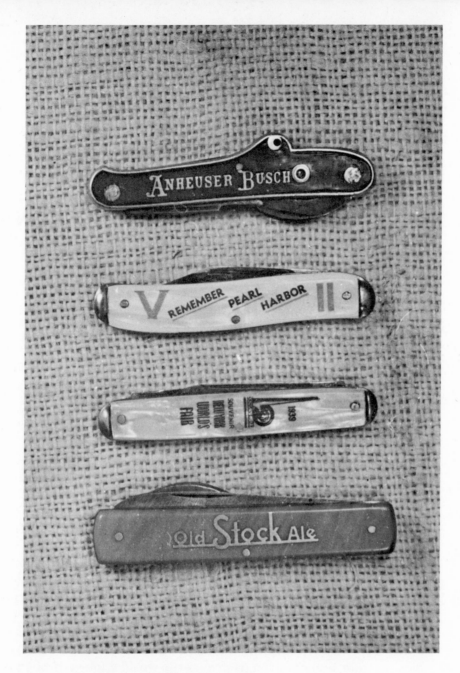

"Remember Pearl Harbor" knife, second from top, is a collectible of World War II vintage. (*Courtesy Ed Bardy, Traverse City, Mich.*)

19 A COLLECTOR'S MISCELLANY

OF the thousands of objects spawned during the imaginatively fertile period of the thirties and forties, there were many that do not fit neatly into pigeonholed categories. Nevertheless, they are collectible and would probably be more widely collected if more persons knew of them.

Among this miscellany — which does perhaps deserve a category of its own — are mementos of two great Worlds Fairs — Chicago's Century of Progress Exposition that opened May 27, 1933, and the New York World's Fair that opened April 20, 1939. The former continued its run until November 12, 1933, and reopened again from May into November 1934. The New York spectacle was open in 1939 until the end of October and again in 1940 from May 11 until October 21. The Golden Gate International Exposition in San Francisco was also held in 1939 but was overshadowed by the more pretentious pomp and pageantry in Gotham.

The affair in Chicago opened during the Depression, but the hard times were not reflected in the attendance: More than 20,000,000 men, women, and children from over the world clicked through the turnstiles, and the fair ended substantially in the black. No international fair in history had been more successful, at least from a financial standpoint.

Spectacular was the word for it. The switch that turned on the lights to herald the fair's opening was activated by the star Arcturus

—the first gesture in a parade of scientific marvels. But, no two ways about it, the stellar attraction of an all-star cast was undoubtedly Miss Sally Rand, a lissome lady with an appealing face who shed her clothing and executed a series of remarkable gyrations, first with fans and subsequently with an oversized ball. Fandancing hasn't been the same since.

The Chicago exposition was exceeded only by that in New York's Flushing Meadow with a first-year attendance of 25,000,000. Its sumptuous displays and exhibits forecast, as it was intended for them to do, the "World of Tomorrow" — and particularly a world in which television was to play an absorbing role. The symbols of this great fair were a huge Trylon and a Perisphere, which were reproduced on millions of souvenirs. Even the great Albert Einstein was induced to participate in a spectacular revelation of scientific mysteries involving the use of cosmic rays, and millions marveled at the first television studio set up on the grounds by the General Electric Corporation. There was something for everyone except the Germans, who did not participate, their Nazi leaders being preoccupied with plans to conquer the world.

Hundreds of thousands of visitors to the two great expositions wanted souvenirs to take home as reminders of a thrilling experience, and there were souvenirs galore, many of them distributed without charge by exhibitors but more that were sold by commercial participants. And one did not actually have to attend these fairs to procure souvenirs of them: Some were sold by gift shops and chain stores around the country, including a Chicago World's Fair watch that was being offered at 98 cents by Montgomery Ward before that exposition's doors were open.

There are several collectors around the country who have been seeking souvenirs and other memorabilia of these two fairs for the past several years, both because the fairs were prophetic of things to come and made an impact upon their times and also because many of the objects hold a peculiar fascination. The fairs' collectible adjuncts include medallions depicting buildings, elongated cents, arm patches stitched with representations of the Trylon and Perisphere, and risque bottle openers in the form of bare-breasted ladies.

Virtually anything associated with the two fairs is collectible now, including souvenir booklets and other printed materials as well as postcards and admission tickets. Available at the Chicago fair was a series of elongated cents that depicted various scenes ranging from that of the Sky Ride to buildings and villages constructed for the fair. Current prices of these have varied from around $4 to $15 each. In a similar category were the tokens from the New York fair with a portrait of George Washington on one side and representations of the Trylon and Perisphere on the reverse.

There were bronze coins and medals from New York and miniature wooden canteens only 2 inches high and souvenir spoons from Chicago.

The semi-nude bottle opener from New York is currently valued at around $25 (bottle caps were removed by the lady's middle). A 7-inch-high plaster cast of an artist at work stemming from the Chicago exhibition is valued at $6.50. Miniature replicas of a Chicago Century of Progress Greyhound bus will bring $15 to $30, and even so relatively inconsequential an item as a soap dish on which Chicago exhibits are illustrated will fetch close to $5.

Other collectibles of these fairs included metal bowls, glass mugs, enameled and other types of rings, mesh bags, tie clips, costume jewelry, metal ash trays, fountain pens (especially those with decals of the Trylon and Perisphere), matchbooks, lighters, compacts, bracelets, lamps, letter openers, playing cards, billfold sets, walking sticks, pocket knives, trays, drinking cup sets, and pencil sharpeners, to mention only a few.

Although I know of no dedicated collectors in the field, the repeal of the Prohibition laws led swiftly to the production of dozens of objects that reflect the end of an era in American history. Congress, in March 1933, at the President's behest legalized the sale of wines and beers that did not exceed 3.2 percent in alcoholic content, and the 21st amendment to the Constitution, repealing the 18th or Prohibition amendment but guaranteeing dry states against the importation of illegal alcoholic beverages, became law on December 5, 1933. Only eight states, the bulk of them in the South, chose to remain "dry."

The result was that bars, taprooms, and cocktail lounges descended like locusts upon restaurants, hotels, and private clubs and the portable home bar made its appearance. So, too, did a multitude of elbow-bending adjuncts. The flourishing business of bootlegging was hard hit in the "wet" states, and many an erstwhile bootlegger became a legitimate businessman — or another type of racketeer. But bootlegging by no means ceased. Some of the populace, ashamed to be seen drinking or buying alcoholic beverages in public, continued to buy from their bootleggers; and the business, of course, continued to thrive in the dry states. In one of these dry states in the South, there was a justice of the peace, who, upon the adjournment of his court each day, promptly opened a bar in a back room of his offices to friends, selling them applejack imported from Virginia at 25 cents a throw.

New types of furniture were created to lend the proper atmosphere of relaxation to cocktail lounges. Enterprising manufacturers were hard-pressed to meet the demand for such things as cocktail shakers, beverage sets, bottle openers and corkscrews, and pocket flasks.

Musical cocktail shakers became the rage. Most of them played *How Dry I Am* upon being lifted. There were musical pottery jugs that were reminiscent of the brown jugs that had housed many a gallon of bootleg whiskey. There were musical decanters of glazed pottery, musical pinch bottles, musical figural whiskey containers, and musical steins. There was a handled pottery musical jug in the shape of a cannonball and a glazed pottery hunter jug with scenes of hunting dogs embossed on its square sides.

There were cocktail shakers and beverage sets of pewter, chrome plate, plated silver, ceramics, glass. Oak keg sets with pouring spigots, hoops of plated copper, and a set of four glasses were being sold in 1934 for as little as a dollar. There was a midget beverage radio whose hinged front panel concealed a removable stoneware keg, two serving trays, and six tumblers. The cabinet was made of gumwood. Interesting, too, was a beverage set in the shape of a set of three books. It housed a Johnny Walker bottle and two 1½-ounce glasses; its front cover was actually a hinged door.

There were glass decanter sets with all types of enameled decorations. A Take a Shot cup set was produced in 1933 with five cups housed inside a metal container in the form of a shell. A Balloon liquor set was made of silverplated metal in the shape of a balloon with simulated mesh covering. The top lifted off to disclose a bottle and glasses. The Cameo Oasis beverage set boasted a stoneware keg astride the hump of a carved wooden camel. Complete with six tumblers, it wholesaled in 1934 for only $2.10.

Beer sets were made in copper, glass, and ceramics, consisting usually of seven pieces, although some added a tray to the pitcher and six mugs or steins.

Novelty bottle openers, corkscrews, and bottle corks were turned out in considerable abundance. A carved wooden monk's figure was fitted inside with a corkscrew and four nickelplated liquor cups. It originally sold for only about a dollar. Old Snifter evoked many a laugh. It was made of metal in the likeness of the so-called "snifter prohibitionist" with hands clasped before him and wearing a tall hat; the figure's nose was used to remove bottle caps, and a cork-screw was concealed in the back. He was available shortly after prohibition's repeal. Imported from Italy was a hand-carved wooden figure of an inebriated man leaning against a lamp post, which contained a corkscrew and bottle opener. These retailed for about $4 in 1933. A variety of other carved wooden figures also held either corkscrews or bottle corks.

There was a metal combination opener–corkscrew in the form of a parrot. Caps were removed in the bird's opened beak. The Big Bad Wolf combination was a metal representation of the wolf himself with a corkscrew tail and jaws for lifting caps.

Figural corks were made in large quantities in Italy and imported to sell for around 35 cents to about $1.50 each. Most were amusing figures. Another novelty was a miniature hand-carved wooden picket fence with three carved wooden heads peering over the top. This was fitted with a cork screw, bottle opener, and cork.

There were flasks in all price ranges and sizes. They were made of silver, plated silver, Britannia metal, and pewter. Some were enameled in colors, and many had a plate on which the owner's initials could be engraved. The majority had hinged screw caps and some came with leather cases. Some sold for two or three dollars and others for $50 or more.

Fancy cup sets were great for outings or brawls. The Barrel set had four telescoping cups fitted inside a squat barrel-shaped container. Sets also were made of Beetleware—the same sort of material of which some of the Orphan Annie mugs were made. Beetleware is a chemical compound having characteristics of both china and glass and durability akin to ivory.

With the scarce glass paperweights turned out in France, Bohe-mia, England, and the United States in the mid-19th century now primarily beyond the financial means of the impecunious collector, novelty paperweights of the thirties and forties are likely to be of interest.

Many of these were in the form of metal figures of animals — bulls, bison, horses, tigers, dogs, elephants, and others. Some were free-standing and others were mounted on bases of various materi-als.

Some figures were offered for use as paperweights, bookends, or doorstops! These included dogs of metal measuring 6 to 6½ inches long and 4½ to 5 inches high. An amusing comic figure paperweight of 1940 was Bozo the Bowler with a metal figure of a bowler torturously bent over and aiming a bowling ball held in both hands. The figure was mounted on a painted metal base. Appealing was an all-metal fish paperwight of chrome over nickel silver. These stood 4¾ inches tall and cost only $1.50.

Even more versions of bookends were produced, and everyone who reads should possess at least one pair. If there is an entire collection devoted to bookends, I have not heard of it. Perhaps the reason is that most individuals are not aware of their variety and downright charm. In the 1930s one could find Art Deco bookends, such as a pair made of copper and incorporating a full-length female figure with a diaphanous garment swirling around her, or a pair with a graceful nude cutout figure and two animals standing beside her. The latter could be either goats or dogs, and I'm not about to take a guess as to which they are. These bookends can now be bought at about $7 to $15 a pair.

There were metal bookends in the shape of coaches, galleons, the London Mail coach, the Liberty Bell, covered wagons, baskets of flowers, cathedrals, a girl at a fountain, books themselves, pirates with treasure chests, Arabian sheiks, cowboys with lariats, Mexican figures with sombreros, ships' wheels, Indians, crouching pairs of dogs, and, of course, the popular figures of Lincoln and Rodin's "The Thinker." There was even a pair of bookends with a cast figure of a football player, ball clutched under one arm and the other outstretched for stiff-arming.

Moreover, there were bookends of earthenware with Hummel-type figures, horses' heads, dogs, and other representations. Many of these were originally quite inexpensive, selling for less than $1.75 a pair, some for under $1, and they could prove fun to collect. And for those who do not think they have appreciated in value, the Art Deco nude bookends mentioned above originally sold for $1.65 a pair; a recent advertisement offered them at $45.

There was a revival in the thirties of the old decorative paper clips that abounded in the late 19th century but were abandoned in the 20th in favor of the small bent wire clips that handle their job effectively but are, of course, utterly devoid of character. The cast metal clips of the thirties were produced in figural shapes and given a brass or bronze finish. A Hagn catalog of 1933 reveals that these were made in the form of owls, frogs, and duck bills. They were 4 to 5½ inches long and had an opening at the top so that, if desired, they could be hung on a nail on the wall of one's office. The 19th century clips of this type are scarce and bring good prices when found. Those of the thirties also seem to be scarce and could provide the basis for a unique collection.

Cast metal tie racks also were fashioned in novel shapes. One said to portray an Egyptian temple actually featured a cast top of three pagodalike miniature buildings. Another was adorned with an Oriental figure design and still another with the head of a Negro boy in a straw hat. The racks were 11 to 13 inches long and had from three to five hooks on which to hang ties. Prices started at a little over a dollar and the more elaborate ones cost about $3.75.

One will encounter a few horn novelties from time to time in some antiques shops. Carving horn is an ancient art, but an array of these novelties were available in the early 1940s. They included numerous ashtrays, vases, and ornamental pieces. In decades past cow and steer horn were used to make such needed articles as powder horns, translucent panels for lanterns, spoons, snuffboxes, combs, ladles, and other household objects. The horn could be bent into desired shapes after heating. Saws, files, and knives were the implements of the trade — plus a vise.

Some modern plastic materials can be confused with horn, but in the early 1940s, Joseph Hagn Co. offered a number of articles characterized as being made of "genuine animal horn," hand-carved. Fish and birds were favorite shapes, although the flower vases were made apparently of complete cleaned horns attached to a base. Prices ranged from less than a dollar (for a half-horn ashtray) to $6.30 for a vase with a horn bird attached. I have in my collection a number of horn objects, including decorative groups and inkstands, some of which were originally made as souvenirs.

Gambling of one type or another has been one of man's favorite pastimes since the dawn of civilization. In the thirties and forties slot machines and punchboards abounded. One encountered them in bars and beer parlors, restaurants, and numerous other establishments catering primarily to males. Save for places such as Las Vegas, the slot machines have been generally outlawed today, and the chances are one may run afoul of the law in most localities if he attempts to indulge in other types of gambling. Both slot machines and punchboards were gambling devices with the odds stacked heavily in favor of the house.

Nevertheless, the slot machines of earlier days are now being collected, and there are a few individuals just starting to collect the punchboards. Miniature slot machines that worked and could be placed in a small area on the counter were available in 1940 and in the thirties at prices that are quite low by comparison with what collectors are offering for them today. There was one intriguing punchboard in the shape of a five-cent slot machine. Called the K-O Vender, it took in $30 when punched out and paid out only $14, thereby netting a gross profit of $16 to the punchboard operator.

A Hit the Ball punchboard paid winners punching slots with slips reading Home Run, Three Base Hit, Double Play and so on. Another type paid winners in cigarettes, and other types paid off winners in other kinds of merchandise. Board names included Poker Kitty, Short and Snappy, Pot Shots, Lucky Pennies, Golden Zephyr, Streamline, Lucky Streak, and numerous others. There were even miniature glass fishbowls filled with tickets. Into the mouths of these fishbowls dipped the hand of many a gambler who felt lucky. He usually wasn't.

The original prices of these boards depended upon how elaborate they were; they ranged generally from 50 cents to about $6. Collectors prefer those that have not been used.

Other types of gambling devices of the period also are collectible. These include Chuck-a-Luck and Bingo cages, roulette wheels, and even certain types of poker racks and chips.

Lithographed tobacco tins, as we have noted, have attracted many collectors. The colorfully lighographed lunch boxes of the thirties merit attention too. This should be especially true of those with lithographed scenes of childhood, and these were still in widespread use in the early thirties when many children took their lunches to school.

Other collectibles which may soon attract collector attention but neglected up to now include comical molded wood novelties (including one of a horse named after the comic strip character Sparkplug); figural tape measures and thermometers; world globes, since the face of the world has been radically altered in recent decades; and athletic trophies.

Happy hunting!

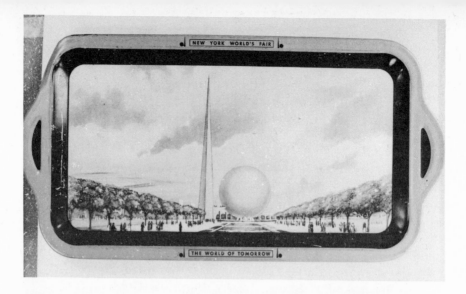

Top and Center: 1939 New York World's Fair Souvenirs, courtesy Ted Hake, Philadelphia. **Below:** Lenox, Inc. designed these pieces exclusively for Ovington's of New York City.

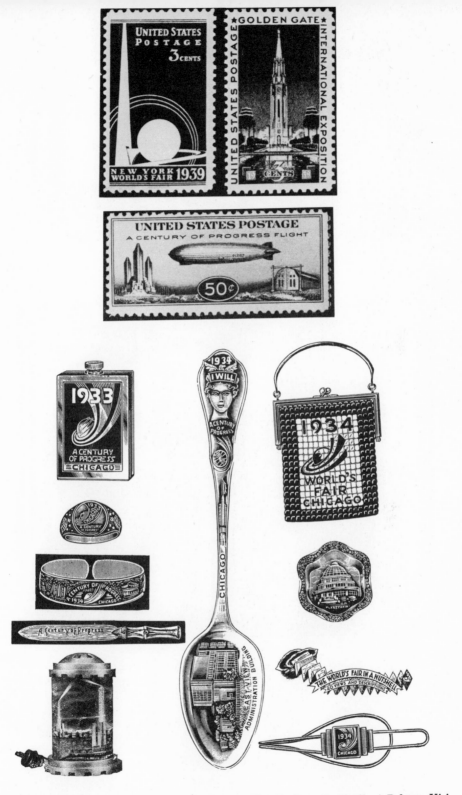

Top: Commemorative postage stamps (*Courtesy Miss Barbara R. Mueller.*) **Below:** Visitors to Chicago World's Fair's second year had a choice of souvenirs such as these.

Top: Group of Dorothy Thorp glasses and a silverplated cocktail shaker. (*From the Collection of Maurice D. Blum and John J. Greer. Photo by Marlin E. Fenical.*) Below: porcelain figural liquor decanter and monk jug played tunes.

Novelty paperweights of the forties.

Bookends of the thirties and forties.

Top: Beverage sets. Below: Cast metal paperclips, bookends, tie racks. (*Courtesy Americana Interstate Corp.*)

Home bar novelties. Top: Musical decanter cocktail shaker and jug. Second Row: Copper beverage set, pottery beer set, musical stein, and decorated earthenware beer set. Bottom: beverage containers with book set. Top Right: "Old Snifter" bottle opener. Below: Carved miniature wooden figures (left) made in Italy. Below Right: Figural corkscrew, and corkscrew and cup set housed in wooden figure.

Top: Carved horn novelties of early forties. **Below:** Pocket flasks.

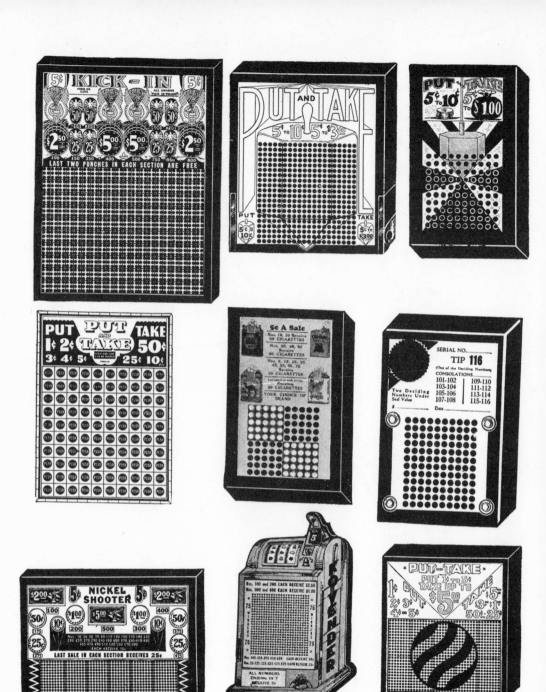

A miscellany of punchboards of the late thirties and early forties.

A
SELECTED
BIBLIOGRAPHY

ART & PHOTOGRAPHY

Battersby, Martin. *The Decorative Thirties.* New York: Walker & Co., 1971.

Brown, Robert K. "Art Deco." *Spinning Wheel,* January–February, 1971.

Cheney, Sheldon. *The Story of Modern Art.* New York: The Viking Press, Inc., 1945.

Copplestone, Trewin. *Modern Art Movements* (revised edition). London: Paul Hamlyn, 1967.

Garwood, Darrel. *Artist in Iowa: A Life of Grant Wood.* New York: W. W. Norton, 1944.

Gilbert, George. *Photographic Advertising from A to Z.* Riverdale, N. Y.: Yesterday's Cameras, 1971.

Gombrich, E. H. *The Story of Art.* New York: Phaidon, Inc. 1961.

Hillier, Bevis. *Art Deco.* New York: Studio Vista/ E. P. Dutton, Inc., 1968.

Minneapolis Institute of Arts. *Art Deco.* Catalog of the Exhibition, July 8–September 5, 1971. Minneapolis. 1971.

Rickards, Maurice. *Posters of the Nineteen Twenties.* New York: Walker & Co., 1968.

Selz, Peter. *Seven Decades; 1895–1965: Crosscurrents in Modern Art.* Washington, D. C.: Public Education Association, 1966.

AUTOGRAPHS

Benjamin, Mary A. *Autographs: A Key to Collecting.* New York: R. R. Bowker, 1946.
Hamilton, Charles. *Scribblers & Scoundrels.* New York: Paul S. Eriksson, Inc., 1968.

BUSINESS ANTIQUES

Bardy, Ed. *Advertising with a Sharp Edge.* Traverse City, Michigan: privately published, 1970.
Cope, Jim. *Soda Water Advertising.* Orange, Texas: privately published, 1971.
Gaylord, Bill. "Advertiques." (A series of articles in various issues of *Western Collector* from 1968 through 1971.)
Kaduck, John M. *Sleepers That Have a Future.* Cleveland, Ohio: privately published, n. d. (1971?).
Mebane, John. *New Horizons in Collecting.* Cranbury, N. J.: A. S. Barnes, 1966.
_____. *Treasure at Home.* Cranbury, N. J.: A. S. Barnes, Inc., 1964.
Rawlinson, Fred. *"Tin Cans."* *The Antiques Journal,* September, 1970.

CERAMICS

Altman, Seymour and Violet. *The Book of Buffalo Pottery.* New York: Crown, 1969.
Crawford, Jean. *Jugtown Pottery, History and Design.* Winston-Salem, N. C.: John F. Blair, Publisher, 1964.
Henzke, Lucile. *American Art Pottery.* Camden, N. J.: Thomas Nelson, Inc., 1970.
Peck, Herbert. *The Book of Rookwood Pottery.* New York: Crown, 1968.
Purviance, Louise and Evan, and Norris F. Schneider. *Zanesville Art Pottery in Color.* Leon, Iowa: Mid-America Book Co.
Schneider, Norris F. *Zanesville Art Pottery.* Zanesville, Ohio: privately published, 1963.

COLLECTIBLES OF COCA-COLA

Garrett, Franklin M. "Those Coca-Cola Collectibles." *The Antiques Journal,* July 1968.
Munsey, Cecil. "Coca-Cola." *Western Collector,* January–February 1971.

ENTERTAINMENT

Bardèche, Maurice, and Robert Brasillach. *History of the Motion Pictures.* New York: W. W. Norton and The Museum of Modern Art.

Chase, Frank, Jr. *Sound and Fury.* New York: Harper & Brothers, 1942.

Hampton, Benjamin B. *History of the American Film Industry from Its Beginnings to 1931.* New York: Dover, 1970.

Knight, Arthur. *The Liveliest Art.* New York: Macmillan, 1957.

Lahue, Kalton C. *Continued Next Week, A History of the Moving Picture Serial.* Norman, Oklahoma: University of Oklahoma Press, 1964.

Mayer, Arthur. *Merely Colossal.* New York: Simon & Schuster, 1953.

Morehouse, Ward. *Matinee Tomorrow.* New York: Whittlesey House/McGraw-Hill, 1949.

Slate, Sam J., and Joe Cook: *It Sounds Impossible.* New York: Macmillan, 1963.

Schickel, Richard. *The Stars.* New York: Dial, 1962.

Spaeth, Sigmund. *A History of Popular Music in America.* New York: Random House, 1948.

Stearns, Michael. *The Story of Jazz.* New York: Oxford University Press, 1956.

Time–Life Books Editors. *This Fabulous Century, 1930–1940.* New York: Time–Life Books; distributed by Little, Brown, 1971.

FURNITURE

Morningstar, Connie. *Flapper Furniture.* Des Moines, Iowa: Wallace–Homestead, 1971.

GENERAL BACKGROUND

Allen, Frederick Lewis. *Since Yesterday.* New York: Harper & Brothers, 1941.

American Heritage Editors. *The American Heritage History of the 20's and 30's.* New York: American Heritage, 1970.

Beard, C. A., and G. H. E. Smith. *The Old Deal and the New.* New York: Macmillan, 1941.

Battersby, Martin. *The Decorative Twenties.* New York: Walker, 1969.

Boardman, F. W., Jr. *America and the Great Depression.* New York: Henry Z. Walck, 1967.

Burns, J. MacG. *Roosevelt: The Lion and the Fox.* New York: Harcourt, Brace, 1956.

Congdon, Don (Ed.). *The Thirties: A Time to Remember.* New York: Simon & Schuster, 1962.

DeVincenzo, Ralph (Coordinating Editor). *Curios and Collectibles: A Price Guide to the New Antiques.* New York City: Dafran House, 1971.

Hurd, C. *When the New Deal Was Young and Gay.* New York: Hawthorne, 1965.

Leighton, Isabelle (Ed.). *The Aspirin Age.* New York: Simon & Schuster, 1949.

Lindley, Ernest K. *The Roosevelt Revolution: First Phase.* New York: Viking, 1938.

Schlesinger, Arthur M., Jr. *The Coming of the New Deal.* Boston: Houghton Mifflin, 1959.

GLASS

Appleton, Budd. *A Guide to Akro Agate Glass.* Kensington, Md.: privately published, 1966.

Avila, George C. *The Pairpoint Glass Story.* New Bedford, Mass.: Reynolds–DeWalt Printing, Inc., 1968.

Emanuele, Concetta. *Heisey Gems.* Sunol, Cal.: privately published, 1968.

———. *Heisey Gems II.* Sunol, Cal. privately published, 1969.

———. *Stems.* Sunol, Cal.: Olive Tree Publications, 1970.

Revi, Albert Christian. *American Art Glass Nouveau.* Camden, N. J.: Thomas Nelson & Sons, 1968.

Skelley, Leloise Davis. *Modern Fine Glass.* New York: Richard R. Smith, 1937.

Steuben Glass. *A Selection of Engraved Crystal* by Steuben. Corning, N. Y.: Steuben Glass, 1961.

Stout, Sandra McPhee. *Depression Glass in Color.* Ephrata, Wash.: privately published, 1971.

Vreim, Halvor. *Norwegian Decorative Art Today.* Oslo, Norway: Fabritius & Sonner, 1937.

Weatherman, Hazel Marie. *Colored Glassware of the Depression Era.* (revised and expanded edition). Springfield, Mo.: privately published. 1970.

Welker, Mr. and Mrs. Lyle, and Lynn Welker. *Cambridge, Ohio, Glass in Color.* New Concord, Ohio: privately published, 1969.

Yeakley, Virginia and Loren. *Heisey Glass in Color.* Newark, Ohio: privately published, 1969.

POLITICS

Bristow, Dick. *The Illustrated Political Button Book.* Santa Cruz, California: privately published, 1971.

Loomis, Herbert D. "Ballyhoo." *The Antiques Journal,* June 1971.

———. "Political Buttons." *The Antiques Journal,* March 1971.

Wearin, Otho D. *Political Buttons in Color.* Leon, Iowa: Mid-America Book Co., 1970.

READING HABITS

Bails, Jerry G. *The Guidebook to Comics Fandom.* Glendale, Cal.: Bill
Spicer, 1965.
Becker, Stephen. *Comic Art in America.* New York: Simon & Schuster, 1959.
Berger, A. A. *Li'l Abner: A Study in American Satire.* New York: Twayne,
1970.
Couperie, Pierre, and Maurice Horn. *History of the Comic Strip.* New York:
Crown, 1968.
Feiffer, Jules. *The Great Comic Book Heroes.* New York: Dial, Inc., 1965.
Harmon, Jim. *The Great Radio Heroes.* Garden City, N. Y.: Doubleday, 1967.
Hogben, Lancelot. *From Cave Painting to Comic Strip.* New York: Chanti-
cleer Press, 1949.
Lupoff, Dick, and Don Thompson (eds). *All in Color for a Dime.* New Ro-
chelle, New York: Arlington House, Publishers, 1971.
Perry, George, and Alan Aldrich. *The Penguin Book of Comics.* Baltimore:
Penguin Books, 1968.
Waugh, Colton. *Comics.* New York: Macmillan, 1947.

SMOKING ACCESSORIES

Davis, Marvin and Helen. *Tobacco Tins.* Ashland, Ore.: Old Bottle Collecting Publications, 1970.
Pettit, Ernest L. *Collectible Tin Containers.* Wyantskill, N. Y.: privately
published, 1970.

TOYS

Hertz, Louis H. *Collecting Model Trains.* New York: Simmons-Boardman
Publishing Corp., 1956.
_____. *The Handbook of Old American Toys.* Wethersfield, Conn.: Mark
Haber & Company, 1947.
_____. *The Toy Collector.* New York: Funk & Wagnalls, 1969.
Whiting, Hubert B. *Old Iron Still Banks.* Manchester, Vt.: Forward Color
Productions, 1968.

TRANSPORTATION

American Motors Public Relations Department. *American Motors Family
Album.* Detroit: American Motors Corp., 1969.
_____. *Rambler Family Album.* Detroit: American Motors Corp., 1961.
Burness, Tad. *Cars of the Thirties.* Philadelphia: Chilton, 1970.
Toland, John. *Ships in the Sky.* New York: Henry Holt, 1947.
Ziel, Ron. *The Twilight of Steam Locomotives,* New York: Grosset & Dun-
lap, 1971.

WALT DISNEY COLLECTIBLES

Feild, Robert D. *The Art of Walt Disney.* New York: Macmillan, 1942.

WORLD WAR II

Baker, L. *Roosevelt and Pearl Harbor.* New York: Macmillan.

Beard, Edward L. (ed.). *Nazi Medals.* Norwood, Ohio: Pioneer Guns, n.d. (1970).

Eisenhower, Dwight D. *Crusade in Europe.* Garden City, N. Y.: Doubleday, 1949.

Morgenstern, G. *Pearl Harbor: Story of the Secret War.* New York: Devin-Adair, 1947.

Poese, Bill. "Made in Occupied Japan." *The Antiques Journal,* November 1971.

INDEX

A SELECTIVE DIRECTORY OF
COLLECTORS CLUBS

This list is designed to give you an idea of the zeal and enthusiasm to be found in collecting things nostalgic. Of necessity it is limited to just a few of the organizations in the nostalgic field. For instance, there are scores of clubs of people who collect antique autos. Each marque has its own group, and to list every club would entail a chapter unto itself! Consult your local library for the most up-to-date listings of associations and organizations; there are several tomes devoted to this subject.

American Aviation Historical Society
P.O. Box 996
Ojai, Calif. 93023

Antique Wireless Association
Main Street
Holcomb, N.Y. 14469

Universal Autograph Collector's Club
3109 Brighton Seventh St., Box 4J
Brooklyn, N.Y. 11235

Antique Automobile Club of
America
501 W. Governor Road
Hershey, Pa. 17033

Classic Car Club of America
P.O. Box 443
Madison, N.J. 07940

Mechanical Bank Collectors of
America
c/o Albert Davidson
905 Manor Lane
Bayshore, N.Y. 11706

United Federation of Doll Clubs
4035 E. Kessler Blvd.,
Indianapolis, Ind. 46220

International Association of Jazz
Record Collectors
c/o Dick Raichelson
124 Sunnyside Park Road
Syracuse, N.Y. 13214

Company of Military Historians
287 Thayer Street
Providence, R.I. 02906

Orders and Medals Society of America
500 A Guys Run
RFD #2
Cheswick, Pa. 15024

Society of Cinema Collectors and
Historians
307 Trensch Drive
New Milford, N.J. 07646

American Pencil Collectors Society
Sterling, Kansas

Photographic Historical Society
P.O. Box 9563
Rochester, N.Y. 14604

American Political Item Collectors
4144 S.E. Clinton St.,
Portland, Ore. 97202

National Political Button Exchange
5008 Deerpark Circle
Fair Oaks, Calif. 95628

Train Collectors Association
9116-210 Place
Queens Village, N.Y. 11428

National Association of Watch and
Clock Collectors
P.O. Box 33
Columbus, Pa. 17512